The Three
Dynamisms
of Faith

LOUIS ROY, OP

The Three Dynamisms of Faith

SEARCHING
FOR MEANING,
FULFILLMENT
& TRUTH

THE CATHOLIC UNIVERSITY
OF AMERICA PRESS
Washington, D.C.

Image on page ii: Three Standing Figures, by Stefano da
Verona, Italian, Verona (?), ca. 1438.

Library of Congress Cataloging-in-Publication Data
Names: Roy, Louis, 1942– author.
Title: The three dynamisms of faith : searching for
meaning, fulfillment, and
truth / Louis Roy, OP.
Description: Washington, D.C. : The Catholic
University of America Press, 2017. |
Includes bibliographical references and index.
Identifiers: LCCN 2017014562 |
ISBN 9780813229799 (pbk. : alk. paper)
Subjects: LCSH: Faith. | Philosophical theology. |
Catholic Church—Doctrines.
Classification: LCC BT771.3 .R69 2017 | DDC 210.1—dc23
LC record available at
https://lccn.loc.gov/2017014562

❧

When the

Son of Man comes,

will he find faith

on earth?

(Lk 18:8)

Contents

ॐ

Acknowledgments

꙳

I am grateful to my students in Boston, Montreal, Ottawa, and Providence, Rhode Island, for their stimulating interest in my views on faith. For having offered comments on a chapter, I want to thank Rev. John Connelly, Prof. Philip A. Cunningham, the late Rev. Daniel Harrington, SJ, Rev. Carleton Jones, OP, Prof. James R. Pambrun, and Prof. James M. Weiss. I am also indebted to John Martino, acquisitions editor of the Catholic University of America Press for philosophy and theology, and to the anonymous reviewers of the whole manuscript for their many suggestions and corrections. I thank the Dominican University College in Ottawa for providing financial aid to allow a graduate student to work with me on the indices of this book. This student is Scott Ventureyra, to whom I am grateful.

Chapter 6 is a reworking and considerable lengthening of "Three Faith Dynamisms," which appeared in *New Blackfriars* 81 (2000): 541–48.

Throughout this volume, unless otherwise indicated, italicization is by the authors themselves. I follow the usual guidelines of inclusive language regarding people, either by employing the plural or by alternating "he" and "she." However, in accord with biblical language, God is referred to as "he." Biblical quotations are from the New Revised Standard Version, in *The New Oxford Annotated Bible* (Oxford: Oxford University Press), at times with slight modifications.

The Three
Dynamisms
of Faith

Introduction

༄

Our contemporary West's humanism is colored by intense psychological preoccupations. It is also marked by a certain indifferentism: indifference to—and distrust of—organized religion with its institutional and doctrinal apparatus.[1] Having distanced themselves from long-established church teachings, many non-churchgoers are simply disaffiliated from any particular Jewish or Christian denomination. Some of them nevertheless maintain they are still "religious." Yet, a fast-growing segment of North Americans reject the label "religious" and prefer to call themselves "spiritual."[2]

Skepticism toward ecclesiastical talk has become prevalent, commencing with the Baby Boom Generation (1946–65). Insofar as Generation X (1966–85) is concerned, many of those who belong to it recall painful facts that fuel their burning conviction that family, society, and church have failed them. The college students of Generation Y (1986–2005, also dubbed the Millennium Generation or the Millennials, since they began graduating from high school around 2000), may be group-oriented rule followers and deferential to professors in order to build up a curriculum vitae that will propel them toward high-paying jobs;[3] and yet few of them are prepared to

1. For helpful data, see Wade Clark Roof, *A Generation of Seekers: The Spiritual Journeys of the Baby Boom Generation* (San Francisco: Harper, 1993). Noteworthy is the title of chapter 8, "It's Hard to Find a Religion You Can Believe Totally In."

2. See, for instance, Linda A. Mercadante, *Belief without Borders: Inside the Minds of the Spiritual but Not Religious* (New York: Oxford University Press, 2014).

3. See Neil Howe and William Strauss, *Millennials Rising: The Next Great Generation* (New York: Vintage, 2000).

1

accept any doctrinal or moral authority. These features also apply to the latest generation—namely, Generation Z. The end result is what has been variously called à-la-carte, cafeteria, or buffet religion.

Based on surveys, Tom Beaudoin notes that the primary question the Baby Boomers raise is, "What is the meaning of life, of my life?" but that the fundamental question of Generation Xers is, "Will you be there for me?" He comments that the latter ask this question about their self, their body, their partners and families, their country, and God.[4] Prompted by this contrast, I would propose these characterizations: the generation that preceded the Baby Boomers insisted on *truth* and authority; the Boomers insist on *meaning*; and the Xers and their successors insist on *fulfillment*—that is, on emotional comfort thanks to warm group relationships and vivid forms of expression (such as music, dance, candles, incense).[5] I am alluding here to the three components of the faith experience—meaning, fulfillment, and truth—that will be explicated in the course of this volume, especially in chapter 6.

Ours is an era in which interest in spirituality is widespread. The sheer bulk of publications, movies, songs, and websites in that field testify to its importance. This human search proceeds in a fragmented, ever-shifting manner, depending on the images and sounds that the media tender to our yearning hearts. People's opinions are tossed about amidst the waves that rush through the channels of mass communication. The present spiritual movements stir by fits and starts, replete as they are with longings and aversions, insights and oversights, tensions, contradictions, and promises.

This book is addressed to cultivated readers who are aware of concerns and entertain questions about hope and meaning. It is the work of a Canadian theologian, and, as such, it has been thought

---

4. Tom Beaudoin, *Virtual Faith: The Irreverent Spiritual Quest of Generation X* (San Francisco: Jossey-Bass, 1998), 140–41.

5. See introduction and conclusion to Richard W. Flory and Donald E. Miller, eds., *GenX Religion* (New York: Routledge, 2000).

out, over several decades, in the context of a postindustrial country. I am fully aware that my perspective has been fashioned by North Atlantic ideas and concerns. However, because the phenomenon of cultural incoherence is now reaching the whole world to a greater and greater extent, my approach, which addresses this phenomenon, is likely to be of interest to non-Westerners. In a well-documented book, Kaya Oakes wrote, "Instead of cleaving to one particular way of believing, many younger people engage in a kind of spiritual mix and match, blending many traditions and adhering strictly to none."[6] Therefore, one of my goals in these pages is to explain how those who seek out meaning or personal fulfillment can move from a collection of rather disjointed and random beliefs, full of gaps and inconsistencies, toward a supple coherence that remains incomplete and yet progressively becomes more truthful, both to human experience and to Christian wisdom.[7]

It may be useful to situate this study with respect to three earlier books of mine. Two of them deal with transcendent experiences, which bring to light the human openness to the infinite in its affective and intellectual dimensions.[8] In those works, a premium is put on religious occurrences, seen as temporary resolutions to our basic unrest. Pride of place is given to their various elements, types, and concepts. A third book focuses on a contemplative state that is more advanced than transcendent experiences.[9] It sets out to re-

---

6. Kaya Oakes, *The Nones Are Alright: A New Generation of Believers, Seekers, and Those in Between* (Maryknoll, NY: Orbis, 2015), 5. The "nones" are those who checkmark the box "none" in answer to surveys that ask whether they belong to a religion.

7. My first attempts at tackling this issue of coherence resulted in a book: Louis Roy, *La foi en quête de cohérence* (Montreal: Bellarmin, 1988), and reissued as *La foi en dialogue* (Ottawa: Novalis, 2006), trans. and rev. as *Coherent Christianity: Toward an Articulate Faith* (Wipf & Stock, 2017).

8. Roy, *Le sentiment de transcendance, expérience de Dieu?* (Paris: Cerf, 2000), and *Transcendent Experiences: Phenomenology and Critique* (Toronto: University of Toronto Press, 2001). The former offers a phenomenology of transcendent experiences and includes a dialogue with psychology; the latter is an essay in philosophy of religion since Kant.

9. Roy, *Mystical Consciousness: Western Perspectives and Dialogue with Japanese Thinkers* (Albany: SUNY Press, 2003).

trieve the source of mysticism according to its students of classical authors (Plotinus, Eckhart, and Schleiermacher), several Western twentieth-century philosophers (principally Lonergan), and a few Japanese Zen practitioners and thinkers (Suzuki, Nishitani, and Hisamatsu). Those three volumes pertain to the field of the philosophy of religion, although they provide insights that can be subsumed by Catholic faith.

This time, however, I will scrutinize the specifically Christian aspect of the spiritual quest—namely, faith in Jesus. Therefore, I will concentrate on a range of reflections as sets of answers to fundamental aspirations and questions. Still, in order not to prolong this enterprise, I will not venture into the theology of grace and salvation, even though faith is enmeshed with these themes in many strands of the New Testament, especially in St. Paul.[10]

Furthermore, my choice of authors as source material is commanded by my basic aim: to reinterpret and update my own tradition, which is Thomist.[11] The thrust of my inquiry is toward an appropriation of what is best and dependable in a medieval and modern tradition on faith. To achieve this goal, this book canvasses, in an original way, a Catholic position on faith, which is at once time-honored and relevant for today. My inspiration comes mainly from the Bible, Thomas Aquinas, John Henry Newman, and Bernard Lonergan. On each of these thinkers, far from claiming to be exhaustive, I will simply present a few constituents of his thought in order to enrich my analysis. At times, Protestant views are introduced, although sparingly, because I want to present them at length in another book (on revelation).

Some will judge my outlook on faith too progressive; I would

---

10. On such themes, see Roy, "Why Is the Death of Jesus Redemptive?" in *Pondering the Passion: What's at Stake for Christians and Jews*, ed. Philip A. Cunningham (Lanham, Md.: Rowman and Littlefield, 2004), 129–39.

11. To reinterpret my Thomist tradition and to be compendious are the reasons I have not introduced Latin or Greek authors, except Augustine on faith as anticipating Aquinas, in chapter 3.

urge them to ponder my exposition and approval of Newman's antiliberal propos. Others will wonder whether my outlook is not too conservative; I shall be at pains to persuade them that authority is desirable in light of affectivity and reason.

The readers will notice more than one way of handling the subject matter: methodological, descriptive, expository, and foundational. The methodological mode justifies the rationale behind the approach adopted; the descriptive mode brings us in contact with lived experience; the expository mode introduces us to notable historical figures; and the foundational mode details the links among the several concepts discovered in the course of our exploration.

The book begins with the present situation (the issue of hope), then listens to voices from the past, and, last, moves back to the present situation. This will be done in three stages. The first, chapter 1, deals with methodological and descriptive approaches; the next includes chapter 2 (methodological and biblical approaches) and chapters 3 through 5 (the historical approach); the third stage is comprised of chapters 6 and 7 (the foundational approach, enriched by the faith wisdom culled from the past).

Chapter 1 begins with the issue of hope, so basic for humankind. The first section justifies a subjective approach to faith—namely, an approach that proceeds from the perspective of self-knowledge: from the perspective of the subject undertaking to know itself *as an individual subject*. The second section envisions the subject *as universal*; it does so by spelling out an assessment of the human condition, which determines the selection of topics and authors throughout the book. The third section submits that the spiritual quest should no longer be seen as an ascent, but as a descent into the depths of our experience, to the point where people reach the most hidden layer of their anxiety. The fourth section ponders in detail the issue of hope, which has always tantalized the human race.

Chapter 2 puts forward a reading of biblical data that meets the concerns of hope. The first section argues that the Bible can be read in response to the desiderata of foundational thinking. The second section lays out salient features of faith and hope in the Bible, particularly in St. Paul. The third section depicts the sad condition of blindness and underscores the theme of illumination in the New Testament. The fourth section describes faith in John's Gospel.

Chapter 3 delineates Thomas Aquinas's conception of faith and places it in interaction with love. Thereafter, the centrality of the First Truth as the ground of certainty is explained. Next, the text weighs how Aquinas assesses the range of human reason. Last, the chapter introduces the three complementary aspects of believing that we find in Aquinas's oeuvre.

Chapter 4 explores John Henry Newman's views on the process that leads to faith. The first section, entitled "Real and Notional Apprehension," elaborates upon the distinction between notional and real assent. The second section, entitled "Assent and Inference," rejects the Enlightenment's obsession with proving belief and proposes an alternative. The third section probes the way Newman fields inference and apprehension into religion. The fourth section expounds what he says about three distortions of faith.

Chapter 5 states that Lonergan's great contribution to an understanding of faith hinges upon two conversions: religious and intellectual. The third conversion—the moral one—is dealt with cursorily, since it is less crucial for an account of faith. Accordingly, chapter 5 highlights the impact of the religious and intellectual conversions upon such an account. The first two sections discuss the interplay between *religious* conversion and the role of the word and of belief. The third and fourth sections touch on objections raised by George Lindbeck and David Tracy. The fifth section has to do with epistemological consequences of *intellectual* conversion in the practice of theology.

Chapter 6 is rather straightforward. It presents the readers with a proposal for a theology of faith: a frame of reference that integrates three fundamental quests—namely, for affective fulfillment, for meaning, and for truth. The exposé of the chapter first characterizes each of these three forces. It then illustrates how they support one another inasmuch as they function in unison, which brings about a mutually enriching balance. It proceeds to expose the distortions that take place whenever one of those dynamisms strives toward hegemony, or whenever two of them enter into an alliance against a third one. Thereafter, it investigates the issue of self-deception. A last section considers how the discovery of Jesus Christ affects each of the three factors.

Chapter 7 evolves in five steps. First, it underlines the significance of the distinction between meaning and truth. Second, stages are differentiated in the process of coming to believe. Third, some light is thrown upon the complementarity of feelings and insights. Fourth, the chapter asks whether religious experience is the main criterion of truth. Fifth, it marks out the various ways according to which religious experience is concretely mediated.

Finally, the pastoral conclusion puts to fruitful use the result of my inquiry as it stresses the concrete advantages of using the basic dynamisms' tripartite representation. It is an exercise in the theological specialty that Lonergan calls "Communications."

A twentieth-century Chinese thinker loved to say, "The further one looks back, the further one is able to see into the future."[12] However, some readers will probably be more curious to know right away my position and less immediately interested, at least at the outset, in the historical chapters of this book. After reading chapter 1 (on hope as the doorway to faith), they may then want to go to chapters 6 and 7 (for a foundational account of faith) and to the pastoral conclusion—which will make the subsequent reading of chapters 2 to 5 easier for them.

12. John C. H. Wu, quoted by his son John Wu Jr., "Centennial Vignettes: Life with Father," in *Merton and the Tao: Dialogues with John Wu and the Ancient Sages*, ed. Christóbal Serrán-Pagán y Fuentes (Louisville, Ky.: Fons Vitae, 2013), 376.

CHAPTER 1

The Issue of Hope as
the Starting Point

The sociologist Peter Berger highlights one of the major differences between premodern and modern societies. In the former, one could find a great measure of fate, inasmuch as the possibilities of changing practices and conducts were restricted. In medicine, in nonscientific techniques, in methods of education, and so forth, there was little room for maneuvering. By contrast, "the modern individual . . . lives in a world of choice. . . . He must choose in innumerable situations of everyday life; but this necessity of choosing reaches into the areas of beliefs, values, and worldviews."[1] This necessity of choosing he calls "the heretical imperative," from the Greek *hairesis*, choice. Interestingly, already in the seventeenth century, John Locke saw the churches as voluntary associations—which is to say that he saw them as based on personal preference.

Even though the spectrum of choices is often narrow in the sense that the objects offered for selection do not significantly differ from each other, Berger is right when he notes the following consequence:

The taken-for-granted manner in which premodern institutions ordered human life is eroded. What previously was self-evident fact now becomes

---

1. Peter L. Berger, *The Heretical Imperative: Contemporary Possibilities of Religious Affirmation* (Garden City, N.Y.: Doubleday, 1979), 19.

an occasion to choose. Fate does not require reflection; the individual who is compelled to make choices is also compelled to stop and think. The more choices, the more reflection. The individual who reflects inevitably becomes more conscious of himself. That is, he turns his attention from the objectively given outside world to his own subjectivity.[2]

Berger also states, "Modernization has brought with it a strong accentuation of the subjective side of human existence; indeed, it may be said that modernization and subjectivization are cognate processes."[3]

The first section of this chapter will adopt and justify this subjective angle of vision as providing great virtualities for faith. The second section will spell out a theological reading of the human condition, in its longing for a founded hope, with a view to determining whether a person marked by this condition is amenable to a fundamental act of faith. The third section will suggest that the spiritual quest should no longer be seen as an ascent, but as a descent into the depths of our subjective experience, to the point where we reach the most hidden layer of our anxiety. The fourth section will show how the question of happiness, especially in relation to the future of the human race, opens up to religious faith.

A SUBJECTIVE APPROACH TO FAITH

I propose an approach to faith that starts with the subjective and only secondarily incorporates objective reasons for belief. By "the subjective" is meant "the anthropological" and, more precisely in these pages, people's concerns and existential questions. As we shall see in detail in chapter 5, the Jesuit Bernard Lonergan advocated such an exploration of human subjectivity, both in philosophy and in theology.

For all the widespread indifference to religion, few individuals have absolutely *no* concerns and questions regarding hope and meaning. This fact warrants a decision to emphasize the subjective and to

---

2. Berger, *Heretical Imperative*, 22.
3. Berger, *Heretical Imperative*, 20.

let other writers discuss the objective—namely, the historical data that justify Christian belief. Only a restricted number of minds are likely to pay more than a cursory attention to a scholarly investigation into the origins of Christianity, whereas the vast majority of our contemporaries may be attracted to a quest for religious self-knowledge.

Accordingly, I am going to trace a moving viewpoint—that is, an ensemble of dynamic factors that are pushing human beings forward on their journeys. A theology of faith attentive to people's spiritual treks differs from the objective apologetics constructed by Roman Catholics and other Christians as a response to the Enlightenment's rejection of belief. Sure enough, I do not want to demean that enterprise, which can have its weight.[4] Although I sincerely think that many elements of that apologetics—that of the manuals—are true and useful, otherwise I find several of its tenets very naïve, even sometimes childish, with a total lack of historical sense.[5] On account of those shortcomings, I, like John Henry Newman, to whose thought a long chapter will be dedicated in these pages, prefer the subjective style, which throws light upon personal quests. As Ian Ker avers, "Newman's own starting point was not a defense of belief in God or the Christian revelation, but rather an examination of the actual mental process by virtue of which somebody is a believer or an unbeliever."[6]

In fact, objective statements such as the existence of God, a providential design for history, the biblical claim that there is revelation, the credentials of Christianity, have a definite effect on the human intellect only to the extent that they are grafted upon subjective horizons. Thus Newman writes:

4. I commend the version of apologetics by Peter Kreeft and Ronald K. Tacelli, *Handbook of Christian Apologetics: Reasoned Answers to Questions of Faith* (San Francisco: Ignatius Press, 2009).

5. For example, the thesis that the miracles of Jesus (including his resurrection, seen as a miracle) could prove his divinity.

6. Ian Ker, *The Achievement of John Henry Newman* (Notre Dame, Ind.: University of Notre Dame Press, 1990), 36.

Although we must maintain most firmly that the truth which faith embraces is not merely subjective, but is one and the same to all, and immutable in anyone who believes rightly, it is nevertheless clear that the ways by which the mind attains to that truth are as many as the diversity of natural temperaments. Therefore, faith progresses subjectively to its object.... I am concerned ... not with reason considered in itself, in the abstract, but with the concrete question of how faith comes to be in particular minds, and of the kind of reasoning that leads to faith, which certainly is not the same in everyone.[7]

Because I wish to attend to the many "ways by which the mind attains to that truth," as Newman puts it, I shall go by his example and draw from his "grammar of assent" instead of expounding on the contents of revelation at length. I shall ask my readers to ponder "*how* we believe" rather than "*what* we believe." Obviously, talking about the former involves lending consideration to the latter. I am not going to avoid presenting the "what"; yet it will be introduced only to the extent that its meaning sheds light upon the "how." In other words, I will not say much about the *objects* of Christian faith and hope, rather concentrating on how people come to be interested in Jesus at all.

Another way of distinguishing the two approaches to faith is elucidated by Jean Guitton. Following upon Gabriel Marcel's distinction between *mystère* and *problème*, Guitton rightly asserts that Jesus is both a mystery and a problem.[8] The first path is typified by Blaise Pascal: it proceeds through the heart and through prayer. The second path is typified by Guitton: it discusses historical and philosophical topics. In fact, the two paths are traveled by both Pascal and Guitton. They are not exclusive of one another. Both will be explored in these pages. Still, my emphasis will be on the gradual access to the mystery of Jesus.

As I hope to make clear in the course of this book, sound reli-

---

7. John Henry Newman, "Proposed Introduction to the French Translation of the University Sermons," in *Three Latin Papers of John Henry Newman*, trans. Carleton P. Jones (Rome: Pontifical University of Saint Thomas Aquinas, 1995), 49.

8. Jean Guitton, *Critique religieuse* (Paris: Desclée de Brouwer, 1968), 427.

gious experience is entirely compatible with an intellectual integrity that displays an unflinching respect for truth and a vigilant pursuit of objectivity. Readers will quickly notice that my line of argument presupposes the intelligibility of reality. Since, in the confines of the present venture, I cannot explicate this fundamental standpoint, let me recommend the perusal of Lonergan's masterpiece, *Insight*.[9] Some of Lonergan's corollaries will be presented later.

READING THE HUMAN CONDITION THEOLOGICALLY

Since Martin Luther, countless people have been pondering the question, what are the human concerns that prepare the way for genuine faith? Such people have been wondering about the basic disquiet, or uneasiness, that triggers extremely varied spiritual journeys. Let us acknowledge this disquiet (as yet unspecified) as our point of departure, and let us consider it as the first trademark of the anthropological locus of theology.

We cannot but be struck by the ambiguity of religious phenomena: at times they are ennobling and at times disadvantageous. More often than not, they are a mixture of both. As a Catholic theologian, I invariably shy away from disparaging religion. In my estimation, Karl Barth's thesis that faith stands in antithesis to religion is untenable. In order to be totally human, faith must integrate the *natural* desire to understand and to be affectively fulfilled—a *religious* desire that most of the time, in our secular societies, precedes the act of faith, since people become aware of it before they decide to believe.

Thus, the starting point of our inquiry is the human condition, both personal and historical, with its hankering for a founded hope. It would be illogical to begin with the Bible only, since we cannot imagine individuals or groups listening to Scripture without their

9. Bernard Lonergan, *Collected Works of Bernard Lonergan*, vol. 3, *Insight: A Study of Human Understanding*, ed. Frederick E. Crowe and Robert M. Doran (Toronto: University of Toronto Press, 1992).

basic human situation in some way impinging upon that listening. Despite the fideists, such as Barth, who hold that theology should commence with faith to the exclusion of any universally shared anthropological doctrine, it must be maintained that the human predicament, however interpreted, is the common ground for both those who recognize and those who do not accept the Bible as the word of God. This human predicament is the anthropological locus of theology, since, for all the varieties of itineraries adopted, whenever divine initiative and human desire meet, we detect greater advancement in terms of insight and commitment.

The Jewish thinker Franz Rosenzweig once wrote:

> We can know that which is contained in the Bible in two ways: (1) by listening to what it says, and (2) by sounding the human heartbeat. (*Both* are "inductions.") *The Bible and the heart say the same thing.* For this reason (and *solely* for this reason) the Bible is revelation.[10]

Theology of faith calls for some elucidation of the *humanum*— namely, the human being's fundamental disquiet in the world, especially with its protest against the inhumane. The Latin poet Terence wrote movingly, "I am a man and I think nothing human is foreign to me" (*Homo sum: Humani nil a me alienum puto*).[11] Without referring to Terence, albeit perhaps having this line in mind, Edward Schillebeeckx speaks of "the *humanum* that we seek," to designate "the true humanity," "the authentically human" whose deciphering key he finds in Jesus of Nazareth.[12] Yet, he adds elsewhere, "We do not have a pre-existing definition of humanity—indeed for Christians it is not only a future, but an eschatological reality."[13]

In keeping with Schillebeeckx's two-sided position, I would

10. Franz Rosenzweig, Letter of May 27, 1921 to Benno Jacob, in *Der Mensch und sein Werk: Gesammelte Schriften* (The Hague: Martinus Nijhoff, 1979), vol. 1, part 2, 708–9.

11. Terence, *The Self-Tormentor*, Act 1, line 77, my translation.

12. Edward Schillebeeckx, *Jesus: An Experiment in Christology*, trans. Hubert Hoskins (New York: Crossroad, 1979), 606–7.

13. Schillebeeckx, *Christ: The Experience of Jesus as Lord*, trans. John Bowden (New York: Crossroad, 1980), 731.

stress, on the one hand, that the spiritual seekers who encounter Christ have their humanness redefined by him during their earthly existence and, on the other hand, that their humanness will be fully glorified and manifested on the last day. Accordingly, at this stage of our research, let us admit that our human nature is imperfectly known in its open-ended desiring. It can be better known in a dialectic between the Holy Scriptures and our questing, wounded nature. And yet, after such a dialectic has been time and again performed, no human being can verily pretend to possess a complete self-understanding. Actually, the final self-interpretation will occur at the last stage of history, when God stamps the bold characters of an overall meaning onto humankind's journey in the universe.

One of Pascal's theses is precisely that without faith, the human individual cannot make sense of his fundamental plight. "[Man] is a monster that passes all understanding."[14] He goes on to confront his reader: "Know then, proud man, what a paradox you are to yourself. Be humble, impotent reason! Be silent, feeble nature! Learn that man infinitely transcends man, hear from your master your true condition, which is unknown to you." He adds, "Without the aid of faith he would remain inconceivable to himself."[15] Even Thomas Aquinas is not optimistic about the capacity of reason deprived of faith.[16] He is just slightly less pessimistic than Pascal.

The anthropological starting place adopted in these pages is not a thoroughgoing anthropocentrism, as found in the immanentism typical of what was dubbed "modernism," which appeared within Roman Catholicism around 1900.[17] It is useful here to recall Maurice Blondel's contradistinction, during the modernist crisis, be-

---

14. Blaise Pascal, *Pensées*, trans. A. J. Krailsheimer, rev. ed. (New York: Penguin, 1995), Pensée 130. This numbering is based on Pascal's first copy, the order of which is followed by Louis Lafuma's edition: Pascal, *Oeuvres complètes* (Paris: Seuil, 1963).

15. Pascal, Pensée 131.

16. As we shall see in chapter 3, in the section entitled, "The Compass of Human Reason."

17. Although he never said that Rahner was a modernist, Hans Urs von Balthasar perspicaciously distanced himself from his anthropocentric method; see von Balthasar, *The*

tween immanentism (which he repudiated) and his own method of immanence. The former amounts to a restrictive ontology that rules out the possibility of a revelation; the latter is a phenomenology that leaves aside questions of ontology and that "treats phenomena as a system to be understood with regard to their internal relations, without any ontological affirmation."[18]

My position has already been aptly stated by a contemporary theologian, Tullio Citrini:

> An anthropological starting point does not of itself necessarily lead to a fundamental theology that is anthropocentric. If man by his nature is "ec-centric," this intentional eccentricity is activated in faith: faith exists in the believer and is the act of a believing subject, but the object to which faith is directed and its center of gravity is not the believer himself but the God who has revealed himself in Jesus Christ.[19]

A final cautionary note is in order: what is being advocated here is not a strict method of *correlation* between human concerns and divine response. Paul Tillich and others may have pressed the data too much, as they sometimes sketched point-by-point parallelisms between human questions and revealed answers.[20] With Marc Dumas, himself inspired by Schillebeeckx, I would rather propose a method of *interrelation*—namely, a dynamic of mutually critical correlations between the Christian traditions and present-day perspectives, which I hope this volume will exemplify.[21]

Moment of Christian Witness, trans. Richard Beckley (San Francisco: Ignatius Press, 1994), 100–13 and 146–52.

18. James LeGrys, "The Christianization of Modern Philosophy according to Maurice Blondel," *Theological Studies* 54 (1993):473, commenting on Maurice Blondel, "Une des sources de la pensée moderne," in *Dialogue avec les philosophes: Descartes, Spinoza, Malebranche, Pascal, Saint Augustin* (Paris: Aubier, 1966).

19. Tullio Citrini, "The Principle of 'Christocentrism' and Its Role in Fundamental Theology," in *Problems and Perspectives of Fundamental Theology*, ed. René Latourelle and Gerald O'Collins, trans. Matthew J. O'Connell (New York: Paulist Press, 1982), 177.

20. See Peter Harrison, "Correlation and Theology: Barth and Tillich Re-examined," *Studies in Religion/Sciences Religieuses* 15 (1986):65–76.

21. See Marc Dumas, "Corrélations d'expériences?" *Laval Théologique et Philosophique* 60 (2004):317–34.

ASCENT OR DESCENT?

This section attempts to bring to light one of the causes that explain the helplessness, for most moderns and postmoderns, of the traditional Catholic approach to faith, which holds that mysticism equates to an ascent. In short, for many minds the chief difficulty of that approach is that it is tied to a hierarchical worldview.

As is well known, in his *Republic* Plato puts in parallel two portrayals: the soul and the city. Both consist of three components: the knowing, the fighting, and the desiring part. To this anthropological-societal structure, Augustine, in *The City of God*, adds a fourth component: the divine. For Plato as well as for Augustine, orderliness and harmony require obedience to the immediate, higher instance, be it within the person, in society, or in the church.

In Dionysius, a sixth-century Christian thinker inspired by Proclus, himself a disciple of the neo-Platonic Plotinus, we find an even more encompassing schema. *The Celestial Hierarchy*, with its archangels and angels, is located above and in continuity with *The Ecclesiastical Hierarchy*.[22] Along this scale of beings, each inferior receives life and light from its immediate superior. Sacred mediators such as bishops stand closer to the invisible realities than others and thus exercise a nobler function, as their grace trickles down to the lower strata.[23] However, Dionysius corrected Proclus's rigorous hierarchy by insisting that being is directly given by God to creatures.[24] He thus indicated the direction I want to take.

This Greek vision, Christianized and amplified by Augustine and

22. See Pseudo-Dionysius, *The Complete Works*, trans. Colm Luibheid (New York: Paulist Press, 1987).

23. Even a scholar quite taken with neo-Platonic mysticism recognizes that "the intellectual culture" behind it "has long disappeared"; see Denys Turner, *The Darkness of God: Negativity in Christian Mysticism* (Cambridge: Cambridge University Press, 1995), 27; see 27–32 and 48–49 for the shortcomings of Dionysius's vision insofar as the doctrine of creation is concerned.

24. See Dionysius, *The Divine Names*, 592A and 825A–B, and *Ecclesiastical Hierarchy*, 372D.

Dionysius, dominated the entire Middle Ages, thanks to its forceful order and beauty.[25] Yet Marcel Gauchet has stressed the inherent instability and fragility of this social-religious hierarchy. Because of its inequality and divisiveness, such a sacred world was bound to lose its enchanting intellectual cogency.[26]

This medieval conception of the world began to crumble in the fourteenth century, when William of Ockham's empiricism typified a novel temper, characterized by a rejection of abstractions or entities not backed by facts. One century later, Nicholas of Cusa replaced the Greek-Christian model of a finite, hierarchical universe with the newly emerging awareness of an infinite universe, understood as an ensemble of mathematical proportions. Another century later, Martin Luther rebelled against the hierarchical nature of the clerical church and abolished the ecclesiastical mediations—namely, the pope's and the bishops' authority. In the seventeenth century, Pierre de Bérulle "proclaimed, against Dionysius the Areopagite, a 'reversal of the hierarchies.' ... Henceforth, for Bérulle, all the hierarchies of angels will adore Jesus, the God-man."[27] In the eighteenth century, hierarchy became synonymous with heteronomy.[28] Both ecclesiastical intermediaries and angelic (good and bad) spirits were perceived as unduly invading the sphere of personal and collective responsibility.

Already in the seventeenth century, however, scientific progress was not without its shadowy side. Meditating upon the existential consequences of the immense universe studied by astronomy, which has nothing to say about human purpose, Pascal observes:

25. For a presentation of the mysticism involved in this hierarchic model as found in Dante, Seyyed Hossein Nasr, and Huston Smith, with very pertinent critical remarks, see Jonas Barciauskas, *Landscapes of Wisdom: In Search of a Spirituality of Knowing* (Lanham, Md.: University Press of America, 2000), chaps. 1 and 2 and conclusion.

26. Marcel Gauchet, *The Disenchantment of the World*, trans. Oscar Burge (Princeton, N.J.: Princeton University Press, 1997), esp. 36–39 on hierarchy.

27. William M. Thompson, Introduction to *Bérulle and the French School: Selected Writings*, trans. Lowell M. Glendon (New York: Paulist Press, 1989), 14.

28. See Louis Roy, "Does Christian Faith Rule out Human Autonomy?" *Heythrop Journal* 53 (2012):606–23.

When I see the blind and wretched state of man, when I survey the whole universe in its dumbness and man left to himself with no light, as though lost in this corner of the universe, without knowing who put him there, what he has come to do, what will become of him when he dies, incapable of knowing anything, I am moved to terror, like a man transported in his sleep to some terrifying desert island, who wakes up quite lost and with no means of escape.[29]

Further on, he adds, "The eternal silence of these infinite spaces fills me with dread."[30]

What picture of the universe does modern science make implausible? In a remarkable article entitled, "Manifestation and Proclamation," Paul Ricoeur describes the world representations based on a sense of the sacred. The hierophanies so well detailed by Mircea Eliade manifest the sacred in spatial and temporal terms. The world is peopled by sacred beings, distributed according to places and times where they can be recurrently found. Ricoeur then entertains the following hypothesis:

One fact of our culture is that we live in a desacralized world. Our modernity is constituted as modern precisely by having moved beyond the sacred cosmos. Nature, for modern persons, is no longer a store of signs. Its great correspondences have become indecipherable to them. The cosmos is mute. Human beings no longer receive the meaning of their existence from their belonging to a cosmos itself saturated with meaning. Modern persons no longer have a sacred space, a center, a temple, a holy mountain, or an *axis mundi.* Their existence is decentered, eccentric, a-centered. They lack festivals, their time is homogeneous like their space. This is why we only speak of the sacred world today as something archaic.[31]

This archaic sense of the sacred, with its spatializations and temporalizations, was given an additional strength by the intellectual

---

29. Pascal, Pensée 198.

30. Pascal, Pensée 201.

31. Paul Ricoeur, "Manifestation and Proclamation," in *Figuring the Sacred: Religion, Narrative, and Imagination,* trans. David Pellauer, ed. Mark I. Wallace (Minneapolis: Fortress Press, 1995), 61. Later in that essay, Ricoeur nuances his somewhat "iconoclastic discourse," as he himself calls it (61).

constructions of the neo-Platonic tradition, mentioned a moment
ago. It is important to register the fact that this synthesis, which
dominated the Middle Ages and lingered on in the Catholic Church
after the Protestant reformation, is no longer viable.[32] Some of the
folk-religion elements, such as pilgrimage places and memorable
dates, are still very much alive; and yet they inescapably pertain to
current pre-Enlightenment configurations that have little effect on
human interests and thought forms. The same must be said of the
speculative gains dear to the Greeks and the medievals: as much as
several of such gains may be permanently valid; nonetheless, they
must be recast in a new worldview.[33]

The English theologian Cornelius Ernst tried to work out such a
recasting. In critical dialogue with Heidegger, he contends:

Once human inwardness is no longer sustained by the myth of a hierarchical cosmos of the spheres beyond which is God, its ultimate revelation
tends to be one of self-enclosed finitude [Heidegger's position]; but there
is no reason why we should not learn to seek God as the source of that
marriage of man and earth which is consummated in the Event of truth,
and which can serve as the sacramental sign of the revelation of the divine
Truth itself. Our encounter with a Man can be the revelation of God; our
inhabitation of the earth can be and is a sacred history.[34]

Religious experiences surface, not in a vacuum, but in cultural
environments, which at once preclude and open up certain possibilities. The all-pervasive interest in post-Einsteinian cosmologies
and in existential anthropologies is here to stay. Philosophy of religion and theology are well-advised to observe the sense of the infi-

32. With the exception of the degrees of beings that correspond to a scale of the sciences, from physics to the human studies, with chemistry, biology, and psychology in between; see Lonergan, *Collected Works*, vol. 3, *Insight*, 229–30, 280–82, 631.

33. Several of my articles are attempts to retrieve past accomplishments. For example,
Roy, "Neither Within nor Outside Time: Plotinus' Approach to Eternity," *Science et Esprit*
53 (2001):419–26; "Notes on Thomas Aquinas," *Budhi: A Journal of Culture and Ideas* (a
Jesuit periodical at Ateneo de Manila University, Philippines) 6 (2002):235–43.

34. Cornelius Ernst, Introduction, *Theological Investigations*, by Karl Rahner (New
York: Crossroad, 1982), 1:xvi–xvii.

nite displayed in those cosmologies and anthropologies. Pascal did just that. Kant, Schleiermacher, Hegel, and the other thinkers whose writings I examined in *Transcendent Experiences* have much to say about the human being's potential for the infinite, through either cosmos-centered or man-centered meditations.[35] Furthermore, the general public's current fascination for the cosmological theories elaborated by physicists and astronomers evinces more than a curiosity regarding the origin and the end of the universe. Many of the scientists who engage in these discussions are convinced that it is the future not only of our planet but also of the human race in the vast cosmos that is at stake. From this vivid awareness, which attests that the intellectual interest in the cosmos springs from the human desire to understand and indeed from anxiety, we may infer that the concern for the cosmological is intimately bonded with the concern for the anthropological.

Tillich rightly states, "Religion is not a special function of man's spiritual life, but it is the dimension of depth in all of its functions [moral, cognitive, and aesthetic]." He adds, "The religious aspect points to that which is ultimate, infinite, unconditional in man's spiritual life. Religion, in the largest and most basic sense of the word, is ultimate concern."[36] For him, God can be discovered afresh in the profundity of the human soul. Surely "depth" psychology, now more commonly called psychoanalysis, has accustomed us to look into our depths, in this case into the unconscious. As will be demonstrated in chapter 6, no authentic faith comes about without some painful wrestling with the issues of religious illusion and self-deception.

In place of neo-Platonism's multi-leveled hierarchy, I would champion a vision inspired by Tillich and composed of two strata: first, the ordinary, called *le quotidien* by French phenomenologists,

35. On the phenomenon of religious experiences detached from ecclesial venues, see also Roy, *Le sentiment de transcendance*, 9–15.

36. Paul Tillich, *Theology of Culture*, ed. Robert C. Kimball (New York: Oxford University Press, 1959), 5–6 and 7–8.

and second, what lies hidden underneath it, as its base—that is, the receptiveness to the divine. We thus encounter the infinite in our finitude. In this representation, the theological-mystical adventure is no longer regarded as an ascent, but as a descent, "to the bottom of a fertile valley," as Thérèse of Lisieux puts it.[37]

Of course, I do not mean to ban the metaphor of ascent, with its glorious history, from Plato to John of the Cross. I simply intend to indicate my preference for the metaphor of descent as more helpful. Nowadays, we come across truth about our divine condition more in Eckhart's descent into our Ground than in Plotinus's ascent toward the One. Some modes of that descent into the abyss are found in the philosophic-mystical experience of nothingness (for instance, in Plotinus, Eckhart, and Heidegger), in Nietzsche's nihilism, and in Zen's "Great Doubt."[38]

An additional reason for this preference is the fact that an authentic experience of God must include, at least at some point, a descent into the hell of evil. The locus of profound faith lies in the depths of undeserved suffering, oppression, betrayal. The harrowing test of hope lies there, at the foot of the cross. The holy is encountered in the curse that afflicts all sinners—a curse vividly felt on Good Friday and deemed by believers, not without some noble hesitation, to have been overcome on Easter Day.[39]

THE QUESTION OF HAPPINESS

If God can no longer be approached in the ancient and medieval representation of a hierarchical cosmos, the major place of encounter must be anthropological, as suggested previously. We notice such a perspective in Aquinas's first five questions of the first section of the Second Part in his *Summa Theologiae*. In these questions,

---

37. Thérèse de Lisieux, *Conseils et souvenirs recueillis par Soeur Geneviève de la Sainte Face* (Paris: Cerf and Desclée de Brouwer, 1979), 26.

38. On those authors and themes, see Roy, *Mystical Consciousness*, chaps. 4, 5, 9, and 10.

39. See Mt 28:17: "Some doubted."

independently of his hierarchical worldview, he shows himself to be thoroughly anthropological as he retrieves and supplements Aristotle's probing of happiness.[40]

Pascal too is very anthropological in his remarks on happiness and unhappiness:

There are only three sorts of people: those who have found God and serve him; those who are busy seeking him and have not found him; those who live without either seeking or finding him. The first are reasonable and happy, the last are foolish and unhappy, those in the middle are unhappy and reasonable.[41]

It is for the third group that Pascal wrote his *Pensées*. Like Aquinas, he proceeds from the problem of happiness to the necessity of the Good as ultimate end. The conclusion of his apologetics is best captured in the following statement: "The true good must be such that it may be possessed by all men at once without diminution or envy, and that no one should be able to lose it against his will."[42] His position stands in sharp contrast with the one adopted by his contemporary Thomas Hobbes, who asserts there is no highest good—namely, no *summum bonum*. For the latter, all individuals ruthlessly compete for the same limited goods, and there ensues "war of every man against every man."[43]

The bishops at the Second Vatican Council continued the gospel-inspired tradition of care for the welfare of the human race when they declared:

The joy and hope, the grief and anguish of the men and women of our time, especially of those who are poor or afflicted in any way, are the joy and

40. For a study of this anthropological factor in Thomas's theological creativity, see Johannes Baptist Metz, *Christliche Anthropozentrik: Über die Denkform des Thomas von Aquin* (Munich: Kösel Verlag, 1962; note Karl Rahner's approval in his "Einführender Essay" to Metz's book, 9–20.

41. Pascal, Pensée 160.

42. Pascal, Pensée 148. A similar statement had already been made by Aquinas in *Summa Theologiae* I-II, q. 28, a. 4, ad 2.

43. Thomas Hobbes, *Leviathan*, ed. Edwin Curly (Indianapolis: Hackett, 1994), chap. 6, §58, chap. 11, §1–3, chap. 13, §§3–9, 13, chap. 15, §3.

hope, the grief and anguish of followers of Christ as well. Nothing that is genuinely human fails to find an echo in their hearts. For theirs is a community composed of people who, united in Christ and guided by the Holy Spirit, press onwards towards the kingdom of the Father and are bearers of a message of salvation intended for all. That is why Christians cherish a feeling of deep solidarity with the human race and its history.[44]

As human beings raise fundamental questions that bear on the meaning and purpose of the universe, of history, and of their personal lives, they are in touch with their depths—namely, with their profound desire to understand and to be committed to values. They are concerned with the prospect of what is to come. The uncertainty of tomorrow is worrisome. They are anxious about the sort of future they are going to experience during their lifetime and, often more pointedly, about the sort of future their sons and daughters and their grandchildren will face. Will the young adults be able to actualize themselves as human beings?[45] Will they be happy? Will they be satisfied by the more and more frequent combination of part-time, low-paying jobs (especially for women)? Will their marital relationships be marked by misunderstandings, quarrels, and rejections? Will it be possible, for parents with young children, to reconcile family and work?

Many also find themselves conjecturing what kind of planet earth and what kind of global society they will bequeath to their children and descendants. Will there be sustainable development? Will true equality, fair competition, honest dialogue, and genuine peace prevail? Will poverty and sickness ever be eradicated? Will natural calamities or human atrocities (such as war and terrorism) ever be forestalled? Moreover, as many of them fight for a promulgation of new laws flowing from human rights and supported by court

44. "Pastoral Constitution on the Church in the Modern World" (*Gaudium et Spes*), no. 1, in *Documents of Vatican II*, ed. Austin P. Flannery, new rev. ed. (Grand Rapids, Mich.: Eerdmans, 1984). I have slightly amended the translation.

45. See Roy, *Self-Actualization and the Radical Gospel* (Collegeville, Minn.: Liturgical Press, 2002).

decisions, they are conscious of gigantic obstacles standing in the way of justice, and they doubt whether people will have the motivation required for their ideals to become reality.

More radically, lucid people entertain misgivings about the survival of the human race. Thus the sociologist Anthony Giddens has discussed "the *inevitability* of living with dangers which are *remote* from the control not only of individuals, but also of large organisations, including states; and which are *of high intensity* and *life-threatening* for millions of human beings and potentially for the whole of humanity."[46] He points out that this "awareness of risk" is shared by wide publics and that it includes "awareness of the limitations of expertise."[47] This worry is revealed by questions such as, can we sensibly aim at discovering a divine support, a reliable fulcrum that would lift humankind's spirit and enhance its pledge to a better future? Is there a far-reaching hope that is held out for humanity?

In the neo-Platonic cultures, hope did not have much weight. For example, in Augustine's *Enchiridion on Faith, Hope, and Love* there are only three chapters on hope, six on charity, and one hundred and five on faith.[48] Aquinas dedicated only six questions of his *Summa Theologiae* to hope, whereas he dwelled on faith for sixteen questions and on charity for twenty-four questions.

By contrast, midway into modernity, hope took on an enormous importance. In the course of the seventeenth century, science secured its method and embarked on engendering technological inventions that made human life less precarious and more enjoyable. Whatever the part of illusion, earthly happiness became a real possibility.[49] Perhaps for the first time in history, people ceased consider-

---

46. Anthony Giddens, *The Consequences of Modernity* (Stanford, Calif.: Stanford University Press, 1990), 131.

47. Giddens, *Consequences of Modernity*, 125.

48. St. Augustine, *The Enchiridion on Faith, Hope, and Love*, ed. Henry Paolucci, trans. J. F. Shaw (Chicago: Regnery Gateway, 1961).

49. See Paul Hazard, *The European Mind (1680–1715)*, trans. J. Lewis May (Cleveland: World, 1967), chap. 5, "Happiness on Earth."

ing the *vetera* (the old ways) as worthy of utter respect and began to prefer the *nova* (the new ways). In *"la querelle des anciens et des moderns,"* that is, in the debate that raged in France at the beginning of the eighteenth century between the Old School and the New School, the latter defeated the former. The spirit of change dislodged classicism's imposition of stability (as found, for instance, in Bossuet).[50] After the American and the French revolutions, and in the course of the industrial revolution, many people came to the conclusion that, thanks to science, technology, and politics, they could bring about considerable social transformations and thus determine their future.

Immanuel Kant formulates the novel import of hope toward the end of his *Critique of Pure Reason* in "On the Canon of Pure Reason," Second Section: "All interest of my reason (the speculative as well as the practical) is united in the following three questions: 1. What can I know? 2. What should I do? 3. What may I hope?"[51] To answer the third question, he constructs a metaphysics that, like his predecessors, situates happiness in the afterlife. His expectations concerning our earthly existence are restricted, as we can see in his musings on an eventual peaceful lawfulness worldwide. Nevertheless, he believes in the progress of the human race based on "a moral predisposition in the human race" or "a tendency and faculty in human nature for improvement."[52]

In *Religion within the Boundaries of Mere Reason* Kant offers a hermeneutics of religion that comes to grips with evil and hope. As regards this approach, Ricoeur writes, "the existential-historical condition of evil constitutes the challenge to which religion brings the

50. Hazard, *European Mind*, chaps. 1–2.

51. Immanuel Kant, *Critique of Pure Reason*, trans. Paul Guyer and Allen W. Wood (Cambridge: Cambridge University Press, 1998), A 804–5, B 832–3.

52. Kant, "The Conflict of the Faculties," Second Part, "An Old Question Raised Again: Is the Human Race Constantly Progressing?" in *Religion and Rational Theology*, trans. Allen W. Wood and George Di Giovanni (Cambridge: Cambridge University Press, 1996), 302 and 304; see also Kant, "Toward Perpetual Peace," in *Practical Philosophy*, trans. Mary J. Gregor and Allen Wood (Cambridge: Cambridge University Press, 1996), 311–51.

reply of an 'in spite of … ,' an 'even though. …' This tie between challenge and reply is the tie of hope." And he acknowledges the price that the Königsberg philosopher is willing to pay: "Kant manifests no interest for the Jesus of history, as we would put it today. The only thing that is important philosophically is the Christ of faith elevated to an idea or an ideal." Christ is an "archetype of a good intention."[53] Would the participle "reduced" be more appropriate than "elevated"?

For nineteenth-century thinkers the future is of the utmost interest. Indeed, the Danish philosopher Søren Kierkegaard writes:

> The person who is expecting something is occupied with the future. … This is precisely the greatness of human beings, the demonstration of their divine origin, that they are able to be occupied with this; because if there were no future, there would be no past, either, and if there were neither future nor past, then a human being would be in bondage like an animal, his head bowed to the earth, his soul captive to the service of the moment. … The ability to be occupied with the future is, then a sign of the nobility of human beings; the struggle with the future is the most ennobling.[54]

Karl Marx's prospects are a far cry from Kant's and Kierkegaard's, as he looks toward a radical political and economic transformation by virtue of which a collective happiness should ensue. As Nicholas Lash proposes in his insightful study of Marx, the issue is "a matter of hope."[55] In my judgment, the still immensely valuable point in Marx's contribution is the fact that consciousness in a great measure depends on one's position and interests in society. Thus a Christian theology of hope should never forget that economic, social, and political hope requires enormous efforts at consciousness-raising. Unfortunately, Marx himself and his disciples were farthest from being immune to self-deception. Virtually all practical applications of his

53. Ricoeur, "A Philosophical Hermeneutics of Religion: Kant," in *Figuring the Sacred*, 76 and 83.

54. Søren Kierkegaard, "The Expectancy of Faith," in *Eighteen Upbuilding Discourses*, ed. and trans. Howard V. Hong and Edna H. Hong (Princeton, N.J.: Princeton University Press, 1990), 17.

55. Nicholas Lash, *A Matter of Hope: A Theologian's Reflections on the Thought of Karl Marx* (London: Darton, Longman, and Todd, 1981), esp. chaps. 6, 17, and 18.

thought were tantamount to betrayals of human hope (in Russia, China, and other Communist countries).[56] This issue of overcoming illusion will be deferred until we come to chapter 6.

Closer to us, Ernst Bloch updates Marx's philosophy and supplements it with extraordinary descriptions of hope. In his magnum opus *The Principle of Hope*, written between 1938 and 1947 and revised in 1959, this learned observer of cultures takes his readers through perceptive, subtle, albeit sometimes cryptic, analyses of an enormous range of phenomena. He depicts fascinating instances of hope in the Bible, in Greek and Roman thought, in medieval writings, in European mores, symbols, beliefs, utopias, geographical explorations, technologies, literatures, paintings, architecture, music, cinema, and psychology, with shorter excursions into the American mind and even into non-Christian religions. All the striking facts he assembles testify to the paramount importance of hope throughout human cultures.

In his masterly "Introduction," Bloch brings together the subjective and the objective sides of hope. "Expectation, hope, intention towards possibility that has still not become: this is not only a basic feature of human consciousness, but, concretely corrected and grasped, a basic determination within objective reality as a whole." Something real in the universe grounds human hope: "The Not-Yet-Conscious in man belongs completely to the Not-Yet-Become, Not-Yet-Brought-Out, Manifested-Out in the world. Not-Yet-Conscious interacts and reciprocates with Not-Yet-Become, more specifically with what is approaching in history and in the world." The "Not-Yet-Become" is also called the "in-Front-of-Us" or the "Novum."[57]

This surely amounts to a bold ontological claim, which Bloch endeavors to justify by having recourse to the Aristotelian notion of matter as the fount of endless possibilities.

56. For a perceptive discussion of Marx's views, with one chapter on liberation theology, see Georges M.-M. Cottier, *Le conflit des espérances* (Paris: Desclée de Brouwer, 1977).

57. Ernst Bloch, *The Principle of Hope*, trans. Neville Plaice, Stephen Plaice, and Paul Knight (Cambridge, Mass.: MIT Press, 1986), 7, 13 and 6; see also 196–205 and 1323–25.

The Authentic or essence is that *which is not yet, which in the core of things drives towards itself, which awaits its genesis in the tendency-latency of process;* it is itself only now founded, objective-real—hope. And its name ultimately borders on "What-Is-in-possibility" in the Aristotelian sense and in a sense which goes far beyond Aristotle, on what is ostensibly the most certain thing there is: matter.[58]

About "the *process-world, the real world of hope* itself," he states, "this remains founded solely in matter, matter which is certainly moved in many forms."[59]

Regrettably, Bloch's hope is grounded neither metaphysically (despite his appeal to Aristotle's notion of matter) nor religiously. As far as the first (philosophical) problem is concerned, why should we assume that the evolutionary process will ever reach any happy outcome? Louis Dupré perceptively criticizes Bloch's position:

Such a concept of hope as *ideal* of the future needs an *ontological* basis if it is to be more than wishful thinking. Bloch fully realizes this and therefore posits what he calls an ontological priority of the future. Yet such a priority presupposes an over-arching unity which connects the future with the present and with the past. Horizontal transcendence can be established with certainty only if there is a *prior* (in the ontological sense) *vertical* transcendence which launches man on his journey into the future.[60]

For Dupré, a "*horizontal* transcendence"—that is, an "ideal of the future"—must be grounded in a "*vertical* transcendence." The latter posits "an over-arching unity" that founds the overall meaning of anthropological time, encompassing the past, the present, and the future. Without this philosophically—that is, rationally—established view of history, human hope cannot be more than a matter of irrational option.[61]

---

58. Bloch, *Principle of Hope*, 1373.

59. Bloch, *Principle of Hope*, 1374; for more detail, see 191 and 206–7.

60. Louis Dupré, "Hope and Transcendence," in *The God Experience*, ed. Joseph P. Whelan (New York: Newman Press, 1971), 222.

61. This kind of option is what Alasdair MacIntyre called "emotivism"; see MacIntyre, *After Virtue*, 2nd ed. (Notre Dame, Ind.: University of Notre Dame Press, 1984).

As far as the second (religious) problem is concerned, we may easily observe that the biblical foundation of hope greatly differs from Bloch's stance. Throughout Israel's history, the religious attitude of hope has been based on an unbreakable covenant between God and the Jewish people. We may also want to note that Bloch's ontological claim has been weakened by the fact that in his lengthy volumes he—himself a Jew—does not address the calamitous issue of the Shoah.[62] In fact, the permanent indeterminateness of Bloch's hope may incur the negative judgment pronounced by Nietzsche against hope: "Precisely because of its ability to keep the unfortunate in continual suspense, the Greeks considered hope the evil of evils, the truly insidious evil: it remained behind in the barrel of evils (Pandora's box)."[63]

In his *Theology of Hope* Jürgen Moltmann takes up Bloch's theme of the Novum.[64] According to Moltmann, God's message in the Bible turns its hearers to the future. Such temporal imagery stands in contrast to the neo-Platonic spatial imagery. As Ghislain Lafont points out, the ancient vertical symbol of "anagogy" as an ascent toward the One has yielded, in the course of modernity, to the horizontal symbol of "eisagogy"—that is, of the "movement towards" an absolute future.[65] This sense of movement explains and supports my decision to speak of religious hope as emerging from our depths and directing us toward a better world.

Moltmann also reminds us that the word of God topples received opinions about what reality can or cannot be. It triggers the emergence of fresh possibilities in human action. "Hope's statements of

62. Except for a brief mention Bloch's Principle of Hope, at 606. For a critical discussion of Bloch's philosophy, see Josef Pieper, *Hope and History*, trans. Richard Winston and Clara Winston (New York: Herder and Herder, 1969), 17, 61–76, and 88.

63. Friedrich Nietzsche, "The Antichrist," §23, in *The Portable Nietzsche*, trans. Walter Kaufmann (New York: Penguin, 1976), 591; see also Hesiod, *Works and Days*, ed. H. G. Evelyn-White (Cambridge, Mass.: Harvard University Press, 1950), 7.

64. Jürgen Moltmann, *Theology of Hope: On the Ground and the Implications of a Christian Eschatology*, trans. James W. Leitch (New York: Harper and Row, 1967), 16.

65. Ghislain Lafont, *Histoire théologique de l'Église catholique* (Paris: Cerf, 1994), 397n1.

promise, however, must stand in contradiction to the reality which can at present be experienced. They do not result from experiences, but are the condition for the possibility of new experiences."[66] Moltmann surely voices an important consideration here. Yet the incompatibility he sees between these two kinds of experience is irreconcilable with my thesis that a modicum of religiousness may facilitate the acceptance of a revelation. As a matter of fact, there are helpful religious experiences, sustained by divine grace, both before and after the assent of faith.

In 1947 two other German thinkers, Max Horkheimer and Theodor Adorno, coauthored an eye-opening study, *Dialectic of Enlightenment*, actually finished in 1944. As an antidote to Bloch's paean to hope, their cultural analyses are sobering. They document self-destructive tendencies that turn progress into its opposite. According to their account, the Enlightenment lapsed into troubling phenomena such as totalitarian mythologies, anti-Semitism, ruthless exercise of power, the positivism of administered societies, the nullification of the individuals in the face of economic forces, and the stultification of the masses due to a succession of amusements. Their thesis maintains that the Enlightenment, in its noble ideals of freedom and advancement, carried the germ of its disquieting regressions, beginning with the Terror that took place right after the French Revolution. They write, "What is at stake is not conservation of the past but the fulfilment of past hopes."[67]

So again the issue of hope becomes apposite and even urgent: can enlightened human reason, associated with good will, really counter the nemesis that political, administrative, and economic achievement carries with it? About twenty years ago the American Edward Tenner revisited the same phenomenon of "unintended conse-

---

66. Moltmann, *Theology of Hope*, 18; see 103.
67. Max Horkheimer and Theodor W. Adorno, *Dialectic of Enlightenment: Philosophical Fragments*, ed. Gunzelin Schmid Noerr, trans. Edmund Jephcott (Stanford, Calif.: Stanford University Press, 2002), xvii.

quences" wrought by technology, more recently in the domains of health, the environment, agriculture, workplaces, and sports.[68]

In one of his last interviews, Hans-Georg Gadamer avowed, "man cannot live without hope, that is the only sentence I would defend without any restriction."[69] And yet we are threatened by an incapacity to hope with firmness. The second half of the twentieth century witnessed the decline of ideologies, and consequently overall thought-worlds are now met with skepticism. Our contemporaries display a powerless indecision on the subject of religious truth. They seem resigned to be surrounded, indeed permeated, by uncertainty. Undoubtedly they experience a hope deficit.

This failure of hope is particularly damaging to the poor—that is, to those who do not benefit from the rewards of the international market. The mounting strength of globalization more and more reduces the possibility of deliberately planned social entities, limited in size, as Jean-Jacques Rousseau and Ivan Illich envisaged them. The liberation theologians remind us that unless we are sensitive to the plight of "non-persons," our feeble readiness to change unfair regulations and structures more often than not amounts to passive wishing or lip service. From the viewpoint of the Christian message of salvation, it is not merely one's own individual prospect or one's own nation's future that is at stake, but principally the quandary of the disadvantaged masses.[70]

The ability to believe in hope has a psychological side that can only be mentioned briefly here. Following W. W. Meissner, who bases his reflections on Erikson, we must point out that the psycho-spiritual attitudes of faith and hope are tied to the resolution of the first psy-

68. Edward Tenner, *Why Things Bite Back: Technology and the Revenge of Unintended Consequences* (New York: Knopf, 1996).

69. Quoted by Jean Grondin, "The New Proximity between Theology and Philosophy," in *Between the Human and the Divine: Philosophical and Theological Hermeneutics*, ed. Andrzej Wiercinski (Toronto: Hermeneutic Press, 2002), 101; originally reported by the newspaper *Rhein-Neckar-Zeitung*, February 11, 2002.

70. On hope, see Roy, *Coherent Christianity*, chaps. 4 and 5.

chosocial crisis of human life—namely, the antinomy between trust and mistrust.[71] During this crisis, the infant does, or fails to, experience the trustworthiness of the mother. There can emerge a basic trust in oneself as well as a capacity to entrust oneself to others. Depending on the extent to which such a trust is established, it is easier or more difficult to respond to the gifts of hope and faith. In hope, one holds fast to the divine promises, sure that one's most profound wishes shall not be deceived. In faith, a judgment of value regarding the trustworthiness of a caring God leads to the acceptance of propositions concerning the divine plan of salvation.

CONCLUDING REMARKS

The theses of this chapter were, first, that there are reasons systematic theology ought to adopt a subjective approach, which, however, does not preclude the inquiring subject's pursuit of objectivity; second, that the method adopted should be anthropological—that is, focused on human living; third, that the overall context in which we weigh the possibilities of faith should be not a hierarchical ascent toward a passively received Truth, but a phenomenological descent into the human depths; and fourth, that the current worry—and for some, the deep anxiety—about the underpinnings of a grounded hope constitute the best starting point for an orderly account of faith. All these elements will contribute to shaping our systematic elaboration.

71. See W. W. Meissner, *Life and Faith: Psychological Perspectives on Religious Experience* (Washington, D.C.: Georgetown University Press, 1987), esp. chap. 4 and chaps. 10–14; and Roy, "Toward a Psychology of Grace: W. W. Meissner's Contribution," *Theological Studies* 57 (1996): 322–31.

CHAPTER 2

The Bible's Challenge to Human Wisdom

༷

In their journey toward faith or toward a more mature faith, a good number of hikers walk with two legs. The first leg is human hope; the second leg is the biblical message addressed to humanity. Trekkers who, without having responded yet to the summons of the Bible, are nevertheless seriously thinking about the human predicament, may be considered (from a Christian perspective) as walking with one leg. Of them, Clement of Alexandria wrote, "Those who do anything or utter anything without the word of truth are like people struggling to walk without a foothold."[1] By contrast, many of the faithful whose lives have been formed by Scripture have the advantage of having met the challenge of listening to the word of God. Such a challenge to human wisdom is most beneficial, since it considerably enlarges the readers' horizon.

Contrary to the way Paul Tillich understood the "method of correlation,"[2] biblical revelation does not give us a set of answers simply to *our* questions. It also puts questions to people of all ages.

---

1. Clement of Alexandria, *The Exhortation to the Greeks*, book I, chap. 7, trans. G. W. Butterworth (Cambridge, Mass.: Harvard University Press, 1982), 169.

2. Paul Tillich, *Systematic Theology* (Chicago: University of Chicago Press, 1951), 1:59–66.

For Christians, the principal question is, of course, "Who do you say that I am?"[3] In his hermeneutical idiom, David Tracy states:

Christian theology is the attempt to establish mutually critical correlations between an interpretation of the Christian tradition and an interpretation of the contemporary situation.... Once that concrete interpretation begins, all earlier situational analyses are also put at risk by the conversation itself. It is not only our present answers but also our questions which are risked when we enter a conversation with a classic text.[4]

The experience of being "put at risk" in one's "situational analyses" amounts to a demanding test. I will try to convey the strength of this challenge by bringing in pertinent scriptural data. The first section asks how the Bible can be read not only devotionally or exegetically, but theologically; we must identify a practice of theology that is apt to relate the components of faith that are discovered in the Bible. Pushing forward the theme of the preceding chapter, the second section of this chapter presents biblical faith from the perspective of hope and describes several of its characteristics. The third section contradistinguishes two basic attitudes in the face of revelation: faith and unfaith, or more precisely blindness and illumination. The fourth section offers a survey of faith according to John's Gospel.

Although several references will be made to St. Paul, there is no specific section on him, because, as I said in my introduction, this would necessitate entering into the theology of grace and salvation—a topic connected with faith, but distinguishable from it. Treating it here, especially given its complexities, would distract from my purposes in this book.

READING THE BIBLE THEOLOGICALLY

For those of my readers familiar with Bernard Lonergan's differentiation of the theological tasks, I want to clarify my input in the col-

3. Mk 8:29a.
4. David Tracy, *A Short History of the Interpretation of the Bible*, by Robert M. Grant and David Tracy, 2nd ed., rev. and enlarged (Philadelphia: Fortress, 1984), 170 and 173.

laborative task of reading the Bible theologically. This task necessitates we engage in historical and contemporary theology—that is, in all the functional specialties, beginning with modern exegesis. However, my enterprise here is mostly a contribution to the specialty he calls "foundations," which is based on the specialties he calls "interpretation," "history," and "dialectic." Let us note that as preparing the ground for the specialty "systematics," "foundations" is already incipiently systematic. This is evident if we pay attention to Lonergan's delineating of the categories already present in foundations, which recur in systematics.[5] So we may consider foundations as the first part of systematics. In this section, I will speak of systematics or as theology in general as requiring biblical scholarship and all the other specialties, with a focus on foundations and systematics.

As a result, this chapter does not take any of the approaches typical of modern exegesis. My treatment of the biblical insights is conditioned by the preoccupations of an author engaged in the part of theology concerned with an orderly presentation of Christian faith, with its conceptual terms and relations. However, Lonergan's understanding of theological method considerably differs from the modern scholastic practice of theology, whose starting point began with council pronouncements. On the contrary, sound theological reflection ever commences with meditation on the Bible and continues with scholarly exegesis. Nevertheless, theology is composed of more than biblical and historical scholarship. It calls for a comprehensive understanding of a given subject matter. Still, it must remain biblical in its own way, which will be discussed shortly.

In accordance with such requirements, a theological inquiry into the Bible ought to proceed in two phases. The first phase consists in reading it as an ensemble of literary texts. The Scriptures

5. See Bernard J. F. Lonergan, *Method in Theology* (1972; repr. University of Toronto Press, 2003), ch. 11, sec. 5–8. I speak of "foundational-systematic" understanding in Roy, "The Viability of the Category of Religious Experience in Bernard Lonergan's Theology," *Method: Journal of Lonergan Studies*, New Series, no. 6 (2015):99–117.

belong to a vast array of genres: narratives, exhortations, confessions of faith, lyric or epic poetry, prayers, symbolic presentations of transcendent experiences, and so forth. I assume that the readers have already examined—or will examine someday—works by exegetes. I don't wish to substitute for those experts, who indeed have helped me enormously in understanding the Bible. Historical criticism gives us information about the actual contexts in which the texts were composed and handed on with many adaptations in the course of approximately seven hundred years (roughly between the year 600 B.C.E. and the year 100 C.E.). Literary analysis makes us appreciate what Cornelius Ernst, inspired by Wittgenstein's notion of "language-game," calls a "web of association," in which one word ("grace," for instance) is creatively linked with other words in order to mean various things.[6]

This first phase—historical criticism and literary analysis—does not immediately warrant a dogmatic comprehension of any component of Christian belief. It is paramount to register the fact that the biblical writings are not meant to directly yield well-defined creeds. Even the very few faith confessions that are fairly clear (for example, 1 Corinthians 15:3–5) contain verbs that do not denote something merely physical (for example, "he was raised" and "he appeared"); therefore, the faith confessions stand in need of interpretation. The church's doctrinal definitions hinged on complicated historical mediations; they were prepared by questions and insights that came up after the apostolic times. During such periods of gestation, the Scriptures usually functioned as guidelines, often negative, from which believers learned at least what not to say. And insofar as what the bishops declared in councils is concerned, its positive content was not the outcome of proof-text quotations, but rather of cultural

---

6. Cornelius Ernst, *Multiple Echo: Explorations in Theology*, ed. Fergus Kerr and Timothy Radcliffe (London: Darton, Longman and Todd, 1979), 21, and Ernst, *The Theology of Grace* (Cork: Mercier Press; Notre Dame, Ind.: University of Notre Dame Press, 1974), 14; see also Roy, "Cornelius Ernst's Theological Seeds," *New Blackfriars* 85 (2004): 459–70.

transpositions steered by a determination to better appropriate their respective faith traditions.

With such conciliar clarifying pronouncements and patristic ruminations, elements of systematic theology began to take shape. This is the second stage, with which we are concerned here. It goes beyond the first stage, in which the several aspects of faith are simply related *to us*, according to Aquinas's "order of discovery," or in what Lonergan calls a "descriptive" manner. By relating the several aspects of faith *to one another*, the second stage—namely, systematics— endeavors to be "the order of teaching," according to Thomas Aquinas's practice, or "explanatory," in Lonergan's sense.[7] Its systematic character will become apparent in chapter 3, on Aquinas, and in subsequent chapters.[8]

Contemporary theology's assignment is not an easy one, given Scripture scholars' quasi-unanimous insistence on the irreducible variety of religious standpoints in the Bible. Taking account of this variety, theologians face the difficult task of avoiding both classicism, which goes along with asserting a spurious uniformity, and radical pluralism, which entails a relativism that most of the time puts an end to exchanging arguments in discussions.[9] Nor can they find in "the canon within the canon" a real solution, because such a canon singles out one principle (or very few principles) that subjugates all other aspects of belief and thus brings about one-sidedness. For instance, Luther's focus on the cross as the canon within the

7. Lonergan, *Collected Works*, vol. 3, *Insight: A Study of Human Understanding*, ed. Frederick E. Crowe and Robert M. Doran (Toronto: University of Toronto Press, 1992), 101, 201, 419, 562; Lonergan, *Method in Theology*, 346.

8. In *Metaphysics and the God of Israel: Systematic Theology of the Old and New Testaments* (Grand Rapids, Mich.: Baker Academic, 2006), Neil B. MacDonald employs "two fundamental explanatory concepts," namely, YHWH's self-determination in his creative, dialoguing, and saving act and Israel's historical experience of YHWH's acting in its life (see esp. 100–101 and 121). MacDonald acknowledges being indebted to Barth, von Rad, Westermann, Childs, Wolterstorff, and others; however, he does not seem to be aware that his metaphysic owes much to Schelling, whose name is not mentioned in his name index.

9. See Roy, *Engaging the Thought of Bernard Lonergan* (Montreal: McGill-Queen's University Press, 2016), study 7.

canon operated inflexibly without lending itself to being relativized and resituated in a larger whole by other believers' experience and by systematics. Without discarding Luther's interpretations, systematicians must complement them by drawing other norms out of the church's reading of the Bible. We shall see presently how it is possible to explicate such norms in a manner that is supple and fruitful.

Adopting the exegete Raymond Brown's distinction between "what Scripture meant" (at the time it was composed) and "what Scripture means" (in the church's post-biblical understanding),[10] we may say that the former is what exegetes have to ascertain about the past (with a varying degree of probability) and the latter is what believers must articulate for today (with uneven success). Accordingly, although systematic theologians take into serious consideration the results of scriptural scholarship, they must avoid being purely biblical—that is, ever staying within the ambit of biblical thought. They cannot rest content with repeating those results or with looking for one-for-one equivalences between biblical affirmations and conceptual statements; given that biblical affirmations and conceptual statements pertain to different language-games, there can be no point-by-point correspondences. Although the notions coined in a systematic treatment of particular topics can reproduce the same themes as in the Bible, they cannot reproduce them in the same order and with the same meanings. What makes them different is the novelty of post-biblical questions and of the insights these questions have triggered.

Present-day theology's duty consists in meeting the issues of our time head-on. This is the reason it has to be innovative, albeit not in the field of doctrines, which are revealed by God, but in the

10. Raymond E. Brown, *The Critical Meaning of the Bible* (New York: Paulist Press, 1981), 37. Brown's distinction was disputed by Marcel Dumais, "Sens de l'Écriture: Réexamen à la lumière de l'herméneutique philosophique et des approches littéraires récentes," *New Testament Studies* 45 (1999):314–16; yet I think the distinction can be maintained, provided "what Scripture meant" includes a plurality of significations, and not only the literal sense.

field of meanings, which it can work out with some leeway. (This distinction between a doctrine and its meaning, or between truth and meaning, will be clarified and employed in chapters 5, 6, and 7.) The task of systematics demands the setting up of a new horizon in which the elements of belief are interconnected.

On the one hand, then, systematics turns out to be constructive, inasmuch as it erects a conceptual frame of reference, a conceptuality (*Begrifflichkeit*), the components of which are drawn from secular culture (Stoicism, Platonism, neo-Platonism, Aristotelianism, modern European philosophies, or one of the myriad non-Western forms of thought). Each of those frameworks specifies one type of theology, with accentuations that diverge from what is stressed by the several biblical currents or by other types of theology. It is necessary to recognize this plurality and, in particular, to be in principle open to conceptual emphases that are not found in Scripture. The fact that a thinker (say, Thomas Aquinas) employs a nonbiblical conceptuality does not make him unfaithful to divine revelation. Justifiably, however, the conceptuality in question must be friendly both to the insights offered by the scriptural writers and to the "available believable" (Paul Ricoeur's *le croyable disponible*) of the culture in which the theologian operates.[11]

On the other hand, theology's mission cannot be tantamount to pure creative thinking on religion à la Hegel—whatever his remarkable suggestions—whose proud reason speculatively reconstructed the contents of Christianity. Rather, theology must humbly put its systematization at the service of a return to the Bible, of a rereading of the Scriptures, which ever remains the primary text. Since it wants to be Christian, theology needs to be permanently anchored in the Bible. It is aware of having to respond to scriptural norms—namely, to principles that regulate any post-biblical account of belief.

So, we must ask, how are biblical norms derived? These norms

11. Ricoeur, "The Critique of Religion," in *The Philosophy of Paul Ricoeur: An Anthology of His Work*, ed. Charles E. Reagan and David Stewart (Boston: Beacon Press, 1978), 220.

are apprehended in prayerful reading of Holy Scripture (*lectio divina*), in liturgy,[12] in preaching and catechesis, in church councils, in lives of the saints, in reflections offered by prominent theologians of the past, especially those who have been held to be trustworthy by the churches (for instance the great synthesizers such as Augustine, Maximus Confessor, John of Damascus, Thomas Aquinas, Gregory Palamas), and in "the consensus of centrist exegetes."[13] Inevitably, however, a certain arbitrariness (hopefully restrained) affects the choice of biblical themes by systematicians. This limitation is due to their praiseworthy effort to address the concerns and questions of their time in a sound process of inculturation.

Biblical norms are often operative in a fashion that is partly unformulated—what Michael Polanyi calls "the tacit dimension," which he sees at work in the scientific enterprise.[14] They make up a rule of faith (*regula fidei*) or a sense of faith (*sensus fidei*), which is the outcome of listening to the voice of the Holy Spirit, as believers meditate on the word of God and on events in their lives.[15] People who are deeply attached to Jesus Christ instinctively know, without the norms having been spelled out in their minds, the essentials (not necessarily the details) of what their faith includes, what it entails, and what it rules out.[16] The identity of any religion calls for discerning which attitudes and doctrines belong to it. Hence the usefulness of defining its meanings in pronouncements that set the boundaries of the acceptable. In contrast to this orthodoxy, heresy amounts to arbitrary choice among tenets available at the marketplace of ideas.

12. See Geoffrey Wainwright, *Doxology: The Praise of God in Worship, Doctrine and Life* (London: Epworth, 1980).

13. As Gerald O'Collins and Daniel Kendall call them (meaning that those exegetes are neither on the right nor on the left of the spectrum), in *The Bible for Theology: Ten Principles for the Theological Use of Scripture* (New York: Paulist Press, 1997), 6, 25–27, and 38.

14. Michael Polanyi, *The Tacit Dimension* (Garden City, N.Y.: Doubleday, 1966).

15. "Dogmatic Constitution on the Church" (*Lumen Gentium*), §12, in *Documents of Vatican II*, ed. Austin P. Flannery, new rev. ed. (Grand Rapids, Mich.: Eerdmans, 1984).

16. See the International Theological Commission, "*Sensus Fidei* in the Life of the Church" (2014).

FAITH FROM THE VIEWPOINT
OF HOPE

Although the authors who contributed to the composition of the Bible did not envisage any eventual scientific handling of their materials, I will now venture, with the intellectual sensitivity of someone involved mostly in the functional specialty named "foundations," to single out scriptural themes that will guide my elaborations as well as my critique of numerous authors throughout this book.

Let us begin, as we did in our preceding chapter, with hope for the future. To the exiled Jews in Babylon, God declares, "I will fulfill to you my promise and bring you back to this place [Jerusalem]. For surely I know the plans I have for you, says the Lord, plans for your welfare and not for harm, to give you a future with hope."[17] Interestingly, from his Jewish standpoint, the author of the Letter to the Ephesians considers the Gentiles as being without hope. To pagans who have become Christian, he writes, "You were at that time [prior to your conversion] without Christ, being aliens from the commonwealth of Israel, and strangers to the covenants of promise, having no hope and without God in the world."[18]

Two Hebrew terms indicate that Jewish faith is very much a matter of hope. The root *batah* conveys the idea of trustworthiness, upon which faith can lean and rest with confidence and security. Thus the Israelites can depend on their mighty Lord and entrust themselves to his support throughout their history, as was the case in their liberation from Egypt. God's response to their plight ("I know their sufferings, and I have come down to deliver them") elicits faith as trust.[19] In turn, the chosen people are called to prove themselves reliable and dependable. This sense is frequent in the Psalms.

17. Jer 29:10b–11. On hope in the Hebrew Scriptures, see Roy, *Coherent Christianity*, chap. 5.

18. Eph 2:12.

19. Ex 3:7c–8a.

The other root, *aman*, suggests the idea of solidity, firmness, and fidelity, based on a God in whom one finds sureness and certainty. Faith (*he'emin*) denotes a constancy based on divine truth or faithfulness (*emet*), which establishes a stable relationship—namely, the covenant. The Eternal One is the faithful par excellence. In a covenantal situation, both God and the people are expected to be faithful—that is, to keep their promises.

The prophet Isaiah tells us that Ahaz, then king of Judah, in great fear of the kings of Aram and of Ephraim, wanted to provide human safeguards, such as fortifications and military alliances. Yet the prophet proclaimed, "It [the capture of Jerusalem] shall not stand, and it shall not come to pass.... If you do not stand firm in faith, you shall not stand at all."[20] And Third Isaiah defines God himself as "faithfulness."[21]

In the New Testament, because of his indefectibly faithful love, Jesus Christ is called "the Amen, the faithful and true witness."[22] This Amen grounds the coming-to-pass of the divine promises:

As surely as God is faithful, our word to you has not been "Yes and No." For the Son of God, Jesus Christ, whom we proclaimed among you, Silvanus and Timothy and I, was not "Yes and No"; but in him it is always "Yes." For in him every one of God's promises is a "Yes." For this reason it is through him that we say the "Amen," to the glory of God.[23]

St. Paul considers Abraham to be "the father of all who believe."[24] He explains:

Hoping against hope, he believed that he would become "the father of many nations," according to what was said, "so numerous shall your descendants be." He did not weaken in faith when he considered his own body, which was already as good as dead (for he was about a hundred years old), or when he considered the barrenness of Sarah's womb. No distrust made

---

20. Is 7:7 and 9.
21. 65:16.
22. Rv 3:14; see Rv 1:5, 19:11; 2 Cor 1:18–20, and 1 Tm 6:13.
23. 2 Cor 1:18–20.
24. Rom 4:11b.

him waver concerning the promise of God, but he grew strong in his faith as he gave glory to God, being fully convinced that God was able to do what he had promised.[25]

Chapter 6 of the Letter to the Hebrews tells us that our hope is grounded in a divine oath:

When God made a promise to Abraham, because he had no one greater by whom to swear, he swore by himself, saying, "I will surely bless you and multiply you." ... When God desired to show even more clearly to the heirs of the promise the unchangeable character of his purpose, he guaranteed it by an oath, so that through two unchangeable things, in which it is impossible that God would prove false, we who have taken refuge might be strongly encouraged to seize the hope set before us. We have this hope, a sure and steadfast anchor of the soul.[26]

Further on in the same letter, the author speaks of the "full assurance of faith."[27] In chapter 11 he defines faith (*pistis*) as "the assurance of things hoped for, the conviction of things not seen" (v. 1), and he proceeds to eulogize the ancestors who had faith. Abraham receives the longest praise (vv. 8–12 and 17–19). "By faith Abraham obeyed ... and he set out, not knowing where he was going" (v. 8). "For he looked forward" to the future (v. 10), and "he considered him [God] faithful who had promised" (v. 11). In addition to the numerous witnesses mentioned, Jesus is presented as "the pioneer and perfecter (*archēgos kai teleiōtēs*, in the Greek nominative) of the faith," since he "endured the cross, disregarding its shame, and has taken his seat at the right hand of the throne of God."[28]

Another trait of Christian faith is that it is a hope founded on the resurrection of Jesus. "If Christ has not been raised, then our proclamation has been in vain and your faith has been in vain."[29] However, the New Testament does not contain any narrative of Jesus ris-

25. Rom 4:18–21.
26. Heb 6:13–14 and 17–19; see Gn 22:16–17 and Ti 1:2.
27. Heb 10:22.
28. Heb 12:2.
29. 1 Cor 15:14.

ing from the dead and moving out of the tomb. Instead, and more modestly, it contains narratives of Jesus appearing to his disciples. One of those reports is particularly indicative, as it notes, "When they saw him, they worshiped him; but some doubted."[30] Before his passion, commenting on lack of faith among the wealthy, Jesus had already sternly stated, "Neither will they be convinced even if someone rises from the dead."[31] Which is to say that after his resurrection, the presence of the transformed Jesus was not evident. Recognizing him as both the same man and the exalted Christ and Lord required more—namely, spiritual illumination.

During their journey with Jesus toward a village called Emmaus, his two companions told him they had put their trust in a certain Jesus and had been immensely disappointed. Seeing that they lacked the kind of insight at the core of faith, Jesus rebuked them: "Oh, how foolish you are, and how slow of heart to believe all that the prophets have declared! Was it not necessary that the Messiah should suffer these things and then enter into his glory?"[32]

In the Synoptics, Jesus asks his disciples to trust God's power at work in himself and to accept his own words. In Luke's Gospel, Mary is the exemplar of the believers: "Blessed is she who believed that there would be a fulfillment of what was spoken to her by the Lord."[33] She identifies with the poor of Yahweh (the *Anawim*) as she proclaims, "My soul magnifies the Lord, and my spirit rejoices in God my Savior, for he has looked with favor on the lowliness of his servant."[34]

These numerous texts from the Bible evidence the intrinsic link between hope and faith. The connecting idea is reliability on the part of a loyal, dependable, indefectible, and powerful God who is faith-worthy because he is trustworthy.

30. Mt 28:17; compare with Lk 24:37–38 and 41.
31. Lk 16:31.
32. Lk 24:25–26.
33. Lk 1:45; see also Lk 11:28.
34. Lk 1:46–48a.

BLINDNESS AND ILLUMINATION

The evangelists Matthew and Luke underscore the difficulty, on the part of "wise and intelligent people," to understand what God has revealed in Jesus Christ:

> Jesus said, "I thank you, Father, Lord of heaven and earth, because you have hidden these things from wise and intelligent people and have revealed them to infants; yes, Father, for such was your gracious will. All things have been handed over to me by my Father; and no one knows the Son except the Father, and no one knows the Father except the Son and anyone to whom the Son chooses to reveal him."[35]

Clement of Alexandria reads verse 25 of this excerpt as follows: "The Educator and Teacher is there naming us little ones, meaning that we are more ready for salvation than the worldly wise who, believing themselves wise, have blinded their own eyes."[36]

St. Paul uncovers such a dynamics of self-deception:

> Those who are perishing ... refused to love the truth and so be saved. For this reason God sends them a powerful delusion, leading them to believe what is false, so that all who have not believed the truth but took pleasure in unrighteousness will be condemned.[37]

St. Paul also starkly highlights the challenge to human wisdom:

> The message about the cross is foolishness to those who are perishing, but to us who are being saved it is the power of God. For it is written, "I will destroy the wisdom of the wise, and the discernment of the discerning I will thwart." ... We proclaim Christ crucified, a stumbling block to Jews and foolishness to Gentiles, but to those who are the called, both Jews and Greeks, Christ the power of God and the wisdom of God. For God's foolishness is wiser than human wisdom, and God's weakness is stronger than human strength.[38]

35. Mt 11:25–27; see also Lk 10:21–22.
36. Clement of Alexandria, *Christ the Educator* (*Paidagōgos*), book I, chap. 6, trans. Simon P. Wood (New York: Fathers of the Church, 1954), 31.
37. 2 Thes 2:10–12.
38. 1 Cor 1:18–19:23–25.

Jesus proclaims the need for conversion (*metanoia*—namely, a change of mind), given the imminent arrival of God's reign: "The time is fulfilled and the kingdom of God has come near; repent and believe in the good news."[39] Matthew sees the kingdom of justice as self-evolving in a progressive development, like a seed that bears fruit, or like yeast mixed with flour that leavens, while some people refuse to join in and will be condemned.[40]

Luke and the author of the book of Revelation both highlight the social reversal that the coming of the kingdom brings about.[41] The second Letter of Peter envisages very dramatic events: on "the day of God ... the heavens will be set ablaze and dissolved, and the elements will melt with fire. But, in accordance with his promise, we wait for new heavens and a new earth, where righteousness is at home."[42] Although New Testament perspectives are so varied that it is impossible to determine in detail the content of that great hope, one thing is certain: the Spirit of the risen Christ already makes a difference within history, and, when Christ returns, he will fulfill the covenant with the faithful.

Hope is inseparable from faith. The Scottish philosopher John Macmurray observes that for Jesus, faith is the opposite of fear.[43] "Have faith" goes hand in hand with "fear not."[44] His point is well taken: "To 'believe,' or to 'have faith,' means not to be frightened. In that case, faith must mean something like courage, or confidence, or trust."[45] Regrettably, however, he does not realize that this faith has an object, be it God, or Jesus, or the good news, even if, in the gospels, the verb "to believe" (*pisteuein*) most of the time has no complement. As Edward O'Connor remarks, "There was no need

39. Mk 1:15.
40. Mt 13, 25.
41. Lk 1:46–55, 6:20–26; Rv 5, 7, 11–12, 14, 18, and 21–22.
42. 2 Pt 3:12–13.
43. Mt 8:26; 14:30–31.
44. Mt 10:26.
45. John Macmurray, *Ye Are My Friends* and *To Save from Fear* (London: Quaker Home Service, 1979), 6.

to spell out in detail to Whom it [the verb "to believe"] referred."[46]
This faith trust is not sightless. Jesus' pedagogy consists in putting
on view symbolic gestures (for instance, meals with sinners), riddles
(for instance, the Temple, which he will rebuild), parables, all of
which offer hints and clues leading to potential insights.[47]

For Luke, however, one of the chief obstacles to faith is greed.

The Pharisees, who were lovers of money, heard all this, and they ridiculed
him. So he said to them, "You are those who justify yourselves in the sight
of others; but God knows your hearts; for what is prized by human beings
is an abomination in the sight of God."[48]

It is clear that the minority of those who amass money, often in a dis-
honest manner, at the expense of the vast majority, and who enjoy
this earthly life in an inordinate way, without respect for other human beings, resent hearing the disciples of Jesus proclaim his radical
message: "Blessed are you who are poor, for yours is the kingdom of
God."[49] And the two parables about rich men are stern warnings.[50]

The Synoptics all agree that among Jesus' listeners, many remained blind. Inspired by Isaiah 6:9–10, Jesus is reported to have
said to those around him, "To you has been given the secret of the
kingdom of God, but for those outside, everything comes in parables, in order that they may indeed look, but not perceive, and may
indeed listen, but not understand, so that they may not turn again
and be forgiven."[51] However, a more serious charge—that of un-
truthfulness—is forcefully expressed in the controversy between
him and the Pharisees, scribes, and lawyers. "Woe to you lawyers!
For you have taken away the key of knowledge; you did not enter
yourselves, and you hindered those who were entering."[52]

46. Edward D. O'Connor, *Faith in the Synoptic Gospels: A Problem in the Correlation
of Scripture and Theology* (Notre Dame, Ind.: University of Notre Dame Press, 1961), 4.
47. Ben F. Meyer, *The Aims of Jesus* (London: SCM Press, 1979).
48. Lk 16:14–15.
49. Lk 6:20.
50. Jn 12:15–21, 16:19–31.
51. Mk 4:11–12.
52. Lk 11:52.

In Matthew 23, Jesus calls the scribes and Pharisees "hypocrites." Raymund Schwager proposes an explanation for their hypocrisy: they refuse Jesus' message without acknowledging that they are behaving in exactly the same manner as their ancestors. At the same time, they disapprove of their ancestors for having rejected the prophets' message.[53]

> Woe to you, scribes and Pharisees, hypocrites! For you build the tombs of the prophets and decorate the graves of the righteous, and you say, "If we had lived in the days of our ancestors, we would not have taken part with them in shedding the blood of the prophets." Thus you testify against yourselves that you are descendants of those who murdered the prophets.[54]

Furthermore, assisted by René Girard's insights into the sources of violence, Schwager detects a murderous intent in Jesus' adversaries:

> The violent remain unconscious of the projection of their own aggressions upon others. But when revelation brings the hidden tendency to light, they are confronted with the decision either to recognize the truth of their own action or to reject the truth out of *deliberate stubbornness* and thus succumb to hypocrisy and deceit. The scribes and Pharisees already had a long history of revelation to look back on and could learn from their fathers' example how human beings succumb to blind violence. The Old Testament writings offered them considerable insight into the mechanism of violence that leads to self-deception. Yet they did not accept the warnings.[55]

More will be said on this issue of self-induced blindness when we introduce similar writings from the Johannine corpus. However, a remark is in order at this point. The New Testament does not teach that this phenomenon of self-deception is confined to the scribes and Pharisees. They are represented here as characters in a drama, thanks to which readers of the gospels may, at least partly, recognize themselves, uncover their hidden misery, and repent. In other words, even though those compositions presuppose a historical substratum,

53. Raymund Schwager, *Must There Be Scapegoats? Violence and Redemption in the Bible*, trans. Maria L. Assad (New York: Crossroad, 2000), 149–54.

54. Mt 23:29–31; see also Mt 32–37a.

55. Schwager, *Must There Be Scapegoats?*, 151.

they are not exact historical data but rather warnings primarily addressed to those who, whether Christians or non-Christians, would read those texts and apply them to their own lives.

Incidentally, it is to Jewish Christians that James issues this admonition:

Be doers of the word, and not merely hearers who deceive themselves. For if any are hearers of the word and not doers, they are like those who look at themselves in a mirror; for they look at themselves and, on going away, immediately forget what they were like. But those who look into the perfect law, the law of liberty, and persevere, being not hearers who forget but doers who act—they will be blessed in their doing.[56]

Overcoming blindness requires an experience of illumination.[57] It is a passage "out of darkness into God's marvelous light."[58] "Once you were darkness, but now in the Lord you are light."[59] This experience coincides with having a share in Christ's resurrection: "Sleeper, awake! Rise from the dead, and Christ will shine on you."[60] Furthermore, there is a specifically Christian form of gnosis—namely, the glory reflected in the suffering Jesus, in the trials of the apostle Paul, and in the reception of the gospel by Paul's addressees—all of these being the mirror or the image onto which the glory is reflected:[61] "It is the God who said, 'Let light shine out of darkness,' who has shone in our hearts to give the light of the knowledge (*gnōseōs*) of the glory of God in the face of Jesus Christ."[62] The light glows inward and outward, both in our hearts and in the face of Jesus Christ. It yields a knowing that is the result of inner and outer conditions.

56. Jas 1:22–24.

57. Heb 6:4; 10:32.

58. 1 Pt 2:9.

59. Eph 5:8. My treatment of the Pauline corpus is selective, since it does not include the dialectic of law and grace, which, if incorporated into this book, would turn it into Christian ethics rather than a theology of faith and revelation.

60. Eph 5:14.

61. See N. T. Wright, *The Climax of the Covenant: Christ and the Law in Pauline Theology* (Minneapolis: Fortress Press, 1992), chap. 9, "Reflected Glory: 2 Corinthians 3:18."

62. 2 Cor 4:6; see also 3:7–4:6.

Because of Paul's general emphasis on faith as knowing, we must not construe "the obedience of faith" as a military obedience,[63] but as "giving ear" and "listening" (as the Greek *hypakoē* and the Latin *oboedire* both suggest) to the good news. For Paul, such listeners receive understanding. Speaking about the faithful, he wishes that "they may have all the riches of assured understanding and have the knowledge of God's mystery, that is, Christ himself, in whom are hidden all the treasures of wisdom and knowledge."[64] Paul here underlines the centrality of Christ for people's hope and faith.

The experience of being challenged by the divine truth manifested in Jesus crucified is dreadfully unsettling. The first two chapters of Paul's First Letter to the Corinthians dramatically reflect the contrast and the clash between human and divine wisdom. Gerd Theissen observes that these chapters evince a formidable intellectual struggle that issues in a complete restructuring of the believers' thought-world. He explains:

An impetus toward restructuring the interpreted world lies in the cognitive dissonance that came into the world through Christ. This dissonance was triggered by the cross. Where an executed man is presented as mediator of salvation, the interpreted world formed by Jewish and Greek traditions must appear disturbed. The cross is a scandal to the Jews since it contradicts the expectation of powerful signs in which God intervenes salvifically. It is foolishness to the Greeks since it contradicts the standards of wisdom.... Seen retrospectively, abrupt dissonances can have liberating effects because they necessitate restructuring and open new perspectives.[65]

Indeed, faith in a man who was crucified is so mind-boggling that its confession is a gift from God: "No one can say 'Jesus is Lord' except by the Holy Spirit."[66] The resurrection of Jesus makes his followers realize that God has confirmed the righteousness of

63. Rom 1:5.
64. Col 2:2–3.
65. Gerd Theissen, *Psychological Aspects of Pauline Theology*, trans. John P. Galvin (Philadelphia: Fortress Press, 1987), 386–87.
66. 1 Cor 12:3.

his cause. "He was revealed in flesh, vindicated in spirit."[67] In his speeches in the Acts of the Apostles, Peter argues that the passion of Jesus, far from being the just retribution for his words construed as blasphemy, took place in keeping with a divine plan of salvation.[68]

Given the intimate connection between the resurrection and Christian baptism, we can appreciate Paul's reaction, in his letters to the Galatians and to the Colossians, to the multiple initiations that some of them were undergoing. Having done research into the mystery cults of the Mediterranean Basin at that time, Luke Timothy Johnson tells us that, according to that Hellenistic religiosity, to be successively initiated into several mysteries was construed as advancing toward greater and greater *perfection*. Hence his translation of Galatians 3:3 as "having begun in the Spirit are you being perfected (*epiteleisthe*) now in the flesh?"[69] He points out that at stake was the unsurpassable character of baptism into the living Christ. For someone who had been baptized, circumcision ("in the flesh") could be seen as a further step toward perfection—which, to Paul's mind, was equivalent to betraying the divine gift of baptism and to denying the ultimate significance of Christ. Johnson's construal of the issue may shed light on the twenty-first-century phenomenon of multiple religious belonging.

Paul also stresses the interpersonal and mystical side of faith:

I have been crucified with Christ; and it is no longer I who live, but it is Christ who lives in me. And the life I now live in the flesh I live by faith in the Son of God, who loved me and gave himself for me.[70]

He relates to "Christ Jesus our hope."[71] Perhaps Kant, who, as we saw in the preceding chapter, asked in an impersonal way, *"What*

67. 1 Tm 3:16.
68. See Acts 2:22–36, 3:13–18, 4:10–12, 10:36–43; see also Paul's speech in Acts 13:26–33.
69. Luke Timothy Johnson, *Religious Experience in Earliest Christianity* (Minneapolis: Fortress Press, 1998), 99; see 78–103.
70. Gal 2:19–20.
71. 1 Tm 1:1.

may I hope?," should have phrased his question in an interpersonal way: "In *whom* may I hope?"[72]

For Paul, adherence to Jesus Christ is given in the strength of hope and love. "In hope we were saved."[73] "Hope does not disappoint us, because God's love has been poured into our hearts through the Holy Spirit that has been given to us."[74] The object of that hope must have seemed startlingly excessive to Paul's readers. He rejoices "because of the surpassing value of knowing Christ Jesus my Lord."[75] He avows, "I consider that the sufferings of this present time are not worth comparing with the glory about to be revealed to us."[76] "This slight momentary affliction is preparing us for an eternal weight of glory beyond all measure, because we look not at what can be seen but at what cannot be seen; for what can be seen is temporary, but what cannot be seen is eternal."[77]

Faith, however, is not reducible to mere trust. Paul also insists on the mediation that he himself exercises—namely, the cognitive authority he has received from the Lord.

We do not wage war according to human standards; for the weapons of our warfare are not merely human, but they have divine power to destroy strongholds. We destroy arguments and every proud obstacle raised up against the knowledge of God, and we take every thought captive to obey Christ. We are ready to punish every disobedience when your obedience is complete.... Now, even if I boast a little too much of our authority (*exousia*), which the Lord gave for building you up and not for tearing you down, I will not be ashamed of it.[78]

---

72. The contrast between the two phrasings is noted by Daniel Procureur, "Parler de l'espérance aujourd'hui," in *La sagesse, une chance pour l'espérance?*, ed. Adolphe Gesché (Paris: Cerf, 1998), 14.

73. Rom 8:24.

74. Rom 5:5.

75. Phil 3:8; see also Phil 7–14.

76. Rom 8:18.

77. 2 Cor 4:17–18.

78. 2 Cor 10:3b–8.

The two aspects of trust and doctrinal fidelity are combined in the recommendation to Timothy:

I know the one [Christ Jesus] in whom I have put my trust, and I am sure that he is able to guard until that day what has been entrusted to me. Hold to the standard of sound teaching that you have heard from me, in the faith and love that are in Christ Jesus. Guard the good treasure entrusted to you, with the help of the Holy Spirit living in us.[79]

This "treasure" (*parathēkē*, "deposit") must be safeguarded against the pretensions of "false knowledge"—namely, the heretical gnosis.[80] In relation to the Hebrew Scriptures, the author reminds Timothy that "from childhood you have known the sacred writings that are able to instruct you for salvation through faith in Christ Jesus. All Scripture is inspired by God and is useful for teaching, for reproof, for correction, and for training in righteousness."[81]

In another New Testament letter, from the incomparable value of the great gift of prophecy, the advice follows:

You will do well to be attentive to this [the prophetic message] as to a lamp shining in a dark place, until the day dawns and the morning star rises in your hearts. First of all you must understand this, that no prophecy of Scripture is a matter of one's own interpretation, because no prophecy ever came by human will, but people moved by the Holy Spirit spoke from God.[82]

This section has quoted a host of New Testament authors to the effect that faith seeking is dialectical—that is, involved in an inner struggle between self-deception and enlightenment. Exploring the antithesis between blindness and illumination has prepared the way for systematic presentations of this two-sided phenomenon in our chapters 4 (on the distortions of faith), 5 (on the biases), and 6 (on self-deception).

---

79. 2 Tm 1:12–14.
80. 1 Tm 6:20.
81. 2 Tm 3:15–16.
82. 2 Pt 1:19–21.

FAITH IN THE LOGOS INCARNATE

The Jesus who talks in the Fourth Gospel—the "Johannine Jesus," as the exegetes call him—is the Logos incarnate.[83] Most likely, his sayings are amplifications of those Jesus pronounced during his lifetime. They are the words that the risen Christ now communicates to his church. Readers are advised to keep this interpretive principle as they come across Jesus' extraordinary claims in John's Gospel.

That gospel employs the verbs *pisteuein* (to believe) and *ginōskein* (to know), while totally omitting the nouns *pistis* (faith) and *gnosis* (knowledge).[84] The verbal expression denotes an activity in the believers, an event in their lives, a movement springing from their depths. Most of the time, Jesus, the Word become flesh, is the object of such believing or knowing, and sometimes God, Jesus' Father. Throughout the gospel, the semantic interpenetration between knowing (*ginōskein*) and believing (*pisteuein*) is remarkable. "They know in truth that I came from you; and they have believed that you sent me."[85]

In the Fourth Gospel, believing is an acceptance of Jesus by the believers or, closer to the Greek, a "receiving" (*lambanein*), as in "all who received him, who believed in his name."[86] Far from being sightless, such belief or acceptance goes along with a definite "knowing," as we have just noted.

Another key verb is *idein* (to see). For example, Jesus talks of "seeing the kingdom of God"[87] as a synonym for "entering the kingdom of God"[88] or of "seeing life."[89] Such "seeing" amplifies one of Matthew's isolated beatitudes: "Blessed are your eyes, for they see, and

83. Jn 1:14.
84. Raymond E. Brown, *The Gospel according to John* (Garden City, N.Y.: Doubleday, 1966), 1:512, 514.
85. Jn 17:8; see Jn 4:41–42.
86. Jn 1:12.
87. Jn 3:3.
88. Jn 3:5.
89. Jn 3:36.

your ears, for they hear."[90] In his gospel, the disciples see the arrival of the kingdom and hear the words of the parables. In John, the component of understanding is increased, as "seeing" conveys the idea that one is given light, "the true light, which enlightens everyone,"[91] the Logos incarnate himself. However, while at times "believing" amounts to "seeing," at other times the former is set in contrast to the latter. Then "seeing" is given an eschatological sense: "Blessed are those who have not seen and yet have come to believe."[92]

In a study of the semantics of seeing and believing, Heinrich Schlier differentiates three types of usage. First, texts in which seeing comes before believing—for instance, John 11:45: "Many of the Jews therefore, who had come with Mary and had seen what Jesus did, believed in him." Second, texts in which seeing occurs after believing—for instance, John 11:40: "Did I not tell you that if you believed, you would see the glory of God?" And third, texts in which seeing and believing are employed as synonyms—for instance, John 6:40: "This is indeed the will of my Father, that all who see the Son and believe in him may have eternal life; and I will raise them up on the last day."[93]

Among the events that are seen—and conspicuously so—in the gospels are the miracles. In the Synoptics, miracles are *dynameis*, "acts of power"—that is, potent actions such as cures. They herald the beginning of God's reign—namely, of an age in which evil is bound to be defeated. In John's Gospel, miracles are "signs" (*sēmeia*, a word that might be rendered more accurately, if perhaps awkwardly, as "meanings"). Their function is not to replace faith, but to infuse faith with a symbolic reference. No author has exemplified this symbolism better than John the Evangelist, whose "signs" point to a higher level of reality.

90. Mt 13:16.
91. Jn 1:9.
92. Jn 20:29.
93. Heinrich Schlier, "Glauben, Erkennen, Lieben nach dem Johannesevangelium," in *Besinnung auf das neue Testament* (Freiburg: Herder, 1964), 2:283, 285–86.

The "works" (*erga*) performed by Jesus, which are put forth as signs (in chapters 1–12), amount to his actions and words. They are more radical than all visible signs to the extent that they more directly bear witness or testify to Jesus' transcendent origin; they authenticate him. His greatest work is his elevation, both on the cross and in the resurrection,[94] at the appointed hour. This "lifting up" of the Son of Man indicates that he is even the "I am" of Exodus 3:14.[95] By working as the Father does, Jesus gives life to the world. Hence the theme of eternal life, the life given by the risen Christ, a theme that recurs in John.[96]

The topic of witnessing (*martyrein*) has just been mentioned. It includes several components. In the first place, *John the Baptist* testifies to the light that Jesus is and declares that he is the Lamb of God, the one on whom the Spirit descended and has remained, and the Son of God.[97]

In the second place, we may rank *the Scriptures*, about which Jesus maintains that they "testify on my behalf."[98] By "the Scriptures," John the Evangelist has in mind, more particularly, Moses.[99]

In the third place, *Jesus* testifies. "The one who comes from heaven is above all. He testifies to what he has seen and heard, yet no one accepts his testimony. Whoever has accepted his testimony has certified this, that God is true."[100] Notice the connection between testifying and truth, to which we shall return in a moment. Throughout John's Gospel, Jesus proclaims what Thomas Brodie calls "his self-identifying relationship to the Father"[101]—that is, his divine sonship and his role as sharing his Father's life with the believers.

---

94. Jn 3:14–15, 13:1, 17:1.
95. Jn 8:28, 8:58.
96. Jn 3:16, 6:47.
97. Jn 1:6–8:19–36; see also Jn 3:22–30 and 5:33–36a.
98. Jn 5:39b.
99. Jn 5:45–47.
100. Jn 3:31b–33.
101. Thomas L. Brodie, *The Gospel according to John: A Literary and Theological Commentary* (New York: Oxford University Press, 1993), 323, 326.

In the fourth place, *the Father* testifies. "If I testify about myself, my testimony is not true. There is another who testifies on my behalf, and I know that his testimony to me is true."[102] Jesus continues: "The works that the Father has given me to complete, the very works that I am doing, testify on my behalf that the Father has sent me. And the Father who sent me has himself testified on my behalf."[103] In fact, the Father and the Son accomplish the same works and thus give testimony in unison. Thus "the works that I do in my Father's name testify to me."[104] Another way of putting it is rendered by the verb "to seal" (*sphragizein*): "It is on him [the Son of Man] that God the Father has set his seal."[105] The Father has accredited Jesus by enabling him to give "the food that endures for eternal life."[106] He has supplied the disciples with credentials so that Peter can say, "We have come to believe."[107]

In the fifth place, *the Spirit* testifies. "When the Advocate comes, whom I will send to you from the Father, the Spirit of truth who comes from the Father, he will testify on my behalf."[108] "When the Spirit of truth comes, he will guide you into all the truth; for he will not speak on his own, but will speak whatever he hears, and he will declare to you the things that are to come."[109]

In the sixth place, *the disciples* of Jesus testify. "You also are to testify because you have been with me from the beginning."[110] The beloved disciple of the Fourth Gospel is presented as the first to bear witness. After reporting that "one of the soldiers pierced his [Jesus'] side with a spear, and at once blood and water came out," he solemnly comments, "He who saw this has testified so that you also

102. Jn 5:31–32; see Jn 8:14–18.
103. Jn 5:36b–37a.
104. Jn 10:25.
105. Jn 6:27b.
106. Jn 6:27a.
107. Jn 6:69.
108. Jn 15:26.
109. Jn 16:13.
110. Jn 15:27.

may believe. His testimony is true, and he knows that he tells the truth."[111] Once the Johannine community was constituted, the testimony became associated with a collective experience of divine life:

We declare to you what was from the beginning, what we have heard, what we have seen with our eyes, what we have looked at and touched with our hands, concerning the word of life—this life was revealed, and we have seen it and testify to it, and declare to you the eternal life that was with the Father and was manifested to us—we declare to you what we have seen and heard so that you also may have fellowship with us; and truly our fellowship is with the Father and with his son Jesus Christ.[112]

We have seen and do testify that the Father has sent his Son as the Savior of the world.[113]

Noteworthy is the fact that, in John's view, those who testify are not independent agents. We have just seen that Jesus speaks of "the works that the Father has given me to complete."[114] In line with his vision of the synergy between the Father and the Son, John contemplates a single work of witnessing, borne by the Father, through the Son, in their common Spirit, whom they both send.[115] Finally, this task is extended to the believers. According to John 12:17, even the crowds testify; but Jesus did not put much stock in their faith, as indicated in John 2:23–25. We notice the same downplaying of human testimony in the case of the Samaritan woman. The narrator writes that "many more believed because of his [Jesus'] word. They said to the woman, 'It is no longer because of what you said that we believe, for we have heard for ourselves, and we know that this is truly the Savior of the world.'"[116] A disciple's witnessing is thus superseded by the direct hearing of the word of God put forth by Jesus.

It is in receiving truth from God that the disciples—and even the

111. Jn 19:34–35.
112. 1 Jn 1:1–3.
113. 1 Jn 4:14.
114. Jn 5:36b.
115. Jn 15:26, 16:13–15, 20:22.
116. Jn 4:41–42.

Baptist—carry out their faithful testimony. This profound concord in bearing witness is conveyed in these lines:

> This is the one who came by water and blood, Jesus Christ, not with the water only but with the water and the blood. And the Spirit is the one that testifies, for the Spirit is the truth. There are three that testify: the Spirit and the water and the blood, and these three agree. If we receive human testimony, the testimony of God is greater; for this is the testimony of God that he has testified to his Son. Those who believe in the Son of God have the testimony in their hearts.... And this is the testimony: God gave us eternal life, and this life is in his Son.[117]

The testimony was visible as the few disciples standing near the cross of Jesus saw blood and water coming out of his side.[118] However, commenting on the just-quoted passage from John's letter, especially on the phrase "those who believe in the Son of God have the testimony in their hearts," Ricoeur speaks of "a nearly complete internalization of testimony." Not utterly complete, presumably because the believers will still need to be taught by the works performed by the Son of God (what Ricoeur calls "the externalization of testimony"). Again we notice here the complementarity between the objective and the subjective sides of faith. He adds, "The testimony that the witness has in himself is nothing other than the testimony of the Holy Spirit, a notion that indicates the extreme point of internalization of testimony."[119]

Another important topic in John is the truth (*alētheia*), which is the act of witnessing as revealing.[120] The Johannine Jesus declares, "I am the way, and the truth, and the life."[121] In a Jewish milieu, he is the truth, not primarily as opposed to falsity, but more prominently as opposed to lies and deceit. I will say more about lies and deceit

117. 1 Jn 5:6–10b.11.
118. Jn 19:34.
119. Ricoeur, "The Hermeneutics of Testimony," in *Essays on Biblical Interpretation*, ed. Lewis S. Mudge (Philadelphia: Fortress Press, 1980), 138, 139.
120. See Ignace de la Potterie, *La vérité dans Saint Jean*, 2 vols. (Rome: Biblical Institute Press, 1977).
121. Jn 14:6.

later in this section. In Jesus we come across the veracious and reliable witness. Thus he says to Pilate, "For this I was born, and for this I came into the world, to testify to the truth. Everyone who belongs to the truth listens to my voice."[122] By listening to Jesus—that is, by paying close attention to his works (words and actions)—one finds the "way," which is "truth" and "life." This experience consists in receiving Jesus who reveals himself as sent by the Father to carry out the great saving deed of love. By the same token, the Son manifests the Father's loving design, and he makes known (*exēgēsato*, "he explicated," John 1:18) who the Father is.

Jesus characterizes himself as "a man who has told you the truth that I heard from God."[123] As Logos—that is, as Word—he reveals.[124] In John's Gospel, truth is neither a divine property nor the reality of God (as in Augustine's *Veritas*); instead, it is a revelation. It is offered in the words Jesus pronounces. "If you abide (*menein*, the all-important verb variously translated as "to stay," "to remain," "to dwell") in my word, you are truly my disciples; and you will know the truth, and the truth will make you free."[125] It is worth observing that Jesus is addressing "the Jews who had believed in him."[126] And yet their faith is incomplete, since they refrain from entirely trusting Jesus, whose word is normative and liberating.[127]

As he is praying to his Father, Jesus states, "The words that you gave to me I have given to them, and they have received them and know in truth that I came from you; and they have believed that you sent me."[128] "I have given them your word."[129] "Sanctify them in the truth; your word is truth."[130] Jesus' truth and words come from the Father: "What I speak, therefore, I speak just as the Father has

122. Jn 18:37b–c.
123. Jn 8:40b.
124. Jn 1:1–18.
125. Jn 8:31b–32.
126. Jn 8:31a.
127. Jn 8:31b–33.
128. Jn 17:8.
129. Jn 17:14a.
130. Jn 17:17.

told me."[131] Finally, the Holy Spirit leads the believers into grasping profound religious meanings: "When the Spirit of truth comes, he will guide you into all the truth."[132] Such guidance or empowerment goes beyond the capacity of the weak human intellect: "It is the spirit that gives life; the flesh is useless. The words that I have spoken to you are spirit and life."[133]

John also introduces the theme of darkness (*skotia*), which Karl Barth describes as "the atmosphere which contends against light and redemption."[134] "The light shines in the darkness, and the darkness did not overcome it."[135] "And this is the judgment, that the light has come into the world, and people loved darkness rather than light because their deeds were evil. For all who do evil hate the light and do not come to the light, so that their deeds may not be exposed."[136] After Satan had entered into Judas and the latter had gone out in order to betray Jesus, the evangelist noted, "It was night."[137]

Therefore, Jesus adjures the crowd, "Walk while you have the light, so that the darkness may not overtake you. If you walk in the darkness, you do not know where you are going."[138] One of the reasons given for living in darkness is concern for one's reputation: "Many, even of the authorities, believed in him. But because of the Pharisees they did not confess it, for fear that they would be put out of the synagogue; for they loved human glory more than the glory that comes from God."[139] In another speech, Jesus asks, "How can you believe when you accept glory from one another and do not seek the glory that comes from the one who alone is God?"[140]

131. Jn 12:50b.
132. Jn 16:13a.
133. Jn 6:63; see Jn 3:6.
134. Karl Barth, *Witness to the Word: A Commentary on John 1*, ed. Walther Fürst, trans. Geoffrey W. Bromiley (Grand Rapids, Mich.: Eerdmans, 1986), 45, 47.
135. Jn 1:5.
136. Jn 3:19–20.
137. Jn 13:30.
138. Jn 12:35b–c.
139. Jn 12:42–43.
140. Jn 5:44.

In addition to this troubling refusal of light, John mentions the worrying possibility for believers of falling back into the darkness— lack of love for one's brother or sister occasions such a fall: "Whoever hates another believer is in the darkness, walks in the darkness, and does not know the way to go, because the darkness has brought on blindness."[141] Those who admit their blindness begin to see, whereas those who think they see are a prey to self-deception: "I came into this world for judgment so that those who do not see may see, and those who do see may become blind."[142] And addressing the latter group, Jesus adds, "If you were blind, you would not have sin. But now that you say, 'We see,' your sin remains."[143]

The drama of faith is staged in terms not only of darkness, but also of the "world" (*kosmos*). Barth defines one of its senses as "the creature in its hardened turning from God and his revelation [is] shut off from revelation because it shuts itself off."[144] "The world did not know him [the Word, who is the true light]."[145] The reason is that "the whole world lies under the power of the evil one."[146] What is wrong with the world? In his letter, John provides an answer: "Do not love the world or the things in the world. The love of the Father is not in those who love the world; for all that is in the world—the desire of the flesh, the desire of the eyes, the pride in riches—comes not from the Father but from the world."[147] Therefore Jesus declares, "I am not asking on behalf of the world, but on behalf of those whom you gave me, because they are yours."[148] "I have given them your word, and the world has hated them because they do not belong to the world, just as I do not belong to the world."[149]

141. 1 Jn 2:11.
142. Jn 9:39.
143. Jn 9:41.
144. Barth, *Witness to the Word*, 63.
145. Jn 1:10b.
146. 1 Jn 5:19b.
147. 1 Jn 2:15.
148. Jn 17:9b.
149. Jn 17:14.

In this long discourse already quoted, Jesus fathoms the profound absurdity of the hatred directed at him and at his disciples:

If the world hates you, be aware that it hated me before it hated you.... If I had not come and spoken to them, they would not have sin; but now they have no excuse for their sin. Whoever hates me hates my Father also. If I had not done among them the works that no one else did, they would not have sin. But now they have seen and hated both me and my Father. It was to fulfill the word that is written in their law, "They hated me without a cause."[150]

Such hatred involves a propensity to act violently.[151] Because Jesus' truth throws light upon the hitherto concealed intentions of his opponents, they react in the following manner: "You are trying to kill me, a man who has told you the truth that I heard from God."[152] And here is the root cause of that will to kill:

You are from your father the devil, and you choose to do your father's desires. He was a murderer from the beginning and does not stand in the truth, because there is no truth in him. When he lies, he speaks according to his own nature, for he is a liar and the father of lies.[153]

The lies exercise the function of covering up false religiosity. "An hour is coming when those who kill you will think that by doing so they are offering worship to God. And they will do this because they have not known the Father or me."[154] The potential subjects of such self-deception are not only the Jewish officials at the time of Jesus ("the Jews" in John's Gospel), but all those whose allegiance is to "the world." And, as was briefly noted when I drew attention to the possibility of falling back into the darkness, even the members of the Johannine community were not immune from that danger. Hence the dire warning: "We must not be like Cain who was from the evil one and murdered his brother. And why did he murder him?

150. Jn 15:18, 15:23–25.
151. See Schwager, *Must There Be Scapegoats?*, 157–63.
152. Jn 8:40a.
153. Jn 8:44.
154. Jn 16:2b–3.

Because his own deeds were evil, and his brother's righteous.... All who hate a brother are murderers."[155]

In contrast to those who belong to the world, the disciples are urged to be loving persons. "I give you a new commandment, that you love one another. Just as I have loved you, you also should love one another."[156] It is the clause "just as I have loved you" that is most exacting. "Having loved his own who were in the world, he loved them to the end."[157] Like a slave, Jesus washed the feet of his disciples.[158] Yet the greatest deed of love on his part is his willingness to give his life. "I am the good shepherd. The good shepherd lays down his life for the sheep."[159]

In John's writings, love, belief, and knowledge are intermingled in a single spiritual experience, thanks to which the members of the community of the beloved disciple are urged to partake together of Jesus' sacrificial love for humankind. John underscores this experiential character: "We have known and believe the love that God has for us."[160] The very observance of God's commandment enables the believers to recognize the authenticity of Jesus' message. "My teaching is not mine but his who sent me. Anyone who resolves to do the will of God will know whether the teaching is from God or whether I am speaking on my own."[161]

Conjoined with the experiential character of faith is its affective factor:

Beloved, let us love one another, because love is from God; everyone who loves is born of God and knows God. Whoever does not love does not know God, for God is love. God's love was revealed among us in this way: God sent his only Son into the world so that we might live through him. In

155. 1 Jn 3:12, Jn 3:15a.
156. Jn 13:34.
157. Jn 13:1b.
158. See Jn 13:3–17.
159. Jn 10:11; see also Jn 10:1–30.
160. 1 Jn 4:16; see Jn 1:3, "what we have seen and heard."
161. Jn 7:16–17; compare with the Samaritans, who declare, "we have heard for ourselves, and we know that this is truly the Savior of the world"; Jn 4:24b.

this is love, not that we loved God but that he loved us and sent his Son to be the atoning sacrifice for our sins. Beloved, since God loved us so much, we also ought to love one another.[162]

As a French exegete explains, "the expression 'to know God' denotes the subjective coming to awareness (*la prise de conscience subjective*) of this divine presence brought about by his action in our soul.... To know God is, therefore, to know Love; it is to become aware of God-Love radiating love in our soul."[163]

This mystical identification of the believing community with the Spirit of Jesus is compared to an "anointing" (*chrisma*, more precisely an "ointment"). "You have been anointed by the Holy One, and all of you know (*oidate*)."[164] "As for you, the anointing that you received from him abides in you, and so you do not need anyone to teach you. But just as his anointing teaches you about all things, and is true and is not a lie, and just as it has taught you, abide in him."[165] By juxtaposing these two units with other texts by John, Ignace de la Potterie shows that the ointment refers to the word of Christ[166] and to "the truth that abides in you."[167] The true disciples have interiorized the message of Christ, and consequently they can discern the truth that now has taken root in them. In contradistinction to those who disbelieve the incarnation and have left the community, the faithful ones are in no need of further teaching and are even said to be impeccable.[168]

162. 1 Jn 4:7–11.

163. M.-E. Boismard, "La connaissance dans l'Alliance Nouvelle d'après la Première Lettre de Saint Jean," *Revue Biblique* 56 (1949): 388. I have adopted, with one correction, Francis Martin's translation of this excerpt from Boismard's article, in Martin, *The Feminist Question: Feminist Theology in the Light of Christian Tradition* (Grand Rapids, Mich.: Eerdmans, 1994), 12.

164. 1 Jn 2:20.

165. 1 Jn 2:27.

166. Jn 8:31–32.

167. 2 Jn 1–2; de la Potterie, "L'onction du Chrétien par la foi," in *La vie selon l'Esprit: Condition du Chrétien*, by I. de la Potterie and S. Lyonnet (Paris: Cerf, 1965), chap. 5, esp. 134–41.

168. 1 Jn 3:6–9.

James Gaffney distinguishes, in the Fourth Gospel, three classes that govern the objects of believing.[169] First, *pisteuein eis* (to believe in), followed by the Greek accusative, indicates that people believe in someone *tout court*—namely, in Jesus (save for two instances—namely, in God or in Him who sent Jesus). The other two classes have to do with statements of Scripture, facts, or persons (for example, what Moses said) that are simply accepted. In the second class, the verb commands the dative; in the third, it is followed by *hoti* ("that"). The latter two groups only suggest a mere assent to some information, with little or no religious understanding and commitment. Nevertheless, this openness may lead to the real and complete faith, which consists in *believing in* Jesus. "To believe in" and "to believe that" are the initiating of a differentiation of the faith experience. Our next chapter will introduce Aquinas's threefold schema—believing in, believing that, and believing *tout court*—based on John, other parts of the New Testament, and on Augustine.

We may close off this section by observing that John's use of verbs, such as "to believe," "to know," "to receive," and "to see," points to the subjective approach to faith, which was underlined at the beginning of chapter 1 and to which we shall return in the concluding remarks of chapter 6. The topics of the signs, of Jesus' works, and of the witnessing prepare the way for the signs of credibility and of credentity, which will be treated in chapter 7. In addition, the themes of darkness, of blindness, of the refusal of light, of the world as antipathetic to faith and as hating the disciples, of the will to kill, and of the devil's lies all demonstrate the ambiguous character of the quest for faith. Finally, John the evangelist also highlights the experiential character of faith and its affective factor—for example, with the vocabulary of "anointing."

169. James Gaffney, "Believing and Knowing in the Fourth Gospel," *Theological Studies* 26 (1965):215–41.

CONCLUDING REMARKS

As we bring this chapter to a close, we may want to draw, from the foregoing presentation, biblical norms for the theology of faith and revelation that will evolve in this book:[170]

- The insight that only God is totally reliable and that our hope is based on his promises and on the signs of his effective presence, visible to the poor in the first place;
- The importance of the exemplar of hope and faith, principally Abraham, "the father of all who believe," and Jesus, "the pioneer and perfecter of faith," both of whom exercise a mediating role with respect to believers;
- The experiential and affective side of biblical religiousness as an ever renewed meeting of God; faith as both trusting and giving credence—that is, as the basis for doctrinal fidelity;
- Faith as a gift actively received or stubbornly denied; sham faith as a self-deception in the absence of love for others; and last,
- Faith as seeing and knowing Jesus the Christ and Son of God and as being illumined by the Holy Spirit in such a way that it can mature and become so interiorized that no dichotomy is felt between objective expressions and subjective appropriations.

This list of norms, derived from the texts garnered in this chapter, is probably not exhaustive, as was remarked at the end of our first section when the impossibility of completely spelling out biblical norms was mentioned. Their role is to guide the elaboration of theologies in such a way that, if some important norm is omitted, theologians should be urged to heed it in their enterprises. The first of such systematic accounts of faith to be delved in is the one worked out by Thomas Aquinas, to which we now turn.

170. These norms are evolved according to the ten principles put forward by O'Collins and Kendall in *Bible for Theology*, but mostly according to the three principles that they enunciate as the principle of biblical convergence, the principle of exegetical consensus, and the principle of metathemes and metanarratives (6–7, 24–28, and 38). These three principles refer to themes and narratives that recur in the Bible.

CHAPTER 3

Thomas Aquinas on the Word Embodied in Christ

༉

This chapter introduces a medieval thinker, Thomas Aquinas, and investigates how he understands several central aspects of the act of faith. Since it is very important to take account of the affective side of faith, we shall begin with his views on the interaction between faith and love. Thereafter, I shall vindicate the centrality of the First Truth, which intellectually grounds faith in a God whose presence, self-revelation, and self-communication are real. Next, we shall ponder the way Aquinas assesses the role and compass of human reason in the faith experience. We shall end with a description of what he considers, following Augustine, as the three fundamental components of the act of believing, which complement one another.

FAITH AND LOVE

In Aquinas's representation, faith should never be dissociated from love. According to his anthropology, the will (*voluntas*) is a rational desire, an inclination of the heart flowing from an apprehension of the good. He situates this interplay in the dynamic climate of the person's finality, where the intellect, which is attracted to the true, informs the will, which is attracted to the good. For instance, prior to the act of faith, unbelievers experience both inquiry (the intellectual movement) and pursuit of happiness (the affective movement).

So the act of faith, which is a kind of knowledge, is conditioned by love:

As a lamp cannot give light unless there is a fire blazing within it, so a spiritual lamp does not give any light unless it is first set ablaze and burns with the fire of love. Therefore, to be ablaze comes first, and the giving of light depends on it, because knowledge of the truth is given due to the blazing of love.[1]

The decision to believe, which is proper to the will, never occurs without the mind being illuminated at the same time. Many other passages in Aquinas's writings suggest that he envisions an interaction between the intellect, which informs the will, and the will, which activates the intellect.[2] In the God-given act of faith, the two faculties are simultaneously operating: "God causes faith in the believer by inclining his will and enlightening his intellect with the light of faith."[3]

The decision to believe is prompted by the will.[4] This point is easily misunderstood because of the late-medieval (hence post-Thomist) and modern construal of the will as an irrational or arbitrary faculty. For instance, Paul Tillich contends that Aquinas is guilty of both intellectualism and voluntarism.[5] First, he thinks that Aquinas accords priority to the "content" (Tillich uses this word

1. Aquinas, *Commentary on the Gospel of St. John*, trans. James A. Weisheipl and Fabian R. Larcher, Part I (Albany, N.Y.: Magi, 1980), no. 812.

2. See, for instance, *Summa Theologiae* (hereafter *ST*), I-II, q. 9 and 10. In this chapter, any quotation announced as I, I-II, II-II, or III, comes from one of the four divisions of the *Summa Theologiae*. Thus I = part 1; I-II = first half of part 2; II-II = second half of part 2; and III = part 3. Translations of Thomas Aquinas's texts are my own, albeit dependent on previous translators.

3. Aquinas, *The Disputed Questions on Truth*, vol. III, trans. Robert W. Schmidt (Chicago: Regnery, 1954), q. 27, a. 3. See also *Commentary on the Gospel of St. John*, Part I, no. 946, where "learning" (*addiscere*) takes place "through affection" (*per affectum*) and culminates in "right action" (*ad rectam operationem*).

4. See *ST* II-II, q. 4, a. 1.

5. Likewise, in *Faith and Knowledge* (Cleveland: Fontana, 1974), 26, John Hick avers that Aquinas's tract on faith rests on an "intellectualist assumption which restricts the entire discussion to propositional truths."

more than once) and consequently is an intellectualist who mistakes faith for belief. Second, Tillich fancies he can connect this presumed intellectualism with a presumed voluntarism in Aquinas: "faith is understood [by Aquinas] as an act of knowledge with a limited evidence and ... the lack of evidence is made up by an act of will."[6]

Tillich correctly points out, however, that "the former [intellectualism] is the basis of the latter [voluntarism]."[7] But his stricture does not apply to Aquinas. What he attacks must have been some modern misrepresentation. Since Aquinas envisions faith as an experience of light, hence of meaning and of credibility, he does not construe it in a conceptualistic fashion. In addition, the act of the will is neither blind nor fanciful, since it too is permeated by intelligent apprehension—to wit, by a definite sense of the extraordinary value of believing in God.[8]

In Aquinas's works we notice a constant interaction between knowing and willing.[9] Knowledge engenders desire, and desire engenders knowledge. "The intellect is properly said to assent (*assentire*)," while "the will is more properly said to consent (*consentire*)."[10] During the process of conversion, as the heart consents to the goodness of the divine Object, the mind assents to its truth. Furthermore, the glow of faith is enhanced by two of the Holy Spirit's gifts—namely, "understanding" and "knowledge."[11]

6. Tillich, *Dynamics of Faith* (New York: Harper and Row, 1957), 35; see also 30–38.

7. Tillich, *Dynamics of Faith*, 35. In *Faith and Belief* (Princeton, N.J.: Princeton University Press, 1979), 280–81n52, Wilfred Cantwell Smith rescues Aquinas from that misrepresentation.

8. Notwithstanding my disagreement with Tillich on his reading of Aquinas, I want to send my readers back to what I have borrowed from his thoughts, in chapter 1 of this volume.

9. See *ST* I-II, q. 9–10. Aquinas balances the cognitive and the affective in religious experience, and he sees the role of the will in the act of faith. Nevertheless, mostly in the *Summa Theologiae* and less in the scriptural commentaries, he does not have recourse to the phenomenology that would allow him to tease out the numerous interactions between the cognitive and the affective.

10. *ST* I-II, q. 15, a. 1, ad 3.

11. *ST* II-II, q. 8, a. 1, and q. 9, a. 1.

One experiences the brightest light when one comes to the conclusion that a person is worthy of being loved and fully trusted. Then one sees that God must be believed. Christian believers perform such judgments of value in regard to God the Father, Jesus Christ, the Holy Spirit, and God's church, which is the body of Christ. But these judgments of value must be preceded by judgments of fact, which are central to the biblical stories and to Catholic belief. Both kinds of judgments are accepted because they have triggered interest in the realities to be believed by giving rise to "a few points for the instruction of our own lives" (*aliqua ad eruditionem uite nostre*), as Aquinas states in his commentary on the Apostles' Creed.[12]

The two defining operations of the human mind (understanding and judging) are spontaneously followed by acts of loving. Being fuller than these intellectual acts, love then permeates and transfigures them. So Aquinas maintains that charity is the form of faith, since "each thing works through its form" and "faith works through charity." He states:

The act of faith is directed to the object of the will, namely, the good, as to its end, and this good, which is the end of faith, that is, the divine Good, is the proper object of charity. Therefore charity is called the form of faith insofar as the act of faith is perfected and formed by charity.[13]

In his nonsystematic works, Aquinas speaks of faith in a holistic way, as an experience. Lecturing on Jesus' invitation, "Come and see," he writes:

In the mystical sense, he [Jesus] says, "Come and see," because the dwelling of God, whether of glory or grace, cannot be known except by experience (*per experientiam*): for it cannot be explained in words.... And so he says, "Come and see": "Come," by believing and working; "and see," by experiencing and understanding.[14]

12. Aquinas, *Sermon-Conferences on the Apostles' Creed*, trans. Nicholas Ayo (Notre Dame, Ind.: University of Notre Dame Press, 1988), Section V, 60–61; Ayo's rendering slightly modified.

13. *ST* II-II, q. 4, a. 3.

14. Aquinas, *Commentary on the Gospel of St. John*, Part I, nos. 292 and 319.

The experience is described as "rest" (*quies*), "stillness" (*vacatio*), and as "tasting the divine sweetness" (*per divinae dulcedinis gustationem*).[15]

In his systematic presentation of the three theological virtues, he considers faith as an intellectual virtue, since it enhances human reason. The two other theological virtues enhance the will. Hope relates humans to God as the still unattained goal of our desire. Charity relates humans to God as already indwelling in our heart.[16]

Thanks to such texts, we can easily see that Aquinas intimately unites faith, hope, and charity in his analyses of the Christian experience.

FIRST TRUTH

Aquinas teaches that faith is said to be grounded in the First Truth —namely, God as revealing.[17] The formal object of faith is compared to the middle term of a demonstration. The middle term appears both in the major and the minor premises, but not in the conclusion. It is the pivot that enables reasoning to tie up subject and predicate in the conclusion. Thus faith assents to propositions (material object) as revealed by God (formal object).

This link between the First Truth (formal object) and the propositions (material object) has two advantages. First, the principal emphasis is laid on the experience of the light thanks to which believers realize that they can totally trust God as truthful without any qualification. "The light of faith makes one see (*videre*) the things that are believed,"[18] or, more precisely, as the rest of reply 3 suggests, *which things* one must believe. "For he [the believer] would not believe if he did not see that they were to be believed (*credenda*), either because of the evidence of signs or because of something else of this kind."[19]

---

15. Jn 1:39; Aquinas, *Commentary on the Gospel of St. John*, Part I, no. 293; see also nos. 289 and 319.
16. *ST* I-II, q. 62, a. 3.
17. *ST* II-II, q.1, a.1.
18. *ST* II-II, q. 1, a. 4, ad 3.
19. *ST* II-II, q. 1, a. 4, ad 2; see a. 5, ad 1.

The second advantage is that Christian beliefs are not devalued, since they convey true judgments made in the light of the First Truth.[20] As Aquinas points out, "The interior act of faith requires a firmness without any doubting, for such firmness proceeds from the infallibility of divine truth, on which faith finds support." He adds, "Faith must be simple, that is, without any mixture of error."[21] People cannot at the same time acknowledge the First Truth and entertain reservations concerning the beliefs that spell it out.

In his commentary on the *Summa Theologiae* Cajetan helpfully explicates Aquinas's thought as he clearly distinguishes the two major steps in the act of faith: the *evidentia credibilitatis*, the credibility of Christian belief, and the *evidentia veritatis*, the apprehension of truth.[22] The former judgment precedes the act of faith; it asserts that the evidence of signs warrants the reasonable and obligatory character of believing Jesus Christ. The latter judgment is the act of faith proper; illumined by the light provided by the Holy Spirit, it asserts with certainty the things that Jesus Christ has revealed.[23]

Aquinas makes room for freedom of conscience in regard to the act of faith. He declares, "Every will at variance with reason, whether the latter is right or erring, is always evil." And he explains:

To believe in Christ is good in itself, and necessary for salvation; but the will does not respond to it except inasmuch as it is proposed by reason.

20. Romanus Cessario rightly insists on the inseparability of the First Truth and the articles of faith; see Cessario, *Christian Faith and the Theological Life* (Washington, D.C.: The Catholic University of America Press, 1996), 57 and 62–63.

21. Aquinas, *Expositio Primae Decretalis*, in *Opuscula Theologica*, ed. Raymundo A. Verardo (Turin: Marietti, 1954), no. 1142; my translation. In further quotations, whenever no translator's name is entered, the translation is mine. We find the same argument in his commentary on the *De Trinitate* of Boethius, q. 3, a. 1, ad 4; English translation: Aquinas, *Faith, Reason and Theology*, trans. Armand Maurer (Toronto: Pontifical Institute of Mediaeval Studies, 1987).

22. Cajetan, *In Summa Theologiae*, II-II, q. 1, a. 4.

23. Bruce D. Marshall overlooks the significance of God-given intellectual light in the judgment of faith, in "Aquinas as Postliberal Theologian," *Thomist* 53 (1989):353–402; see also Roy, "Bruce Marshall's Reading of Aquinas," *Thomist* 56 (1992):473–80, with a rejoinder from Bruce D. Marshall, 499–524.

Consequently, if it is proposed by reason as something evil, the will responds to it as to something evil; not as if it were evil in itself, but because it is evil accidentally, through the apprehension of reason.[24]

Aquinas bases the necessity of such faith judgments on the functioning of the human mind.[25] In contrast to the divine mind, which is completely simple because intuitive, the human mind is complex because discursive. A truth-bearing statement (the *enuntiabile*) expresses a judgment, which apprehends the truth by combining (saying, "Yes, it is") or dividing (saying, "No, it is not"). In this article, we encounter the oft-quoted sentence "the act of the believer does not reach its end in a statement, but in a reality" (*actus autem credentis non terminatur ad enuntiabile, sed ad rem*). He continues, "Through them [*enuntiabilia*, the statements] we have knowledge of realities."[26]

This position assumes that truth resides in the mind, more precisely in the mental act whereby we judge that something is such. For Aquinas, (1) although truth begins with the senses, it is not primarily a matter of perceiving (empiricism); (2) it is not primarily a matter of understanding (a Platonic grasping of the forms, an idealist construction of concepts, or an apprehension of meaning in religious experience); (3) truth lies in correct judgments: building upon what has been perceived (data) and what has been understood (idea, hypothesis), we reflect on the latter by asking, "Is it so?" At the end of this reflective process, we reach a definite objectivity, which can be qualified as either certain or more or less probable. Yet this progression is typical only of the natural order. In the supernatural order, while those operations are not absent, they are nevertheless complemented by another—quite decisive—factor, which we have already introduced: the First Truth.

Let us now try and fathom the depths of truth as Aquinas sees

24. *ST* I-II, q. 19, a. 5.
25. *ST* II-II, q. 1, a. 2.
26. *ST* II-II, q. 1, a. 2, ad 2.

them. He accepts Aristotle's intellectual virtue called *nous* (in Greek), *intellectus* (in Latin), and usually translated as "understanding." It consists in grasping the first principles of knowledge. Such principles are not purely logical rules; they are dynamic in that they operate throughout any intellectual process. In Aquinas's transposition, Aristotle's "understanding" (= the *natural* principles) is matched, in the *supernatural* order, by the first principles of faith. So we find this parallelism: the first principles of faith are to the contents of faith what understanding is to science.

Granted by the revealing God, the first principles of faith generate an increase in the believer's knowing power (*intellectiva virtus*),[27] as well as an attraction to God as First Truth, an instinctive adjustment of one's mind to revealed truth—namely, "an interior instinct (*interior instinctus*) that incites and moves us to believe," "a wonderful joy and love of the truth, which is the very Son of God himself."[28] It is also called "an instinct of the mind (*mentis instinctus*) by which the human heart (*cor*) is moved by God to assent to the realities that pertain to faith."[29] We must never forget that the medieval *mens*, usually rendered as "mind" but better rendered as "human spirit," most of the time comprises both the intellect and the will. Accordingly, both reason and the heart intrinsically want to believe, since what is revealed is directly connected with the pursuit of the ultimate end.[30]

The Aristotelian and Thomist phrase "first principles" is misleading insofar as it suggests something static and thematic. Rather, the phrase designates the dynamic and unthematic source of our intellectual life. For Aquinas, it is exemplified in numerous cases of *intentio*. Since Franz Brentano and Edmund Husserl, this na-

27. *ST* I, q. 12, a. 2.

28. Aquinas, *Commentary on the Gospel of St. John*, Part I, no. 935. In the *Quaestiones Quodlibetales*, ed. Raymundo Spiazzi (Turin: Marietti, 1956), Quodlibetum 2, a. 4, a. 1 (incl. ad 1–3), Aquinas speaks of an *interior instinctus* and of a *vocatio interior*, quoting Jn 6:45 and Rom 8:30.

29. Aquinas, *Super Epistolam ad Romanos Lectura*, no. 707, in *Super Epistolas S. Pauli Lectura*, ed. Raphael Cai (Turin: Marietti, 1953).

30. *ST* I-II, q. 10, a. 1; q. 62, a. 3.

tive movement of our minds has been termed "intentionality."[31] As conditioning all our acts, this intelligent striving toward knowing is immediate and unformulated. Far from being an object of intuition or perception, it is in itself merely conscious (as yet unobjectified) in our raising and answering questions. It becomes formulated only when we pay attention to it and try to understand it. Sebastian Moore dubs it "knowing-by-doing," or "knowing-in-doing."[32] It accompanies all our operations, from bodily awareness to transcendent loving. Even if it can eventually be differentiated, it is basically one dynamism—namely, our conscious human spirit. In meditation, however, we can go beyond images, feelings, and concepts and reach this desire as unspecified, as just wanting, as the still point.

We are aware of light within our soul, and through it we participate in God as truth. Although we enjoy no direct intuition or apprehension of God as First Truth,[33] God's presence is real, and it is mediated by our consciousness of an unknown font of light. This consciousness is a telling element in our structural openness to the Mystery, which Aquinas calls "the preambles of faith, which we must necessarily know in [the act of] faith."[34] Interestingly, Mahatma Gandhi testifies to a very similar conviction:

I have always known God as Truth. There was a time when I doubted the existence of God, but even at that time I did not doubt the existence of Truth. This Truth is not a material quality but is pure consciousness. That alone holds the universe together. It is God because it rules the whole universe.... For me this is almost a matter of direct experience. I say "almost" because I have not seen face to face God Who is Truth. I have had only a glimpse of Him. But my faith is unshakeable.[35]

31. See Roy, *Mystical Consciousness*, 3–10.
32. Sebastian Moore, in an unpublished reflection, entitled, "Knowing by Being and Doing" (February 16, 1989).
33. See *ST* I, q. 88, a. 3, with ad 1.
34. More literally: "which are necessary in the science of faith" (*Commentary on the "De Trinitate" of Boethius*, q. 2, a. 3). This indicates that most of the time, those preambles are discovered, not before, but in the act of faith. For Aquinas, philosophical truths are like water changed into the wine of faith (ad 5).
35. Mahatma Gandhi, *The Essential Writings of Mahatma Gandhi*, ed. Raghavan Iyer

In his commentary on John's Gospel, Aquinas construes the phrase "the true light, which enlightens everyone" in a generous ecumenical way, which would include Gandhi's vivid experience of truth. Aquinas writes, "God is truth itself, and no one speaks the truth except insofar as he is enlightened by him. So Ambrose says: 'Every truth, by whomsoever spoken, is from the Holy Spirit.'"[36]

For Aquinas, human participation in the First Truth is finite, but, as soon as it is graced, it becomes an actual share in infinite life. We believe in a God who bestows his life to us. His light and his love are vouchsafed to our *natural* human spirit, even though it must be elevated by grace. It is our "natural light" (*lumen naturale*) that is "strengthened by an infusion of graced light (*luminis gratuiti*)."[37] In this article, Aquinas also introduces the objective side of revelation, which we receive through the prophets: "At the same time phantasms are divinely formed in the human imagination, which, as appears in prophetic visions, are more expressive of the divine realities than those we obtain naturally from the sensible things."

Nevertheless, since the distinction "natural/supernatural" is theoretical, and therefore post-experiential, the divine gifts of faith, hope, and charity are not *experienced* as purely natural or as purely supernatural. We are simply conscious that our fundamental human dynamism is illumined and pulled toward absolute goodness. In this situation, the natural virtue of religion functions as a means to the supernatural end (union with God), which is already imperfectly achieved through faith, hope, and charity.[38]

Moreover, Aquinas holds that faith is not a sightless adherence, because it is an experience of incipient and increasing light along our intellectual journey toward fuller meaning, as indicated by the famous phrase *fides quaerens intellectum*, "faith seeking understand-

---

(Delhi: Oxford University Press, 1993), 234; see also Roy, *Engaging the Thought of Bernard Lonergan*, study 13, entitled "A Comparison with Gandhi."

36. Aquinas, *Commentary on the Gospel of St. John*, Part I, no. 1250.

37. *ST* I, q. 12, a. 13.

38. *ST* II-II, q. 81, a. 1 and a. 5.

ing." The gift of faith has two aspects: thinking (*cogitare*), expressed in inquiry (*inquisitio*), and adherence to truth (*cum assensione*).[39] The first aspect has to do with our mind's first operation—namely, our desire to understand. "When someone has a will prompt in believing, he loves the believed truth, thinks about it (*excogitat*), and embraces reasons for it if he can find them."[40] It is out of love that a person engages in this search for understanding, which amounts to an intellectual unrest, an incessant quest for meaning. Such craving is bound to be never fully satisfied on earth, given the immensity of divine mystery. The second aspect has to do with our mind's second operation—namely, our assent to truth. It brings about certitude and rest in truth.

The two aspects are present in this remark: "It would be impossible to assent by believing what is proposed without understanding it in some way. However, the completion of understanding follows upon the virtue of faith; and that completion of understanding is itself followed by a kind of certainty of faith."[41] To these two aspects we must add a third, which Aquinas calls *sacra doctrina*. We have then three kinds of knowing: first, the credibility that precedes faith; second, the certainty that is accorded in the act of faith; and third, the catechistic or theological apprehension that comes after the act of faith (faith seeking understanding).

Faith certainty is grounded in the divine origin of the truth that is communicated. He writes, "Only to God appertains the fact of knowing himself perfectly as he is. Therefore no one can truly talk or think about God unless this is revealed by God."[42] "Sacred doctrine is held in the light of divine knowledge, which cannot be misled."[43] The reply to the first objection introduces a penetrating distinction:

39. *ST* II-II, q. 2, a. 1.

40. *ST* II-II, q. 2, a. 10.

41. *ST* II-II, q. 8, a. 8, ad 2.

42. Aquinas, *In Librum Beati Dionysii de Divinis Nominibus Expositio*, ed. Ceslai Pera (Turin: Marietti, 1950), no. 13.

43. *ST* I, q. 1, a. 5.

What is in itself the more certain may seem to us the less certain on account of the weakness of our intelligence.... Hence the fact that some people happen to have doubts about articles of faith is not due to the uncertain nature of the realities, but to the weakness of human intelligence.[44]

This text allows for the coexistence of two states of mind: absolute certitude in our judgments of faith and doubting—that is, lack of intellectual certitude in our apprehensions of meaning. Doubting is ruled out in our judgments and yet is at times unavoidable on the level of understanding.

By contrast, Paul Tillich's existentialist rendering of this issue in terms of meaninglessness and courage to be, while phenomenologically enriching, nonetheless fails to incorporate the complete certainty that derives from having embraced judgments of truth coming from God.[45] He seems to confuse two things: on the one hand, the state of doubting, which cannot be dissociated from the awareness that we lack full clarity and thus ask questions and, on the other hand, a doubting that amounts to radical uncertainty and insecurity.[46] For Aquinas (and for Newman, as we shall note in chapter 4), the latter form of doubt is incompatible with faith in Christ, the Word of God. Indeed, he writes, "The believers have a simple knowledge of the truth without any doubt or inquiry (*absque dubitatione et inquisitione*), according to a certain immutable identity, since it stays in truth in the same, immutable, manner."[47]

Here in this excerpt from his commentary on Dionysius,[48] Aquinas considers Hebrews 11:1 as the adequate definition of faith. We may render his Latin version as "faith is the substance of realities (*rerum*) to be hoped for, the evidence of realities that do not appear." The definition consists of two components, one affective and the

44. *ST* I, q. 1, a. 5, ad 1. This text is supported by *ST* II-II, q. 4, a. 8, and other reflections by Aquinas.
45. Tillich, *The Courage to Be* (New Haven: Yale University Press, 1952), 171–78.
46. Tillich, *Systematic Theology*, vol. 2 (1957), 72–73, and vol. 3 (1963), 239–40.
47. Aquinas, *In Librum Beati Dionysii de Divinis Nominibus Expositio*, no. 737.
48. As well as in *ST*, II-II, q. 4, a. 1.

other intellectual. The first one is a matter of hope—that is, "the relation of the act of faith to its end"; the second one is a matter of assent—that is, "the firm adhesion of the intellect to the non-evident truth of faith." The fact that, for Aquinas, this adhesion is much more than theoretical is confirmed by a remark taken from his commentary on Ephesians 3:16: "We receive him [the Spirit] through a faith which is most strong because it is the substance of the realities we hope for—that is, it makes these desired realities exist within us."[49] Elsewhere he boldly avers, "We should hope from God for nothing less than himself."[50]

The logical-epistemological side is unmistakable in Aquinas's treatment of truth. And yet, in a faith environment, a remarkable warmth accompanies the enjoyment of truth. He writes that "those who are captivated by his [the Father's] greatness ... are also drawn by the Son, through a wonderful joy and love of the truth, which is the very Son of God himself." He continues, "we find our pleasure in truth, happiness, justice, eternal life: all of which Christ is!"[51]

THE COMPASS OF

NATURAL REASON

Aquinas sees faith as perfecting human reason. Influenced by chapter 1 of Paul's Letter to the Romans, he claims that divine wisdom is perceptible in the natural world. Notwithstanding the validity of the proofs for the existence of God, he contends that without revelation it is extremely difficult, indeed practically impossible, to secure an exact knowledge of God. In his *Summa Contra Gentiles* he distinguishes two kinds of truth on the subject of God: "Some truths about God exceed all the ability of the human reason. Such is the truth that God is triune." He could have added incarnation,

49. Aquinas, *Commentary on Saint Paul's Epistle to the Ephesians*, trans. Matthew L. Lamb (Albany, N.Y.: Magi, 1966), chap. 3, lecture 4.

50. *ST* II-II, q. 17, a. 2.

51. Aquinas, *Commentary on the Gospel of St. John*, Part I, no. 935.

redemption, and participation in divine life through the sacraments. He continues, "But there are some truths which the natural reason also is able to reach. Such are that God exists, that He is one, and the like."[52] The first kind of truth surpasses the whole ability of human reason; the second kind doesn't, and yet it also needs to be revealed. It is the Holy Spirit who reveals both kinds.[53]

In an earlier writing, Aquinas makes a brief case for the indispensability of belief even on the natural plane.

Because in human society one person must make use of another just as he does himself in matters in which he is not self-sufficient, he must take his stand on what another knows and is unknown to himself, just as he does on what he himself knows. Hence, belief (*fides*) is necessary in human society, one person believing what another says.[54]

According to Aquinas, if the religious truths that reside *within* the compass of human reason were not revealed, three awkward consequences would follow. First, few people would possess the knowledge of God. Three considerations support this fact: want of intellectual talent, lack of time, and indolence. The second awkward consequence is that even in the case of those with ample leisure, vital truths, which indicate the origin and the direction of human life, would be discovered only after a great deal of time. And third, the truths would be either held with doubt or mixed with error.[55] Aquinas may have had in mind his favorite philosopher, Aristotle, whose "First Mover" did not possess the attribute of providence: the Stagirite's God had no interest in becoming abreast of the contingent events of our human history. Actually, in the context of a homily, where he permitted himself to be dismissive, Aquinas declared, "God enlightens the intellect through faith. This is the great-

---

52. Aquinas, *Summa Contra Gentiles*, trans. Anton C. Pegis (Notre Dame, Ind.: University of Notre Dame Press, 1975), book I, chap. 3, par. 2; see chap. 4; see also *ST* I, q. 1, a. 1.

53. See *ST* I-II, q. 109, a. 1, ad 1.

54. Aquinas, *Commentary on the "De Trinitate" of Boethius*, q. 3, a. 1; Maurer's translation slightly emended.

55. Aquinas, *Summa Contra Gentiles*, book I, chap. 4, par. 2–5; see *ST*, II-II, q. 2, a. 4.

est teaching. Having a little bit of faith is more than knowing every-thing that all philosophers in the world have known."[56]

Insofar as the religious truths that reside *beyond* the compass of human reason are concerned, Aquinas's argument turns on the ut-most importance of an ultimate end—what we nowadays call the meaning of human life or the evolution of the universe. At the very beginning of the *Summa Contra Gentiles*, he writes:

> The ultimate end of the universe must be the good of an intellect. This good is truth. Truth must consequently be the ultimate end of the whole uni-verse, and the consideration of the wise person aims principally at truth. So it is that, according to his own statement, divine Wisdom testifies that he has assumed flesh and come into the world in order to make the truth known: "For this I was born, and for this I came into the world, to testify to the truth."[57]

Aquinas has an acute awareness of the treasure offered by Christi-anity and, correspondingly, of the great lacuna that would plague humankind, had there been no revelation and no knowledge of the ultimate end.

Inspired by the thought of St. Paul, Aquinas makes it clear that "it is useless to look for genuine wisdom except in Christ" and that "all science resides in Christ."[58] He declares that "Christian faith ... especially boasts in the cross of our Lord Jesus Christ."[59] Elsewhere he offers the following explanation: "There [in the cross] an obvious sign of divine friendship is shown.... For nothing shows His mercy to us as much as the death of Christ."[60] Commenting on St. Paul's First Letter to the Corinthians, he stresses that in regard to God's design for the destiny of the human race, both philosophical reasons

---

56. Sermon 21, in Aquinas, *The Academic Sermons*, trans. Mark-Robin Hoogland (Washington, D.C.: The Catholic University of America Press, 2010), 317.

57. Jn 18:37; Aquinas, *Summa Contra Gentiles*, book I, chap. 1, par. 2.

58. Aquinas, *Super Epistolam ad Colossenses Lectura*, nos. 82 and 84, in *Super Epistolas S. Pauli Lectura*.

59. Aquinas, *De Rationibus Fidei*, Caput 1, no. 949, in *Opuscula Theologica*, vol.1.

60. Aquinas, *Commentary on Saint Paul's Epistle to the Galatians*, trans. F. R. Larcher (Albany, N.Y.: Magi, 1966), chap. 6, lecture 4.

and rhetorical arguments are inadequate.[61] He repeatedly asserts that divine wisdom revealed in Christ transcends the capacities of the human mind.[62] Likewise, Christ's resurrection (which no one ever watched) lies beyond human understanding. It is only through the appearances of Jesus that his disciples gained access to the mystery of his glorious transformation and wonderful presence.[63]

As an illustration, Aquinas cites this belief: "The preaching of Christ's cross contains facts that seems impossible to human wisdom, for instance, that God could die or that the Almighty could fall into the hands of the violent."[64] By contrast, the believers "recognize in the cross of Christ the power of God through which the devils are defeated, sins are remitted, and human beings are saved."[65] Such an act of recognition is at once a divine gift and a human operation.

There is also another aspect of Jesus that draws people to him:

No one was converted when John [the Baptist] praised the dignity of Christ, saying, he "ranks ahead of me," and "I am not worthy to unfasten the strap of his sandal." But the disciples followed Christ when John talked about Christ's humility and about the mystery of the incarnation; and this is because we are more moved by Christ's humility and the sufferings he endured for us.[66]

Contemplating Christ has a strong impact upon our hearts.

The knowledge (*notitia*) acquired through faith both illumines the intellect and delights the affectivity (*affectum*), because it says not only that God is first cause, but also that he is our Saviour, our Redeemer, who loves us, and that he became incarnate for us. All these things enkindle our affectivity.[67]

Christ is also at the center of the scriptures:

61. Aquinas, *Super Primam Epistolam ad Corinthios Lectura*, no. 77, in *Super Epistolas S. Pauli Lectura*.

62. See, for example, *Super Primam Epistolam ad Corinthios Lectura*, no. 86.

63. See ST III, q. 55, a. 1, a. 2, a. 5, & a. 6.

64. Aquinas, *Super Primam Epistolam ad Corinthios Lectura*, no. 47.

65. *Super Primam Epistolam ad Corinthios Lectura*, no. 60; see also no. 47.

66. Aquinas, *Commentary on the Gospel of St. John*, Part I, no. 285.

67. Aquinas, *Super Secundam Epistolam ad Corinthios Lectura*, no. 73, in *Super Epistolas S. Pauli Lectura*.

The word of God leads to Christ, since Christ himself is the natural Word of God. But every word inspired by God is a certain participated likeness of that Word. Therefore, since every participated likeness leads to its original, it is clear that every word inspired by God leads to Christ.[68]

Combining 1 Corinthians 3:11 and Ephesians 3:17, Aquinas sums up his views on Christ by stating that the sole "foundation" (*fundamentum*) is "Jesus Christ, who dwells in your hearts through faith." And drawing from Matthew 7:25, he adds that this foundation "possesses the solidity of a rock."[69] In addition to being the object of belief, Christ is also the one we believe.

Because whoever believes assents to the word of the one he believes, in any form of belief what seems primary (*principale*) and, as it were, the end, is the one whose word is assented to, those things by holding to which a person wishes to assent to the other are secondary (*secundaria*). Thus the person who rightly has Christian faith voluntarily assents to Christ in those matters that truly belong of his teaching.[70]

Faith is directed to Christ in an interpersonal relationship. And yet the Holy Spirit also plays a crucial role in the understanding that is part and parcel of the faith experience.

Just as the effect of the mission of the Son was to lead us to the Father, so the effect of the mission of the Holy Spirit is to lead the faithful to the Son.... And so the effect of this kind of mission [of the Spirit] is to make us sharers in the divine wisdom and knowers of the truth. The Son, since he is the Word, gives teaching to us; but the Holy Spirit enables us to grasp it.[71]

Aquinas's view of the Christian relationship with Christ has a pronounced affective side, as in this sentence: "To know Christ's love is to know all the mysteries of Christ's Incarnation and our Redemption. These have poured out from the immense charity of God; a charity exceeding every created intelligence."[72]

68. Aquinas, *Commentary on the Gospel of St. John*, Part I, no. 820.
69. Aquinas, *Super Primam Epistolam ad Corinthios Lectura*, nos. 151–52.
70. *ST* II-II, q. 11, a. 1.
71. Aquinas, *Commentary on the Gospel of St. John*, Part I, no. 1958.
72. Aquinas, *Commentary on Saint Paul's Epistle to the Ephesians*, chap. 3, lecture 5.

THREE ASPECTS OF BELIEVING

Many centuries before Aquinas, Augustine stressed in a sermon the superiority of belief in Christ (*credere in Christum*) to the mere belief that Jesus is the Christ (*credere Christum esse*). The former requires that someone also hope in Christ and love him; the latter is an assent that even the demons can make.[73] In his commentary on the Gospel according to John, again Augustine places much more weight upon "faith working through love" (quoting Galatians 5:6) than on "believing him [Christ]" (*credere ei*). He explains that believing in Christ means "by believing to go into him" (*credendo in eum ire*)—thus forcefully expressing the movement of faith in love toward Christ.[74] Last, in another sermon, he brings together the three sides of faith, as he points out:

It [the Apostles' Creed] does not say, "I believe that God [is such and such]"; or, "I believe God," although these also are necessary for salvation. It is one thing to believe him (*credere illi*), another thing to believe that he [is such and such] (*credere illum*), and still another thing to believe in him (*credere in illum*). To believe him is to believe that what he says is true; to believe that he [is such and such] is to believe that he himself is God; to believe in him is to love him.[75]

Drawing from three Latin phrases employed by Augustine, Aquinas articulates the three aspects of believing in a more systematic manner than his predecessor.[76] First, the *credere in Deum*, "to believe

---

73. St. Augustine, *Sermones ad populum*, CXLIV, Caput II, §2, PL 38, 788; *Sermons III/4 on the New Testament*, trans. Edmund Hill, ed. John E. Rotelle (Brooklyn, N.Y.: New City Press, 1992), 430–31.

74. Augustine, *In Joannis Evangelium*, XXIX, §6, on Jn 7:17, PL 35, 1631; *Homilies on the Gospel of John*, in *Nicene and Post-Nicene Fathers*, ed. Philip Schaff, First Series, 2nd printing (Peabody, Mass.: Hendrickson, 1995), 7:185.

75. Augustine, *Sermo de Symbolo*, PL 40, col. 1190–91; the English rendering is mine, since, even after consulting with three specialists in Augustine's works, I was unable to locate a published English translation.

76. See Peter Lombard's *Sentences*, book 3, dist. 23, which quotes Augustine. In his commentary on the *Sentences*, Aquinas introduces Augustine's three acts of faith and felicitously clarifies the *credere in Deum*, which he explicates as "tending towards God by

in God," where the Latin preposition *in* suggests an impulsion into or unto God, a thrust of the human affectivity in its journey toward God; this is the voluntary side. The other two phrases refer to the intellectual side. So we have, second, the *credere Deum*, "to believe that," which is to say that the human intellect affirms its beliefs as propositions (for instance, "I believe that God created the universe"). And third, there is the *credere Deo*, "to believe God," with faithfulness and fidelity.[77]

In other words, the *credere in Deum* expresses the act of consenting. The other two phrases express the act of assenting. Thus *credere Deum* means to believe that God is such and such (= the material object); the *credere Deo* means to believe God (= the formal aspect). In his commentary on Romans, Aquinas claims that the *credere Deo* is more properly the act of faith—namely, its species.[78] And in his commentary on John, he elaborates:

> It is one thing to say: "I believe that God [is such and such]" (*credere Deum*), for this indicates the object. It is another thing to say: "I believe God" (*credere Deo*), for this indicates the one who testifies. And it is still another thing to say: "I believe in God" (*credere in Deum*), for this indicates the end. Thus God can be regarded as the object of faith, as the one who testifies, and as the end, but in different ways.[79]

The *credere in Deum* is affective, whereas the first two phrases are facets of knowledge. *Credere Deum* is a matter of receiving the revealed propositions both in their symbolic and in their conceptual garb. *Credere Deo* refers to the ground of such an acceptance—to wit, the First Truth. Jesus Christ is the First Truth, the Word embodied in a human nature and thus become visible. To quote Aquinas

---

loving" (*amando in eum tendere*); see Aquinas, *Scriptum super Libros Sententiarum*, book 3, dist. 23, q. 2, a. 2, sol. 2, no. 149, in Maria Fabianus Moos's edition (Paris: Lethielleux, 1933).

77. *ST* II-II, q. 2, a. 2; see also q. 1, a. 1.

78. Aquinas, *Super Epistolam ad Romanos Lectura*, no. 327.

79. Aquinas, *Commentary on the Gospel of St. John*, Part I, no. 901 (translation slightly emended).

again, "He [Christ] was also full of truth, because the human nature in Christ attained to the divine truth itself, that is, that this man should be the divine Truth itself.... Thus it is said: 'In whom all the treasures of wisdom are hidden' (Col 2:3)."[80]

In Aquinas's view, the decision to believe, which generates the unconditional assent of the mind—the formal characteristic of faith—is preceded and followed by intelligent and affective apprehensions. Christians yearn to love and to be loved by the God they have discovered in Jesus and in their brothers and sisters (*credere in Deum*). Still, the decision to believe is far from being blind: Christians see in Jesus Christ what God is and what man is called to be (*credere Deum*). At the same time, they are receptive to the truths revealed by God: they believe God (*credere Deo*).

CONCLUDING REMARKS

The first section of this chapter demonstrated that, far from being anti-intellectual or "para-intellectual," faith can enhance the human search for affective fulfillment and for understanding. I also provided an account of why Aquinas holds First Truth as the keystone of the act of faith: his justification consists in philosophically explaining, in an Aristotelian manner, how it is that believing rests on the very basic principles of thinking. I then examined the considerations he adduces to defend his realistic view of the limitations of human reason; those limitations have to do with the several hurdles that most of the time impede people's search for truth. Finally, I showed that he joins, in a balanced synthesis, the three elements of the faith experience: "to believe in God," "to believe that," and "to believe God." As we saw in chapter 2, the presence of these three aspects is already noticeable in the Gospel according to John, albeit in a less systematic way than in Aquinas's works. Moreover, I will insist again on their complementarity when I propose, in chapter 6, an actualization of these three components of faith for today.

80. *Commentary on the Gospel of St. John*, Part I, no. 188.

CHAPTER 4

John Henry Newman

AN APOLOGY FOR
CHRISTIANITY

ॐ

Throughout his life, John Henry Newman (1801–90) was concerned with the challenge that the rationalism of his time, which he often called "liberalism," addressed to Christianity. In this chapter, therefore, we shall concentrate on aspects of his thought that shed light on his account of the faith process—a process he viewed as much broader and deeper than any rationalist methodology. In this respect, most innovative and valuable are his notions of "real apprehension" and "inference."

One of his groundbreaking works, *An Essay in Aid of a Grammar of Assent*, is composed of two parts, as Edward Caswall of the Birmingham Oratory noted, in a kind of shorthand, after he had a conversation with Newman: "Object of the book twofold. In the first part shows that you can believe what you cannot understand. In the second part that you can believe what you cannot absolutely prove."[1] Accordingly, we shall begin with the first part of his *Grammar*, entitled, "Assent and Apprehension," where the distinction

---

1. Quoted by C. Stephen Dessain, "Cardinal Newman on the Theory and Practice of Knowledge: The Purpose of the *Grammar of Assent*," *Downside Review* 75 (1957):3.

between real and notional apprehension is expounded; this distinction explains why faith, being the outcome of real apprehensions, does not require, in most believers' minds, notional apprehensions that are systematically correlated. Then we shall go to the second part, entitled "Assent and Inference," where the Enlightenment's obsession with proof of belief is dismissed in favor of an approach that is very similar to the kind of informal reasoning we find in everyday life. Afterward, we shall study the chapter in which he situates inference and apprehension in the field of religion.[2] Finally, another section will examine what Newman thought of three distortions affecting faith.

REAL AND NOTIONAL APPREHENSION

Newman does not clearly differentiate apprehension and assent. He does not have to, since assent always incorporates some apprehension and since he is eager to put forward another distinction—that is, between two kinds of apprehension, real and notional.[3] Yet, under the influence of Lonergan, for whom insight (apprehension) and judgment (assent) are two distinct intellectual acts, I prefer speaking of *apprehension* as occurring most of the time prior to assent.[4]

In preparatory notes for the *Grammar*, Newman distinguishes the two kinds of apprehension:

2. On the plan of the book, see John Henry Newman, *An Essay in Aid of a Grammar of Assent*, 384, 300. In this chapter, page numbers are given to two editions, preceded by *GA*: first to the eighth edition of the *Grammar* by Longmans, Green, and Company, London and New York, 1889, reedited by I. T. Ker (Oxford: Clarendon Press, 1985), with references to the 1889 edition in the margins, and second to the edition published by University of Notre Dame Press in 1979. Each of those fairly recent editions is preceded by an insightful introduction, by I. T. Ker and Nicholas Lash, respectively.

3. For helpful comments on Newman, see Charles C. Hefling Jr., "Newman on Apprehension, Notional and Real," *Method: Journal of Lonergan Studies* 14 (1996):55–84.

4. Let us notice, however, that apprehension is not always a full act of understanding: "Apprehension then is simply an intelligent acceptance of the idea, or of the fact which a proposition enunciates" (*GA*, 20, 36).

The apprehension, which is thus a condition of Assent to a proposition, is of two kinds, apprehension of its meaning and of its object; the former of these is mainly an act of pure intellect, the latter an act of experience, present or past and of memory in aid of experience; and according, and so far as, the apprehension is of the former or the latter kind, so is the assent languid or energetic.[5]

And he provides an illustration:

Hagar said in the desert "Thou, God, seest me."[6] She spoke of a fact, which she contemplated by a quasi-image—it was not a mere intellectual idea— but in a philosopher or a child "the Omniscience of God" stands for a notion which he has formed in his mind from many other notions, and which he could hold quite as well, if he had no experience of God's omniscience, as if he had.[7]

In the *Grammar* itself, he contrasts real and notional apprehension:

I have said that our apprehension of a proposition varies in strength, and that it is stronger when it is concerned with a proposition expressive to us of things than when concerned with a proposition expressive of notions; and I have given this reason for it, viz. that what is concrete exerts a force and makes an impression on the mind which nothing abstract can rival.[8]

Real apprehension is voiced as a proposition about (concrete) individuals whereas notional apprehension is voiced as a proposition about (abstract) generalities. The former is vivid and is usually associated with assent; the latter is logical and is usually associated with inference.[9]

In a sermon, apropos of real apprehension, Newman uses the verb "to realize" as an equivalent of "to feel": people "feel them [their 'excellences' or qualities] in that vivid way which we call realizing." He

5. Newman, *The Theological Papers of John Henry Newman on Faith and Certainty*, ed. J. Derek Holmes (Oxford: Clarendon Press, 1976), 135.

6. Gn 16:13.

7. Newman, *Theological Papers*, 137. A notion is "an intellectual view," as Newman says in *Discourses Addressed to Mixed Congregations*, 6th ed. (London: Burns and Oates, 1881), discourse IX, "Illuminating Grace," 177.

8. *GA*, 36, 49; see 9–12, 29–31; 23–30, 38–44; and 36–41, 49–52.

9. *GA*, 12, 31; 40, 51–52.

adds, "When men realize a truth, it becomes an influential principle within them, and leads to a number of consequences both in opinion and in conduct."[10]

About real assents, he writes:

They are of a personal character, each individual having his own, and being known by them. It is otherwise with notions; notional apprehension is in itself an ordinary act of our common nature. All of us have the power of abstraction, and can be taught either to make or to enter into the same abstractions; and thus to co-operate in the establishment of a common measure between mind and mind.[11]

In notional apprehension, reasoning is prominent; in real apprehension, the role of the imagination is paramount, for it touches the heart:

The heart is commonly reached, not through the reason, but through the imagination, by means of direct impressions, by the testimony of facts and events, by history, by descriptions. Persons influence us, voices melt us, looks subdue us, deeds inflame us. Many a man will live and die upon a dogma: no man will be a martyr for a conclusion.[12]

No wonder, then, that Newman singled out the pregnant phrase *Cor ad cor loquitur* ("Heart speaks to heart") and, as cardinal, inscribed it on his coat of arms.[13]

Concrete images influence the affections and passions and through them bring about "energetic" assents and deeds. The imagination stimulates the human faculties from which behavior proceeds.[14] Its importance in ethics and religion is immense.

10. Newman, *Parochial and Plain Sermons* (San Francisco: Ignatius Press, 1987), part VI, sermon 18, "Subjection of the Reason and Feelings to the Revealed Word," 1340.

11. *GA*, 83, 82.

12. *GA*, 92–93, 89.

13. Newman must have found it in St. Francis de Sales, who wrote "*cor cordi loquitur*," a phrase he quotes in *The Idea of a University*, ed. Martin J. Svaglic (Notre Dame, Ind.: University of Notre Dame Press, 1982), 308; or the earlier edition (London: Longmans, 1912), 410.

14. *GA*, 82, 81–82; 89, 86.

Belief, … being concerned with things concrete, not abstract, which variously excite the mind from their moral and imaginative properties, has for
its objects, not only directly what is true, but inclusively what is beautiful,
useful, admirable, heroic; objects which kindle devotion, rouse the passions, and attach the affections; and thus it leads the way to actions of every
kind, to the establishment of principles, and the formation of character, and
is thus again intimately connected with what is individual and personal.[15]

An objection may be opportune here: aren't the most profound
convictions based on something deeper than the imagination or the
affections? Isn't fidelity to God often without vivid images and without consolation? In a couple of sermons, Newman cautions against
relying on "excited feelings" that he says are typical of the beginning
of Christian life and that after a while are no longer present to stim-
ulate us.[16] In the *Grammar* he simply highlights the fact that concrete and moving representations facilitate real apprehensions and
assents. Regrettably, at least in those sermons, he fails to point out
that they recur, even during advanced stages of the spiritual journey.
Just think of the poems composed by John of the Cross, with their
intensely affective metaphors.

Real apprehensions make people sensitive and attuned to realities ("things," in Newman's vocabulary) to which they would otherwise remain indifferent.

To the devout and spiritual, the Divine Word speaks of things, not merely of notions. And again, to the disconsolate, the tempted, the perplexed,
the suffering, there comes, by means of their very trials, an enlargement
of thought, which enables them to see in it what they never saw before.
Henceforth there is to them a reality in its teachings, which they recognize
as an argument, and the best of arguments, for its divine origin.[17]

In this last sentence, what does Newman mean by "reality"? I would
say: significant truth for the person concerned. All together, the

15. *GA*, 90, 87.
16. Newman, *Parochial and Plain Sermons*, part I, sermon 8, "The Religious Use of Excited Feelings," and sermon 14, "Religious Emotion."
17. *GA*, 79, 79.

imagination, the emotions, and the mind produce what Robert Holyer felicitously calls "a sense of reality."[18] Especially when Newman's "things" are persons (Christ and his followers), the concreteness of the events that place them on a visible stage, so to speak, engenders a vivid sense that they are momentous for the personally engaged observer.

A few paragraphs further on, however, Newman prudently cautions:

The fact of the distinctness of the images, which are required for real assent, is no warrant for the existence of the objects which those images represent. A proposition, be it ever so keenly apprehended, may be true or may be false. If we simply put aside all inferential information, such as is derived from testimony, from general belief, from the concurrence of the senses, from common sense, or otherwise, we have no right to consider that we have apprehended a truth, merely because of the strength of our mental impression of it.[19]

As we shall find out in a while, Newman's approach to religious belief is composed of both real apprehension and inference. Without the latter, the former would be misleading. In his philosophical notes, he defines our imaginative faculty: "Imagination is the habit or the act of making mental *images*." Then he declares, "Mere imaginations cannot be matter of *judgment*, i.e. of assent or dissent, because you cannot affirm or deny without grounds—and hence there is no basis of knowledge at all."[20]

Newman also stresses the complementarity of notional and real assents. Aquinas's "believing that" and "believing in" should always

18. Robert Holyer, "Religious Certainty and the Imagination: An Interpretation of J. H. Newman," *Thomist* 50 (1986): 411. This article critically and sympathetically completes M. Jamie Ferreira, *Doubt and Religious Commitment: The Role of the Will in Newman's Thought* (Oxford: Clarendon Press, 1980).

19. *GA*, 80, 80.

20. Newman, *The Philosophical Notebook of John Henry Newman*, vol. 2, *The Text*, ed. Edward Sillem, rev. A. J. Boekraad (Louvain: Nauwelaerts, 1970), 152. Vol. 1 is Sillem's "General Introduction to the Study of Newman's Philosophy"—a huge mine of information.

be paired. We might say that real assents are the marrow of religious experience, while notional assents constitute the hard part of the bones— namely, the theological enterprise. Real apprehensions are acts of religion, while notional apprehensions are activities of theology.[21] There is no "contrariety and antagonism between a dogmatic creed and vital religion."[22] "The propositions ... are useful in their dogmatic aspect as ascertaining and making clear for us the truths on which the religious imagination has to rest."[23]

Our author states two things. First, "there is nothing to hinder those who have even the largest stock of such notions [notional apprehensions] from devoting themselves to one or other of the subjects to which those notions belong, and mastering it with a real apprehension." Second, "religion may be made a subject of notional assent also."[24]

Further on, Newman gives five "instances of the change of Notional Assent into Real."[25] When real assent becomes notional, does it cease to be real? And when notional assent becomes real, does it cease to be notional? Not necessarily. At the end of chapter 1, Newman informs us that "in the same mind and at the same time, the same proposition may express both what is notional and what is real."[26] We observe great flexibility in the human mind. For instance, an assent can cease being real and become merely notional. Without disparaging theological reasoning, Newman nonetheless remarks:

Questioning, when encouraged on any subject-matter, readily becomes a habit, and leads the mind to substitute exercises of inference for assent, whether simple or complex. Reasons for assenting suggest reasons for not assenting, and what were realities to our imagination, while our assent was

---

21. *GA*, 98, 93.
22. *GA*, 120, 108.
23. *GA*, 120, 109.
24. *GA*, 55, 62.
25. *GA*, 75, 76.
26. *GA*, 11, 30; see 26, 41; 35, 47.

simple, may become little more than notions, when we have attained to certitude.[27]

By underlining the complementarity between real and notional apprehension and between religion and theology, Newman qualifies the contrast he portrays between them. As will be shown presently, he wants to chart the path toward faith that people actually take—a path at variance with the scientific manner of reasoning. Yet, unfortunately, he does not question the conceptualistic account of science that the moderns worked out. He simply puts the notional in its place instead of indicating what is its function *within* religious experience itself. Nevertheless, despite several commentators who presume to detect a dualistic epistemology in Newman's works, real and notional apprehension differ less than they think.[28] He is aware that real apprehension requires at least a modicum of notional apprehension, since there can be no insight into the significance of a concrete thing or person without some general idea that conveys that significance.[29] Thus he writes:

In the proposition "Sugar is sweet," the predicate is a common noun as used by those who have compared sugar in their thoughts with honey or glycerine; but it may be the only distinctively sweet thing in the experience of a child, and may be used by him as a noun singular.[30]

Regrettably, however, Newman does not display the manner in which common and singular nouns are integrated into the adult's thinking.[31]

27. *GA*, 217, 178.
28. For example, Jay Newman, *The Mental Philosophy of John Henry Newman* (Waterloo, Ont.: Wilfrid Laurier University Press, 1986), chap. 2.
29. I tackled this issue in Roy, "Interpersonal Knowledge according to John Macmurray," *Modern Theology* 5 (1989):349–65.
30. *GA*, 11, 30.
31. In "A Neglected Argument for the Reality of God (1908)," in *The Essential Peirce: Selected Philosophical Writings*, ed. Peirce Edition Project (Bloomington: Indiana University Press), 2:434–50, Charles Sanders Peirce puts forward an argument that resembles Newman's real apprehension in that it is based on the human heart's admiration for the beauty of three "Universes of Experience." They are: all mere ideas; the Brute Actuality of

In this section, I have employed myself in rendering, as much as possible, the phenomenological wealth in Newman's descriptions of the real and notional apprehension. By and large, they correspond to Aquinas's "to believe in" and "to believe that." Both are indispensable in the process of hoping and of putting one's faith in God.

INFERENCE BASED ON

CONVERGING EVIDENCE

We now move to part two of the *Grammar*. One of the brilliant achievements of this work consists in having abandoned the modern problematic regarding belief—a problematic adopted by both the Christian apologists and their opponents. For them, the principal question was whether one could prove the fact of biblical revelation. The *Grammar* goes to the root of the matter by demonstrating that the whole debate rested on a concept of proof that is out of place, both in daily experience and in religion.

Newman notices this concept of proof in a fellow Englishman, John Locke. Reacting to his critics, Newman exclaims, "Let those who think I ought to be answered, those Catholics, first master the great difficulty, the great problem, and then, if they don't like my way of meeting it, find another."[32] This "great difficulty" is Locke's view of reason and of its role in the process of coming to believe. Even though Locke recognizes what he himself calls "the reasonableness of Christianity," still, for him, faith amounts to a personal adhesion to propositions, which falls short of demonstrability. To his mind, then, intellectual honesty requires that religious assents be always qualified by the provisional nature of the inference.[33] In the nineteenth century, W. K. Clifford and others transferred Locke's point

---

things and facts; and the active power to establish connections between different objects (435). For Peirce, the one who muses on the three Universes may see his whole conduct shaped "into conformity with the hypothesis that God is Real and very near" (446).

32. Newman, *The Letters and Diaries of John Henry Newman*, ed. Charles Stephen Dessain et al. (Oxford: Clarendon Press, 1973), 25:280.

33. John Locke, *An Essay concerning Human Understanding* (1700), ed. Peter H.

more expressly into the field of religion, belabored it, and hardened it. The outcome is that all faith judgments are merely probable, albeit sometimes highly probable, and yet never absolutely certain. In chapter 6 of the *Grammar*, Newman replies that Locke's position unwarrantedly presumes *formal demonstrability* as the yardstick. Over against the latter, Newman broadens the Enlightenment's understanding of "reason" by introducing another kind of reasonable ascertainment: *informal* inference. Pace Locke, informal inference leads to judgments that brook no *degrees* of assent: our judgments can legitimately be held as unconditional even in the absence of formal proofs. Moreover, they may remain intact long after the process of inferring was made—to wit, when the reasons one entertained have been forgotten. Often those reasons have never been made explicit.[34] They may even defy logical analysis. As Michael Polanyi has observed, many of the steps taken by scientists are not methodically conscious. This philosopher of science has underscored the vital role of tacit, inarticulate knowing: "We can know more than we can tell."[35] There is informal inference even in science.

Section 1 of chapter 6 is concerned to underscore the fact that in ordinary life most of our assents are simple—that is, unanalyzed. Still, even these assents are categorical. In section 2 of the same chapter, the author points out that "complex or reflex assents" are made consciously and deliberately.[36] The process of inferring that culminates in such assents takes place in an orderly and logical manner. The stages of the argument are explicitly identified and related.

Nidditch, 4th ed. (Oxford: Clarendon Press, 1975), book IV, chap. 16, "On the Degrees of Assent."

34. Newman's University Sermon 13, entitled "Implicit and Explicit Reason," expounds this distinction; see Newman, *Fifteen Sermons Preached before the University of Oxford* (Notre Dame, Ind.: University of Notre Dame Press, 1997).

35. Polanyi, *Tacit Dimension*, 4. For a Polanyian reading of Newman, see Martin X. Moleski, *Personal Catholicism: The Theological Epistemologies of John Henry Newman and Michael Polanyi* (Washington, D.C.: The Catholic University of America Press, 2000).

36. In his *Theological Papers* (64–72) Newman calls the simple assent an *intuition* and the complex assent a *contuition*.

JOHN HENRY NEWMAN

Certitude attaches to them inasmuch as they are reflective. "Certitude … is the perception of a truth with the perception that it is a truth, or the consciousness of knowing, as expressed in the phrase, 'I know that I know.'"[37] The conviction is a *certitude*, whereas the proposition or truth is a *certainty*.[38] The two sides, subjective and objective, are inseparable. Let us be clear that both simple and complex assents may be certain as assertions, even though their contents may be qualified. "When I assent to a doubtfulness, or to a probability, my assent, as such, is as complete as if I assented to a truth; it is not a certain degree of assent. And, in like manner, I may be certain of an uncertainty."[39] For instance, a twentieth-century scientist would say, "I hold without any doubt that Einstein's theory of relativity is very probably true."[40]

Newman defines informal inference as "the method by which we are enabled to become certain of what is concrete." It consists in "the cumulation of probabilities, independent of each other, arising out of the nature and circumstances of the particular case which is under review; probabilities too fine to avail separately, too subtle and circuitous to be convertible into syllogisms, too numerous and various for such conversion, even were they convertible."[41]

As instances of judgments reached through informal inference, let us single out Newman's statements that "Great Britain is an island" and that "I, in my own particular case, shall die." The first statement flows from "negative arguments and circumstantial evidence." "Numberless facts, or what we consider facts, rest on the truth of it; no received fact rests on its being otherwise."[42]

The second statement is called "antecedent probability, which is

37. *GA*, 197, 163.
38. *GA*, 196, 162.
39. *GA*, 175, 147.
40. For a more detailed treatment than Newman's, see Lonergan, *Collected Works*, vol. 3, *Insight*, index, "Unconditioned, virtually."
41. *GA*, 288, 230.
42. *GA*, 295, 235.

101

by itself no logical proof."[43] It points to the probability that something is or will be a fact. Newman observes, "Many of our most obstinate and most reasonable certitudes depend on proofs which are informal and personal, which baffle our powers of analysis, and cannot be brought under logical rule."[44]

Elsewhere Newman distinguishes formal and informal proof:

Argumentation is chiefly of two kinds: it gives either extrinsic or intrinsic reasons for what it wants to prove. Intrinsic reasons are those that derive from what strictly pertains to the matter which is to be proved, whereas extrinsic reasons are those that appeal to what is prior to the matter in question, and has a greater extension. For example, let us suppose that someone has been murdered. Investigators seek two kinds of evidence. On the one hand, a suspect is known to consort with murderers; to have been tried for the same crime before. On the other hand, he is known to have blood on his clothes; to have had an item of the victim's clothing on his person when he was apprehended; to have been loitering at the scene of the crime about the time it was committed....

These extrinsic kinds of argumentation are therefore called "verisimilitude," "antecedent probability," or "presumption." Only intrinsic argumentation is called "proof."[45]

He comments:

In regard to this distinction, it should first be said that whereas *proof* makes a thing evident, *presumption* gives it greater credibility.... However, even though presumption cannot by itself yield credibility, it still has considerable power to make the matter to be proved credible (that is, by making the evidence highly credible) when even minimal *proof* is offered.[46]

As I. T. Ker reports, Newman proposes three helpful comparisons. The first one is an arch: "I liken [the proof of religion] to the mechanism of some triumph of skill, tower or spire, geometrical

43. *GA*, 299, 237.
44. *GA*, 301, 239.
45. Newman, "Proposed Introduction to the French Translation of the University Sermons," in *Three Latin Papers*, 51.
46. Newman, "Proposed Introduction," 52.

staircase or vaulted roof, where ... the weight is ingeniously thrown in a variety of directions, upon supports which are distinct from, or independent of each other." He provides another analogy: it is like a "bundle of sticks, each of which ... you could snap in two, if taken separately from the rest."[47] Or again: "The best illustration ... is that of a *cable* which is made up of a number of separate threads, each feeble, yet together as sufficient as an iron rod." He defends the validity of such an informal proof: "An iron rod represents mathematical or strict demonstration; a cable represents moral demonstration, which is an assemblage of probabilities.... A man who said 'I cannot trust a cable, I must have an iron bar,' would *in certain given cases*, be irrational and unreasonable."[48] In keeping with Newman's metaphor of the cable, then, while specific arguments are directed against particular threads, belief is based on the cable—namely, on the whole antecedent probability.

Basil Mitchell clarifies the nature of a probable proof by declaring that it is not a series of buckets set inside each other, each of which is leaky.[49] He says this in reply to Anthony Flew, who denounced "the Ten-leaky-buckets-Tactic, applied to arguments none of which hold water at all." The point is well taken. Having remarked that any piece of evidence can be apprehended in more than one way, Clyde Nabe comments, "A leaky bucket is present when there are other ways of understanding the evidence which make a good deal more sense than the one which we are calling a leaky bucket understanding." In contrast, the basic condition for not having a series of leaky buckets is as follows: "When such pieces of evidence are put together in one particular way they make more sense than when they are put together in some other way." Each piece must be worthy of serious consideration, but their being pasted together must also make sense. Hence Nabe concludes:

47. Newman, *Letters and Diaries*, 19:460 and 24:146; quoted by I. T. Ker, "Editor's Introduction," in *GA*, xxvii–xxviii.

48. Newman, *Letters and Diaries*, 21:146.

49. Basil Mitchell, *The Justification of Religious Belief* (London: Macmillan, 1973), 40.

A probable argument is one in which each piece *does* work, and where each piece has some important strength of its own; it is just that no one piece can carry all of the weight by itself. To accomplish this task, other pieces are necessary; the work is finally accomplished *together* by individual pieces all of which contribute in a positive way, and all of which are valuable in their own right.[50]

In a nineteenth-century treatise on astronomy, its author concedes that he cannot offer a direct demonstration that the earth rotates about its axis, and he appeals to a cluster of reasons based "upon *different* principles." Having quoted this phrase in his *Grammar*, Newman notes that even scientists often have to work with "independent probabilities in cumulation."[51] Nabe remarks that Newman too starkly opposes scientific and practical reason (I would add, *most of the time* he does, notwithstanding the exception just mentioned). Nabe gives an apposite example from science itself, which confirms Newman's view concerning method in astronomy:

That this is hardly unique to religion is not hard to show. The history of the development of evolutionary theory is replete with the formation of hypotheses in quite different realms of nature. Over the course of a century or two, geology, paleontology, anthropology, genetics, ecology, and ethology have each developed hypotheses which work together to support a theory of evolution. That theory, while not particularly convincing perhaps on the basis of the work in any *one* of those fields of investigation becomes highly probable when they are taken together.[52]

In a much less articulated fashion, wise people rest content with probable evidence regarding their everyday assumptions. As Bishop Joseph Butler, whose thought exercised an enormous influence upon Newman, remarked, "To us, probability is the very guide of life."[53] Inspired by intelligent human experience, one has a right to

50. Clyde Nabe, *Mystery and Religion: Newman's Epistemology of Religion* (Lanham, Md.: University Press of America, 1988), 43.

51. *GA*, 318, 252.

52. Nabe, *Mystery and Religion*, 51.

53. Joseph Butler, *The Analogy of Religion, Natural and Revealed, to the Constitution and Course of Nature* (London: George Bell and Sons, 1878), 73.

believe what one cannot absolutely prove. In light of British common law, Nicholas Wolterstorff thus paraphrases Newman: "Our beliefs ... are innocent unless proven guilty."[54]

To justify this attitude, Newman looks for another model of reason. He finds it in Aristotle's notion of practical wisdom—namely, in *phronesis*. Besides scientific inquiry, human beings engage in deliberation. The former consists in speculative reasoning, whereas the latter consists in applied reasoning. This is one of Newman's brilliant insights: the realization that religious inference is like common sense, not like science. As Aristotle himself declared, ethics does not function in the same manner as mathematics.[55] In the process of coming to believe, *phronesis* operates in this way: "What does that subtle *phronesis* or wisdom in determining *when* we ought to be certain &c. It has two offices—1. to bring together ALL the arguments, however subtle. 2. and next, to determine their place and worth whether separately or in combination."[56]

Newman transposes this Aristotelian notion from the field of practical truth into the field of what people hold as factual truth.[57] He moves from ethics to religion, from the issue of what is to be done in general to the issue of what is to be believed. Still, faith remains in the sphere of "what is to be done." The end result of the religious quest is a decision that *does* something—that is, that triggers an assent accompanied by many existential and moral implications. While the object of assent is truth, the will's decision to assent nevertheless pertains to "the way of practice." Newman states, "The moral sense is an assent to a thing as right."[58] Moreover, about mat-

54. Nicholas Wolterstorff, "Can Belief in God Be Rational If It Has No Foundation?" in *Faith and Rationality: Reason and Belief in God,* ed. Alvin Plantinga and Nicholas Wolterstorff (Notre Dame, Ind.: University of Notre Dame Press, 1983), 163.

55. Aristotle, *Nicomachean Ethics,* book 1, section 3, 1094b, and section 7, 1098; book 2, section 2, 1104a. This Aristotelian model of practical reason is transposed by Hans-Georg Gadamer into the field of hermeneutics; see Gadamer, *Truth and Method,* trans. Joel Weinsheimer and Donald G. Marshall, 2nd rev. ed. (New York: Crossroad, 1989), 312–24.

56. Newman, *Philosophical Notebook of John Henry Newman,* 2:163.

57. *GA,* 354, 277n1.

58. Newman, *Theological Papers,* 120.

ters of life and death it is vital to make up one's mind: "In many cases indeed it is not necessary to be certain … ; but in other cases it is imperative, or it is a duty to be certain."[59]

In Newman's treatment, Aristotle's *phronesis* becomes the "illative sense," defined as the "power of judging and concluding, when in its perfection."[60] He explains that

The sole and final judgment on the validity of an inference in concrete matter is committed to the personal action of the ratiocinative faculty, the perfection or virtue of which I have called the Illative Sense, a use of the word "sense" parallel to our use of it in "good sense," "common sense," a "sense of beauty," &c.[61]

In Lonergan's words, "By definition the … illative sense proceeds along ways unknown to syllogism from a cumulation of probabilities—too manifold to be marshaled, too fleeting to be formulated—to a conclusion that nonetheless is certain."[62] The adjective "illative" derives from the Latin *illatus*, past participle of *inferre*, to infer, to carry in, to perform the mental act signaled by the word "hence."

The antecedent probability of inferring and of assenting to some philosophical or religious truth derives from a person's outlook on reality. Newman's reflections on David Hume make this clear. Hume's repudiation of miracles tallies with his view that the necessary laws of nature cannot be violated,[63] whereas Newman's reply assumes that the belief in divine providence and revelation opens someone to the possibility that miracles may very well occur. Newman spells out his own presuppositions as he introduces them with three "supposing…."[64]

Given the particular horizons that situate people's expectations,

59. Newman, *Theological Papers*, 121; see also *Fifteen Sermons*, 298.
60. *GA*, 353, 276.
61. *GA*, 345, 271.
62. Lonergan, "The Form of Inference," in *Collected Works*, vol. 4, *Collection*, ed. Frederick E. Crowe and Robert M. Doran (Toronto: University of Toronto Press, 1988), 3.
63. *GA*, 306, 242–43; see 81, 81.
64. *GA*, 306–7, 243.

certain events do or do not make sense to them. Assents can be either facilitated or hampered by "the moral state of the parties inquiring or disputing,"[65] by "the influence of moral motives in hindering assent to conclusions."[66] "For instance, as to the emotions, this strength of assent may be nothing more than the strength of love, hatred, interest, desire, or fear, which the object of the assent elicits, and this is especially the case when that object is of a religious nature."[67] In the case of negative emotions regarding the object of the proposed assent, we could speak of "antecedent improbability," as Avery Dulles does, in an allusion to Newman. Dulles acknowledges that "the affirmations of Christian faith must seem implausible to all who do not experience the power of God's word in Christ."[68]

In University Sermon 10 Newman affirms that "it [faith] is mainly swayed by antecedent considerations." He avows, "Faith is influenced by previous notices, prepossessions, and (in a good sense of the word) prejudices."[69] And the preacher adds:

I do but say that it is antecedent probability that gives meaning to those arguments from facts which are commonly called the Evidences of Revelation; that, whereas mere probability proves nothing, mere facts persuade no one; that probability is to fact, as the soul to the body; that mere presumptions may have no force, but that mere facts have no warmth. A mutilated and defective evidence suffices for persuasion where the heart is alive; but dead evidences, however perfect, can but create a dead faith.[70]

Newman's "antecedent considerations" and "prejudices" are called by Gadamer the "fore-meanings and prejudices"—namely, the prejudgments that orient our attitude to a text or to anything that solicits our recognition. They may "have either a positive or a negative value"

65. *GA*, 320, 253.
66. *GA*, 169, 143.
67. *GA*, 185, 154–55.
68. Avery Dulles, *The Craft of Theology: From Symbol to System*, new expanded ed. (New York: Crossroad, 1995), 67 and 68.
69. *GA*; Newman, *Fifteen Sermons*, 187.
70. *GA*, 200.

and consequently be legitimate or objectionable, helpful or unhelp-
ful. The issue is "how to distinguish the true prejudices, by which we
understand, from the *false* ones, by which we *misunderstand*."[71] The
latter can be overcome, albeit not easily.

INFERENCE AND REAL ASSENT

IN CHRISTIANITY

We still have to trail Newman, this time in his application of the notions of inference and real assent to Christianity. Insofar as inference
is concerned, it is in Butler that he found the idea of an accumulation of probabilities as a valid ascertainment of the truth both in
"common matters" and in "religion." He quotes Butler at length:

> Probable proofs, by being added, not only increase the evidence, but mul-
> tiply it.... The truth of our religion, like the truth of common matters, is to
> be judged by the whole evidence taken together ... ; in like manner, as if in
> any common case, numerous events acknowledged, were to be alleged in
> proof of any other event disputed; the truth of the disputed event would
> be proved, not only if any one of the acknowledged ones did of itself clearly
> imply it, but though no one of them singly did so, if the whole of the ac-
> knowledged events taken together could not in reason be supposed to have
> happened, unless the disputed one were true (319, 252–53).[72]

This is an excerpt from *The Analogy of Religion*, a work that Butler published in 1736, at an epoch when the religious controversies
were mired in the stark antithesis of undeniable proof/no proof at
all. The insightful Butler allows Newman to adopt a middle position
between these two unreasonable treatments of belief. The case for
belief rather resembles the evidence adduced at a judicial trial. The
jury can weigh evidence that amounts to high probability and that
warrants definite conclusions.

In a religious quest, however, at some point an individual comes

<hr>

71. Gadamer, *Truth and Method*, 269, 270, 298–99; see also 277. On the concept of
"horizon," see 302.

72. Newman, *Fifteen Sermons*, 319, 252–53. Quoting Butler, *Analogy of Religion*, 306–8;
I have followed Butler's punctuation, which differs from Newman's.

to the conclusion that believing has now become a matter of obligation for her or for him. Newman thus wrote to Mrs. William Froude,
"Faith then is not a conclusion from premises, but the result of an
act of the *will*, following upon a *conviction* that to believe is a *duty*."[73]

After the act of faith has been made, religious tenets are accompanied by certitude. Newman claims that assents to divine revelation rule out any doubting. "Ten thousand difficulties do not make
one doubt."[74] Difficulties are encountered by the intellect, which, to
the extent that it cannot solve a problem, undertakes what he calls
an "investigation." Assents take place on a higher level, the level
of judgments accepted by faith. Newman notes that these assents
can stay firm despite lack of light, despite losing particular reasons
or grounds to support a particular belief. "Arguments against the
grounds of our certitude about any object have no direct power to
destroy our certitude, even though we confess we cannot answer
them, as daily experience shows;—they are but directed against the
grounds."[75] He explains:

Such a state of mind [certitude], it is plain, cannot be immediately dependent on the reasons which are its antecedents, and cannot rightly be
referred back to them as its producing cause. If it were the direct result of
sight, or testimony, or argument, then, as it has been gradually created by
them, so might it be gradually destroyed, and each objection would weaken
it according to its own force.[76]

Lest this position might seem irrational, just remember that for
the Newman of the *Grammar*, if faith is unable to get along with "inquiry," it is perfectly compatible with "investigation." As regards the
latter, he writes:

I say, there is no necessary incompatibility between thus assenting and yet
proving,—for the conclusiveness of a proposition is not synonymous with

73. Newman, *Letters and Diaries*, 12:228; emphases are Newman's.
74. Newman, *Apologia pro Vita Sua: Being a History of His Religious Opinions*, ed. Martin J. Svaglic (Oxford: Clarendon Press, 1967), 214.
75. Newman, *Theological Papers*, 122–23.
76. Newman, *Theological Papers*, 123–24.

its truth. A proposition may be true, yet not admit of being concluded;—
it may be a conclusion and yet not a truth. To contemplate it under one
aspect, is not to contemplate it under another; and the two aspects may
be consistent, from the very fact that they are two *aspects*. Therefore to set
about concluding a proposition is not *ipso facto* to doubt its truth; we may
aim at inferring a proposition, while all the time we assent to it.[77]

In contrast, inquiry is induced by doubting:

I have been speaking of investigation, not of inquiry; it is quite true that
inquiry is inconsistent with assent, but inquiry is something more than the
mere exercise of inference. He who inquires has not found; he is in doubt
where the truth lies, and wishes his present profession either proved or dis-
proved. We cannot without absurdity call ourselves at once believers and
inquirers also.[78]

Despite the different epistemic frameworks, Newman's "investigation" amounts to Aquinas's "thinking" (*cogitare*), engaging in an
"inquest" (*inquisitio*), as we found out in chapter 3. Likewise, Karl
Rahner alludes to "many intellectual difficulties" in the minds of the
believers. He submits, "But such difficulties are too particular and—
compared to the reality of existence—too slight objectively speaking to be used as the basis for decisions about the ultimate questions
of life; they are not weighty enough to be allowed to determine the
whole, unspeakably profound depths of life." With his usual lucidity
and honesty, he continues: "The real argument against Christianity
is the experience of life, this experience of darkness, ... these ultimate experiences of life causing the spirit and the heart to be som-
ber, tired and despairing."[79] We shall see presently that Newman is
also aware of this enormous difficulty as he treats the third channel
of natural religion.

Chapter 10 of the *Grammar* tackles the issue of Christianity's
credentials and brings together the two concepts of real apprehen-

77. *GA*, 190, 158.

78. *GA*, 191, 159.

79. Karl Rahner, "Thoughts on the Possibility of Belief Today," in *Theological Investigations*, trans. Karl-H. Kruger (Baltimore: Helicon Press, 1966), 5:5, 6.

sion and inference; section 1, entitled "Natural Religion," establishes the threefold natural basis for Christianity's supernatural revelation: "our own minds, the voice of mankind, and the course of the world." These are the "three channels" through which the human race has come to know God.[80] They amount to real apprehensions.

The first channel is "our own mind"—namely, "Conscience."[81] Newman summarizes here what he wrote in his chapter 5, section 1, to which he refers. There he has initiated something new. Instead of belaboring the proofs for the existence of God—the much-traveled notional route—he prefers to "show how we apprehend Him, not merely as a notion, but as a reality."[82] He endeavors "to explain how we gain an image of God and give a real assent to the proposition that He exists."[83] In the variegated feeling that is associated with conscience (for instance, "grief, regret, joy, or desire"; "self-approval and hope, or compunction and fear"), he locates "the materials for the real apprehension of a Divine Sovereign and Judge." "The feeling of conscience … is twofold:—it is a moral sense, and a sense of duty; a judgment of the reason and a magisterial dictate."[84] "Thus conscience has both a critical and a judicial office." The first side amounts to "a rule of right conduct"; the second side offers us "a sanction of right conduct."[85] The former was emphasized in Aristotle's ethics, whereas the latter was stressed in Kant's morals. For Newman, conscience helps us to picture God as a living Person both as the originator of specific ethical norms (the Sovereign) and as the one to whom we are accountable (the Judge).

The second channel of natural religion is "the universal testimony of mankind"[86] about the sin that caused "a degraded, servile con-

80. *GA*, 389, 303.
81. *GA*, 389, 303.
82. *GA*, 104, 97.
83. *GA*, 105, 97.
84. *GA*, 105, 98.
85. *GA*, 106, 99.
86. *GA*, 389, 303.

dition" and that "requires expiation, reconciliation, and some great change of nature."[87] The "sense of sin," a "vivid sense"[88] (notice the real apprehension here) is accompanied by hope—a concern I emphasized in chapters 1 and 2. Humanity's "rites of deprecation and of purification" convey "some hope of attaining to a better condition than their present."[89]

The third channel is "the history of society and of the world"[90]—namely, providence. Newman discerns in this history an "established order of things." And yet he honestly puts forward the objection that "His [the Creator's] control of this living world is so indirect, and His action so obscure.... What strikes the mind so forcibly and so painfully is, His absence (if I may so speak) from His own world. It is a silence that speaks."[91] Furthermore, paying attention to "the amount of suffering, bodily and mental, which is our portion in this life," Newman asks about the cause of evil and about our moral impotence.[92]

He concludes that long segment on natural religion with a paragraph that sums up the long-established Catholic inclusivist position:

Such, then, in outline is the system of natural beliefs and sentiments, which, though true and divine, is still possible to us independently of Revelation, and is the preparation for it; though in Christians themselves it cannot really be separated from their Christianity, and never is possessed in its higher forms in any people without some portion of those inward aids which Christianity imparts to us, and those endemic traditions which have their first origin in a paradisiacal illumination.[93]

We now come to Newman's approach to supernatural religion. In the second section of chapter 10, entitled "Revealed Religion," he tells us that, since "I am suspicious then of scientific demonstrations

87. *GA*, 392, 305.
88. *GA*, 392, 305.
89. *GA*, 394, 307.
90. *GA*, 389, 303.
91. *GA*, 396–97, 309.
92. *GA*, 398, 310.
93. *GA*, 408, 317.

in a question of concrete fact, in a discussion between fallible men
… I am going to attempt to prove Christianity in the same informal
way in which I can prove for certain that I have been born into this
world, and that I shall die out of it."[94] This can be achieved thanks
to "an *accumulation* of various probabilities."[95] His way of proving is
not a formal, philosophical one. In the case of concrete individuals
whose "principles are of a personal character, … the validity of proof
is determined, not by any scientific test, but by the illative sense."[96]
Needless to say, such "principles … of a personal character" depend
in a large measure on the input of the imagination, on its affective
consequences, and on the real apprehensions that are thus triggered.

Earlier in his career, in his University Sermon 12, Newman rela-
tivizes the efficacy of the available evidence in order to insist on the
decisive role of an individual's personal conceptions as he considers
the Christian message:

What he thinks likely to be … depends surely on nothing else than the
general state of his mind, the state of his convictions, feelings, tastes, and
wishes…. If he is indisposed to believe, he will explain away very strong
evidence; if he is disposed, he will accept very weak evidence.[97]

Indeed,

the antecedent judgment, with which a man approaches the subject of religion, not only acts as a bearing this way or that,—as causing him to go out
to meet the evidence in a greater or less degree, and nothing more,—but,
further, it practically colours the evidence, even in a case in which he has
recourse to evidence, and interprets it for him.[98]

Concerning the relation between love and evidence, Dulles points
out that in Newman's apologetics, love is not "a substitute for rational
grounds." He continues:

94. *GA*, 410, 319.
95. *GA*, 411, 320.
96. *GA*, 413, 321.
97. Newman, *Fifteen Sermons*, 226.
98. Newman, *Fifteen Sermons*, 227.

I take him to mean rather that where such love is present, sincere inquirers will be able to find sufficient evidence for at least a rudimentary faith in God. If they are privileged to encounter a religion accredited by divine signs, they will be able to recognize and embrace it. But if their hearts are hardened, the evidence will be wasted upon them.[99]

In chapter 10, section 2, no. 1, of the *Grammar*, Newman returns to his position on the antecedent probability of believing. He uncovers some of the erroneous presumptions (negative prejudices, Gadamer would say) hindering people from even considering "the Evidences of Christianity."[100] On the contrary, the persons who are likely to believe are "those who are imbued with the religious opinions and sentiments which I have identified with Natural Religion."[101] For instance, he writes:

One of the most important effects of Natural Religion on the mind, in preparation for [being] Revealed, is the anticipation which it creates, that a Revelation will be given.... This presentiment is founded on our sense, on the one hand, of the infinite goodness of God, and, on the other, of our own extreme misery and need—two doctrines which are the primary constituents of Natural Religion. It is difficult to put a limit to the legitimate force of this antecedent probability.[102]

The context is the contrast that Newman draws between his perspective and William Paley's excessive confidence in argumentation. Newman prefers to count on the affective preparation that enables a person to greet revelation.

They who have no religious earnestness are at the mercy, day by day, of some new argument or fact, which may overtake them, in favour of one conclusion or the other. And how, after all, is a man better for Christianity, who has never felt the need of it or the desire? On the other hand, if he has longed for a revelation to enlighten him and to cleanse his heart, why may

99. Dulles, *Newman* (New York: Continuum, 2002), 59.
100. *GA*, 417, 324.
101. *GA*, 416, 323.
102. *GA*, 422–23, 328. This argument recurs in Lonergan, *Collected Works*, vol. 3, *Insight*, chap. 20, section 2, "The Existence of a Solution."

he not use, in his inquiries after it, that just and reasonable anticipation of its probability, which such longing has opened the way to his entertaining?[103]

Let us now focus on Newman's examination of Edward Gibbon's thesis concerning the five "human causes," which presumably would explain the rise of Christianity: "the zeal of Christians, inherited from the Jews, their doctrine of a future state [= immortality], their claim to miraculous power, their virtues, and their ecclesiastical organization."[104]

Newman's reply consists in questioning the contention that these traits of Christianity actually caused its being adopted by many people. These "five characteristics of Christianity … neither did effect such conversions, nor were adapted to do so."[105] Instead, he suggests that "the wonder is, what made them come together"—namely, "their combination," "their coincidence."[106] Moreover, such remarkable combination was itself made possible by something anterior—that is, a real apprehension. In other words, what grounded the early disciples' belief in Jesus Christ are not the five characteristics, but rather the real apprehension of what he meant for them.

Newman wants to replace Gibbon's conjectures with the facts about which the New Testament talks. In a rhetorical manner, he counters:

It is very remarkable that it should not have occurred to a man of Gibbon's sagacity to inquire, what account the Christians themselves gave of the matter. Would it not have been worth while for him to have let conjecture alone, and to have looked for facts instead? Why did he not try the hypothesis of faith, hope, and charity? Did he never hear of repentance towards God, and faith in Christ?[107]

103. *GA*, 425, 330.
104. *GA*, 457, 354; Edward Gibbon, *The History of the Decline and Fall of the Roman Empire*, vol. 1 (New York: Allen Lane/Penguin, 1994), chap. 15.
105. *GA*, 459, 355.
106. *GA*, 457, 354.
107. *GA*, 462, 357–58.

What is it, then, that made such a difference in the expectations of the first followers of Christ the Savior? It was the "description of the life, character, mission, and power of that Deliverer, a promise of His invisible Presence and Protection here, and of the Vision and Fruition of Him hereafter." More concretely, Jesus managed "to have imprinted the Image or idea of Himself in the minds of His subjects individually." Solely this image could have been "the original instrument of their conversion."[108] Indeed, it is "this central Image"— namely, "the Thought of Christ"—that brought about the dynamic interplay of the five characteristics.[109] Newman supports his claim with several texts from the New Testament.[110]

Still, while I agree that "this Thought or Image of Christ was the principle of conversion and of fellowship,"[111] I am skeptical with respect to Newman's other thesis "that among the lower classes, who had no power, influence, reputation, or education, lay its principal success."[112] With due deference to Newman, contemporary scholarship makes us aware that the biblical writers were articulate thinkers and that their readers needed a certain sophistication so as to be able to appreciate the New Testament.[113] It is nevertheless true that the genius of Catholicity consists in uniting all the social classes into one communion.

In University Sermon 7, he avers, "The Gospel, by affording us, in the Person and history of Christ, a witness of the invisible world, addresses itself to our senses and imagination."[114] In University Sermon 12, he argues that reason is not equipped to fully protect faith from the aberrations of credulousness.

108. *GA*, 464, 359.
109. *GA*, 465, 359.
110. *GA*, 466, 360–61.
111. *GA*, 465, 360.
112. *GA*, 466, 360.
113. See Rodney Stark, *The Rise of Christianity: A Sociologist Reconsiders History* (Princeton, N.J.: Princeton University Press, 1996).
114. *GA*; *Fifteen Sermons*, 121–22.

The safeguard of Faith is a right state of heart. This it is that gives it birth; it also disciplines it. This is what protects it from bigotry, credulity, and fanaticism. It is holiness, or dutifulness, or the new creation, or the spiritual mind, however we word it, which is the quickening and illuminating principle of true faith, giving it eyes, hands, and feet. It is Love which forms it out of the rude chaos into an image of Christ.[115]

He adds, "We *believe*, because we *love*." He explains: "The divinely-enlightened mind sees in Christ the very Object whom it desires to love and worship,—the Object correlative of its own affections; and it trusts Him, or believes, from loving Him."[116] Finally, he cites the famous metaphor according to which, as we shall observe later on in Lonergan and Rousselot, "Love … is the eye of Faith."[117]

University Sermon 2 is more explicit regarding what the believers precisely find in Christ:

Above all, in the New Testament, the Divine character is exhibited to us, not merely as love, or mercy, or holiness (attributes which have a vagueness in our conceptions of them from their immensity), but these and others as seen in an act *of self-denial*—a mysterious quality when ascribed to Him, who is all things in Himself, but especially calculated (from the mere meaning of the term) to impress upon our minds the personal character of the Object of our worship.[118]

Thanks to our meditating on "the life of Christ," "Revelation meets us with simple and distinct *facts* and *actions*.… Facts such as this are not simply evidence of the truth of the revelation, but the media of its impressiveness."[119] By contemplating the actions of Jesus, particularly his ultimate act of self-denial during his passion, our minds are "impressed"—that is, they receive insights into the

---

115. *GA; Fifteen Sermons*, 234.

116. *GA; Fifteen Sermons*, 236. The Christological character of human faith is emphasized in sections 17–23 of University Sermon 12.

117. Newman, *Fifteen Sermons*, 238. Augustine speaks of "the eye of faith," for instance, in Letter 130 to Proba, chap. 5, in *Letters 100–155*, trans. Roland Teske (Hyde Park, N.Y.: New City Press, 2003), 186.

118. Newman, *Fifteen Sermons*, 25–26.

119. Newman, *Fifteen Sermons*, 27.

significance of those facts for us.[120] Elsewhere, Newman says that "the picture of our Lord" is mirrored in the saints: "The Christian has a reflexion of it in his own mind to help him, and a Catholic is familiar with multiplied and recent copies of it in the Lives of the Saints."[121] We must note that Gibbon mentions the zeal and virtues of the Christians—namely, those Newman here calls "the saints." However, what is missing in Gibbon's account is the centrality of Jesus, with whom the Christians are intimately related and thanks to whom his five characteristics are combined.

In a meditation on "the mental sufferings of our Lord," dated 1855, Newman contemplates the face of Jesus:

I see the figure of a man, whether young or old I cannot tell. He may be fifty or He may be thirty. Sometimes He looks one, sometimes the other. There is something inexpressible about His face which I cannot solve. Perhaps, as He bears *all* burdens, He bears that of old age too. But so it is; His face is at once most venerable, yet most childlike, most calm, most sweet, most modest, beaming with sanctity and with loving-kindness.[122] His eyes rivet me and move my heart. His breath is all fragrant, and transports me out of myself. Oh, I will look upon that face for ever, and will not cease.

And I see suddenly some one come to Him, and raise his hand and sharply strike Him on that heavenly face. It is a hard hand, the hand of a rude man, and perhaps has iron upon it. It could not be so sudden as to take Him by surprise who knows all things past and future, and He shows no sign of resentment, remaining calm and grave as before; but the expression of His face is marred; a great weal arises, and in a little time that all-gracious Face is hid from me by the effects of this indignity, as if a cloud came over It.

A hand was lifted up against the Face of Christ. Whose hand was that? My conscience tells me: "thou art the man." I trust it is not so with me now. But,

---

120. See Roy, "The Passion of Jesus: A Test Case for Providence," *New Blackfriars* 79 (1998):512–23.

121. Newman, *Philosophical Notebook*, 2:171.

122. Notice "beaming with sanctity" and "fragrant"; elsewhere, Newman associates sanctity with beauty and fragrance: "they [people who convert] are touched and overcome by the evident sanctity, beauty, and (as I may say) fragrance of the Catholic Religion"; Newman, "Faith and Doubt," in *Discourses Addressed to Mixed Congregations*, 234.

O my soul, contemplate the awful fact. *Fancy* Christ before thee, and *fancy* thyself lifting up thy hand and striking Him! Thou will say, "It is impossible: I could not do so." Yes, thou hast done so. When thou didst sin wilfully, then thou hast done so.[123]

In a sermon, after introducing a similar meditation on the scourged Jesus, Newman equates such contemplation with the highest real apprehension:

Taking into account, then, that Almighty God Himself, God the Son, was the Sufferer, we shall *understand* better than we have hitherto the description given of Him by the Evangelists; we shall see the *meaning* of His general demeanour, His silence, and the words He used when He spoke, and Pilate's awe at Him.[124]

And in another sermon, Newman broadens his vista: "Thus in the Cross, and Him who hung upon it, all things meet; all things subserve it, all things need it. It is their centre and their interpretation."[125]

This section has displayed how Newman envisions the combination of real apprehension and informal inference in Christianity. The former provides the affective concern and motivation that allow the latter to proceed without being intimidated by a rationalist demand—that is, by an intellectual movement that would require a strict proof. Rather than working according to a cogent scientific model, the inference that is affordable is based on converging evidence, as in law and common sense.

THREE DISTORTIONS OF FAITH

Newman shares John Calvin's and Joseph Butler's doctrine of the three offices of Christ: he is priest, prophet, and king. In his preface to the third edition of his *Via Media*, he transfers Christ's three

---

123. Newman, *Meditations and Devotions* (London: Burns and Oates, 1964), 10–11.

124. Newman, *Parochial and Plain Sermons*, part VI, sermon 6, "The Incarnate Son, a Sufferer and Sacrifice," 1223; italics are mine.

125. Newman, *Parochial and Plain Sermons*, part VI, sermon 7, "The Cross of Christ the Measure of the World," 1231.

offices to the church as the body of Christ. So the church is endowed with three functions: sacerdotal, prophetical, and regal. Newman envisions the first as ministering to the experience "of unresisting suffering, of self-sacrificing love, of life-giving grace," which touches "our emotional nature."[126] Regarding the second one—the prophetical capacity—he states that "the instrument of theology is reasoning." He adds that the church also needs the third function—namely, "a rule."[127] In that preface, Newman's goal is to acknowledge and clarify inevitable conflicts among the faithful people's piety, the theologians' pronouncements, and the bishops' rulings about appropriate forms of Christian belief and behavior. However, most pertinent is his conviction that all three roles are indispensable to the church.[128]

Newman recognized actual conflicts among the three functions of the church—that is, among the sacerdotal, the prophetical, and the regal. Throughout his life, he deprecated the specific distortion that may blight each of these functions. For him, emotionalism may affect the sacerdotal, rationalism may affect the prophetical, and authoritarianism may affect the regal. Let us see how he identified the three distortions and managed to steer clear of them.

First, for all his evangelical sensibility, he could not brook the emotionalism of those who pitted the heart against the head or feeling against rational claims. "From the age of fifteen, dogma has been the fundamental principle of my religion: I know no other religion; I cannot enter into the idea of any other sort of religion; religion, as a mere sentiment, is to me a dream and a mockery."[129] He repudiated the position, held in the evangelical movement, "that Religion

---

126. Newman, "Preface to the Third Edition," in *The "Via Media" of the Anglican Church*, ed. H. D. Weidner (Oxford: Clarendon Press, 1990), 56–57 and 25.

127. Newman, "Preface to the Third Edition," 25.

128. See Lash, *Theology on Dover Beach* (London: DLT, 1979), 89–108, and *Easter in Ordinary: Reflections on Human Experience and the Knowledge of God* (Charlottesville: University Press of Virginia, 1988), 136–40 (with comments on earlier texts by Newman).

129. Newman, *Apologia pro Vita Sua*, 54.

consists, not in knowledge, but in feeling or sentiment."[130] He did not agree to a view of faith as "not an acceptance of revealed doctrine, not an act of the intellect, but a feeling, an emotion, an affection, an appetency." He rejected the opinion "that Religion was based, not on argument, but on taste and sentiment, that nothing was objective, every thing subjective, in doctrine." He objected to those who thought "that Religion, as such, consisted in something short of intellectual exercises, viz., in the affections, in imagination, in inward persuasions and consolations, in pleasurable sensations, sudden changes, and sublime fancies."[131] He clearly showed that in the long run, Christian practice cannot draw much vigor from religious emotions.[132]

In the second place, quite early on as well, Newman strongly resisted the rationalism (which he also called "liberalism" or "latitudinarianism") that was gaining strength in the Church of England. Here is the way he introduced the issue in 1835:

Rationalism is a certain abuse of Reason; that is, a use of it for purposes for which it never was intended, and is unfitted. To rationalize in matters of Revelation is to make our reason the standard and measure of the doctrines revealed; to stipulate that those doctrines should be such as to carry with them their own justification; to reject them, if they come in collision with our existing opinions or habits of thought, or are with difficulty harmonized with our existing stock of knowledge. And thus a rationalistic spirit is the antagonist of Faith; for Faith is, in its very nature, the acceptance of what our reason cannot reach, simply and absolutely upon testimony.[133]

Newman explicated what he meant by rationalism as "a certain abuse of reason" in a scientific age:

130. Newman, *Idea of a University*, Svaglic, 21; Longmans, 27.

131. Newman, *Idea of a University*, Svaglic, 21; Longmans, 28.

132. Newman, *Parochial and Plain Sermons*, part I, sermon 9, "The Religious Use of Excited Feelings."

133. Newman, "On the Introduction of Rationalistic Principles into Revealed Religion," in *Essays Critical and Historical* (London: Longmans, Green, 1910), 1:31. Later, he spelled out the tenets of liberalism into eighteen propositions; see his *Apologia pro Vita Sua*, Note A, "Liberalism." See also Newman, *An Essay on the Development of Christian Doctrine* (Notre Dame, Ind.: University of Notre Dame Press, 1989), 357–58.

Besides thus keeping us from the best of guides, it [confidence in our own reasoning powers] also makes us fools, because it is a confidence in a *bad* guide. Our reasoning powers are very weak in all inquiries into moral and religious truth. Clear-sighted as reason is on other subjects, and trustworthy as a guide, still in questions connected with our duty to God and man it is very unskilful and equivocating. After all, it barely reaches the same great truths which are authoritatively set forth by Conscience and by Scripture; and if it be used in religious inquiries, without reference to these divinely-sanctioned informants, the probability is, it will miss the Truth altogether.[134]

These lines are almost an echo of Aquinas's remarks on the limitations of reason, which were presented in chapter 3.

Such rationalism, however, rarely exists today in its pure form. More often than not, it is diluted into relevancy: to be acceptable, beliefs must be immediately relevant. Newman observed that by and large "both the one party and the other [evangelical and latitudinarian] found themselves in agreement on the main point, viz ... that Religion was based, not on argument, but on taste and sentiment."[135] Since such relevance is adjudicated by both the mind and the heart, we have here an alliance of meaning and affectivity against authority. So the contemporary version of rationalism, which I have just dubbed relevancy, is paradoxically mixed with irrationalism. This inconsistent—and alas viable!—blend of rationalism and irrationalism breeds presumptions that orientate a somewhat arbitrary choice of beliefs. It is hostile to any normative determinations coming from outside. Newman noted the disdain, impatience, fear, and anger with which dogma is met: "A man who fancies he can find out truth by himself, disdains revelation. He who thinks he *has* found it out, is *impatient* of revelation. He fears it will interfere with his own imaginary discoveries, he is unwilling to consult it; and when it does interfere, then he is angry."[136]

134. Newman, *Parochial and Plain Sermons*, part I, sermon 17, "The Self-Wise Inquirer," 139. On "the force of public opinion" and "the power of false creeds to fetter the mind and bring it into captivity," see part V, sermon 9, "Christian Sympathy," 1028–29.

135. Newman, *Idea of a University*, Svaglic, 21; Longmans, 28

136. Newman, *Parochial and Plain Sermons*, sermon 17, 138.

He lucidly diagnosed that disease. For instance, regarding those who "skip over things in Scripture," he comments, "they do not judge, they do not examine, they do not go by Scripture; but they take just so much of Scripture as suits them, and leave the rest. They go, not by their private judgement, but their private prejudice, and by their private liking."[137]

Moreover, he accentuated the believer's obligation not to entertain doubts regarding faith, because doubting would jeopardize the personal relationship with Jesus Christ. He explained: "Take an instance; what would you think of a friend whom you loved, who could bargain that, in spite of his present trust in you, he might be allowed some day to doubt you?" And he elaborated:

He [our "loving Lord"] has poured on us His grace, He has been with us in our perplexities, He has led us on from one truth to another, He has forgiven us our sins, He has satisfied our reason, He has made faith easy, He has given us His Saints, He shows before us day by day His own Passion; why should I leave Him? What has He ever done to me but good? Why must I re-examine what I have examined once for all?[138]

Corresponding to this duty of individuals not to reexamine the reasons that led them to Christ, Newman drew attention to the fact that the bishops, along with the pope, have the obligation to clarify Christian belief whenever necessary. According to him, not only has the church received divine revelation, but the Holy Spirit has vouchsafed it the capacity to guarantee definite truths. In this consists its infallibility. It sifts the manifold interpretations that emerge across the centuries, it highlights the right ones, and it discards the wrong ones. Its power of infallibility, as he put it in his *Apologia*, is the only "working instrument ... for smiting hard and throwing back the immense energy of the aggressive, capricious, untrustworthy intellect."[139]

---

137. Newman, *Faith and Prejudice and Other Unpublished Sermons*, ed. Birmingham Oratory (New York: Sheed and Ward, 1956), sermon 4, "Prejudice and Faith" (1848), 57 and 58.

138. Newman, *Discourses Addressed to Mixed Congregations*, discourse XI, "Faith and Doubt," 219 and 224.

139. Newman, *Apologia pro Vita Sua*, 220.

In the third place, Newman did not overstress the role of authority in the church.[140] He called the third office a "fellowship," "a social interchange of thought,"[141] thereby signifying that the church's tradition, far from being reducible to an authoritarian exercise, consists in a sharing of wisdom. Furthermore, taking into consideration the European temper in the 1860s, he personally did not favor the promulgation of the pope's infallibility by the First Vatican Council. Clearly he was not against this doctrine, and yet he did not think its solemn declaration would be opportune. He foresaw that although this dogma was meant to delimit the range of the pope's infallibility,[142] it would in fact be met by misunderstanding on the part of Protestants and would reinforce ultramontanism in the Catholic Church—that is, the propensity to absolutize the power of the pope.[143] As Dulles observes, "Even in his most ardent apologias for Roman primacy one can detect a subtle undercurrent of criticism. Wary of despotism and ultramontane power politics, Newman was strongly committed to the inviolability of conscience, the dignity of the laity, and the freedom of theological investigation."[144]

In his "Letter Addressed to His Grace the Duke of Norfolk," Newman made clear that the pope's authority rests on the Creator-given human conscience: "Did the Pope speak against Conscience in the true sense of the word, he would commit a suicidal act. He would be cutting the ground from under his feet." Newman therefore stated,

---

140. Except perhaps in some passages of Newman, *Discourses Addressed to Mixed Congregations*, where the voice is authoritarian, although his overall point in discourse X, "Faith and Doubt," about avoiding "to pick and choose" (197) is well taken.

141. Newman, *Philosophical Notebook*, 2:167, 169.

142. This is the gist of Newman's interpretation in *A Letter Addressed to His Grace the Duke of Norfolk on Occasion of Mr. Gladstone's Recent Expostulation* (London: Pickering, 1875), esp. section 8, "The Vatican Council" and section 9, "The Vatican Definition." Earlier in 1864, he propounded the same restrictive view of infallibility regarding the dogma of the Immaculate Conception; see his *Apologia pro Vita Sua*, 226–29.

143. In retrospect, who can say whether Newman was right or wrong in this prudential judgment? I personally hold that the Holy Spirit guides the church even in the timing of its conciliar pronouncements.

144. Dulles, *Newman*, 151.

"On the law of conscience and its sacredness are founded both his authority in theory and his power in fact."[145] This antecedence of conscience implies that the decision to assert and accept authority is taken by the conscience, be it the pope's conscience or the people's conscience. Therefore, he ended with the remark, "Certainly, if I am obliged to bring religion into after-dinner toasts (which indeed does not seem quite the thing), I shall drink—to the Pope, if you please,—still, to Conscience first, and to the Pope afterwards."[146]

He also underscored the duty, on the part of bishops, of consulting the faithful in matters of doctrine. He maintained that

the tradition of the Apostles ... manifests itself variously at various times: sometimes by the mouth of the episcopacy, sometimes by the doctors, sometimes by the people, sometimes by liturgies, rites, ceremonies, and customs, by events, disputes, movements, and all those other phenomena which are comprised under the name of history.[147]

Due consideration must be paid to the living tradition, which includes the beliefs and practices of the faithful.

Our analysis of the three deformations of the act of believing will be amplified in chapter 6, where connections are made between Aquinas's three aspects of faith, Newman's description of the three distortions that has been presented in this section, and a contemporary, more psychological, account of the phenomenon.

CONCLUDING REMARKS

To round out this chapter, I want to return to one of the principal themes of this book and to underline the intertwining of the

145. Newman, chapter 5, "Letter Addressed to His Grace the Duke of Norfolk on Occasion of Mr. Gladstone's recent Expostulation," in *Conscience, Consensus, and the Development of Doctrine: Revolutionary Texts by John Henry Cardinal Newman*, ed. James Gaffney (New York: Doubleday, 1992), 451.

146. Newman, chapter 5, "Letter Addressed to His Grace," 457.

147. Newman, *On Consulting the Faithful in Matters of Doctrine*, ed. John Coulson (New York: Sheed and Ward, 1961), 63; see Coulson's excellent introduction, which provides the historical context and an analysis of Newman's text.

subjective and objective sides in Newman's case for Christianity. His argument is conducted as an informal inference in which both the personal factor and the historical information play an essential role.

Subjectively, antecedent probability means the likelihood that someone will assent to a fact, depending on that person's general assumptions about reality and on that person's anticipation of a particular event (for example, a miracle or divine revelation). Objectively, antecedent probability means the likelihood that something did or will happen (for example, the resurrection of Jesus and our resurrection) or, to put it differently, the likelihood that x is a fact, or that y will be the case (for instance, that Great Britain is an island, or that I shall die). The support for belief accumulates as real apprehensions and the evidences of Christianity feed each other in a kind of symbiosis. The summit of this process is reached when the *subjective* real apprehensions occur in the *objective* presence of Jesus Christ, as depicted in scripture and exemplified in the lives of the saints.

It is easy to notice what Newman's discussion of the process of believing adds to Aquinas's rich treatment of faith: the necessity of making a case for Christian faith in a nineteenth-century English culture that had become in a great measure secular. With his description of real apprehension and with his analysis of inference based on converging evidence, Newman presents an apologetic that is modern, since it is inspired both by a psychology of faith and by British law. Furthermore, he very lucidly uncovers three distortions that not infrequently occur in religion—namely, the emotionalism that may affect the priestly function, the rationalism that may affect prophecy, and the authoritarianism that may affect authority.

To end this chapter, I would submit, in a symbolic mode, that two frescos by Fra Angelico, which can be seen at the San Marco Museum in Florence, exemplify the respective strength of real and notional apprehension. In one of them, next to the entrance to the church, St. Dominic, kneeling and weeping, tenderly embraces the foot of the cross; he is affectively one with his suffering Savior. The other painting, on the wall of the chapter room, depicts a crucifixion with many saints in the foreground; among them, St. Thomas Aquinas stands at a distance, with an intent gaze; holding a book, he is pondering the deep theological significance of the death of Jesus.

CHAPTER 5

Bernard Lonergan

HUMAN INTENTIONALITY

AND FAITH

༅

Bernard Lonergan (1904–84) was, in my estimation, the premier Roman Catholic theologian of the twentieth century. Basically a Thomist, he nevertheless displayed remarkable creativity in the areas of epistemology, method, and historical consciousness.[1] His contribution to a theology of faith hinges upon two conversions: religious and intellectual. Accordingly, after briefly characterizing a third kind of conversion, the moral one, which is less important here for a theology of faith, this chapter shows the impact of religious and intellectual conversion.[2] The first two sections discuss the interaction between *religious* conversion and the role of the word and of belief; the third and fourth sections weigh the criticisms addressed to Lonergan by George Lindbeck and David Tracy; the last section has to do with epistemology in light of *intellectual* conversion. In chapter 6

---

1. For a brief presentation of Lonergan, the context of his thought, with a few of his main themes, see Roy, *Coherent Christianity*, chap. 13, "Bernard Lonergan: A Theologian in Dialogue." See also Roy, *Engaging the Thought of Bernard Lonergan*, and the interviews given by Lonergan in *Caring about Meaning: Patterns in the Life of Bernard Lonergan*, ed. Pierrot Lambert, Charlotte Tansey, and Cathleen Going (Montreal: Thomas More Institute, 1982).

2. On the three conversions, see Lonergan, *Method in Theology*, 237–43.

a section on self-deception will describe a fourth type of conversion, submitted by Robert Doran: the psychic conversion, of which Lonergan approved.

Before getting more specific on conversion, let us observe that it does not amount to a mere development. Following Joseph de Finance, Lonergan draws a distinction between a horizontal and vertical exercise of freedom: "A horizontal exercise is a decision or choice that occurs within an established horizon. A vertical exercise is the set of judgments and decisions by which we move from one horizon to another." Then Lonergan goes beyond de Finance as he subdivides the vertical exercise into two kinds:

Now there may be a sequence of such vertical exercises of freedom, and in each case the new horizon, though notably deeper and broader and richer, none the less is consonant with the old and a *development* out of its potentialities. But it is also possible that the movement into a new horizon involves *an about-face*; it comes out of the old by repudiating characteristic features; it begins a new sequence that can keep revealing ever greater depth and breadth and wealth. Such an about-face and new beginning is what is meant by a conversion.[3]

So, all four types of conversion—religious, moral, intellectual, and psychic—are an about-face, not a mere development.

Since moral conversion is less directly joined up with faith than religious and intellectual conversion, I will simply consign my characterization of it to one paragraph. Nonetheless, it has a significant function to exercise in encouraging a well-directed hope and in assisting a religious quest.

Moral conversion consists in becoming attuned to values and in preferring the attraction of values to other satisfactions whenever they conflict. It draws from religious experience the motivation required for the overcoming of individual, group, and general bias.[4]

---

3. Lonergan, *Method in Theology*, 237–38; italics are mine.
4. On bias, see Lonergan, *Collected Works*, vol. 3, *Insight*, 244–67, and Roy, *Engaging the Thought of Bernard Lonergan*, study 14, section entitled "A Wounded Humanity."

Individual bias is the pursuit of self-interest at the expense of others. Group bias is the pursuit of interests shared by a group or class to the detriment of other groups or classes. General bias affects any society whose common sense confines its horizon to what looks practical in the short term. In order to counter bias and foster progress, people have recourse to religious traditions where they find enlightenment and renewal of their willingness to act rightly.

INTENTIONALITY AND

RELIGIOUS CONVERSION

Lonergan distinguishes between four levels of human intentionality: experience, understanding, judgment, and decision. On the first level, we perceive; on the second, we receive insights; on the third, we make judgments; and on the fourth, we decide. Access to truth requires the acceptance of our fourfold desire (labeled "the transcendental notions"): to register all observable data; to understand everything that is intelligible; to reach sound judgments; and to take decisions. Whenever a person knows oneself as involved in one's intentionality, this self-knowledge enables one to be a responsible agent.

Chapter 4 of his book *Method in Theology* introduces the theme of self-transcendence.[5] It is the tendency among human beings to go beyond the strict limitations of their habitat and to learn how to live in a world mediated by meanings and values. People transcend themselves inasmuch as they ask questions *for understanding*, which makes them discern intelligible patterns in the data perceptually collected; inasmuch as they ask questions *for reflection*, which makes them determine the truth of their hypotheses; and inasmuch as they ask questions *for deliberation*, which makes them assess values, courses of actions, and religious commitments. Elsewhere, Lonergan calls this development a movement "from below upwards."[6]

5. Lonergan, *Method in Theology*, 104–5.

6. Lonergan, "Natural Right and Historical Mindedness," in *A Third Collection: Papers by Bernard J. F. Lonergan*, ed. Frederick E. Crowe (New York: Paulist Press, 1985), 180.

One ascends a scale, so to speak, constituted by four levels: experience, understanding, reflection, and deliberation. Hence his four transcendental—that is, cross-cultural—precepts: "Be attentive, Be intelligent, Be reasonable, Be responsible," to which he later adds a fifth, "Be in love."[7]

He points out, "The transcendental notions, that is, our questions for intelligence, for reflection, and for deliberation, constitute our capacity for self-transcendence. That capacity becomes an actuality when one falls in love. Then one's being becomes being-in-love." Among the various kinds of love—all situated on the fourth level of human intentionality—the love of God is supreme. Lonergan is fond of quoting Romans 5:5, "God's love flooding our hearts through the Holy Spirit given to us."[8] Exegetes of St. Paul note the rich ambiguity of the genitive "love of God" (*hē agapē tou Theou*) in this verse of the Letter to the Romans: it means both God's love for us and our love for God. We could encompass the two senses in the phrase "God's love in us."

Such is what Lonergan equivalently calls "religious conversion" or "religious experience." When a person has received this extraordinary gift, she initiates a movement "from above downwards," which complements the first movement, "from below upwards."[9] This second movement proceeds from a summit—namely, the apex of the soul as imbued with divine love. Then one is attuned to the judgments of value (on the fourth level) and judgments of fact (on the third level) handed on by a religious heritage; one tries to understand the meaning conveyed by these judgments (on the second level); and at the end of this descent, one embodies such meanings in words, symbols, artefacts—that is, in newly created data (on the first level).

Subsequently, in the same chapter of *Method*, Lonergan employs a distinction between the inner and the outer word.[10] Of the latter,

7. Lonergan, *Method in Theology*, 231 and 268, respectively.
8. Lonergan, *Method in Theology*, 105.
9. Lonergan, "Natural Right and Historical Mindedness," 181.
10. Lonergan, *Method in Theology*, 112–19 and 123.

he writes, "By the word is meant any expression of religious meaning or of religious value."[11] Of the former, he writes:

Before it enters the world mediated by meaning, religion is the prior word God speaks to us by flooding our hearts with his love. That prior word pertains, not to the world mediated by meaning, but to the world of immediacy, to the unmediated experience of the mystery of love and awe.[12]

What is this prior, inner word? I would venture to say that it covers a twofold experience. First, an affective state that transcends our ordinary states: "being in love in an unrestricted fashion"—that is, "being in love without limits or qualifications or conditions or reservations."[13] Second, a distinctive quality of consciousness, as indicated by the phrase "a *conscious* dynamic state of love, joy, peace."[14] This particular quality consists in a fulfillment: "Being in love with God is the basic fulfilment of our conscious intentionality."[15] As already mentioned, Lonergan situates such consciousness "on the fourth level of intentional consciousness": "It is this consciousness [on the fourth level] as brought to a fulfilment."[16] The two sides of religious experience are concomitant: love and the consciousness that permeates it. In other words, the transcendent love is felt.

Even so, such consciousness differs from knowledge: "The dynamic state is conscious without being known."[17] Lonergan offers a definition of faith: "Faith is the knowledge born of religious love." He distinguishes between two kinds of knowledge: "Besides the factual knowledge reached by experiencing, understanding, and verifying, there is another kind of knowledge reached through the discernment of value and the judgments of value of a person in love."[18]

Commenting on Pascal's famed phrase "the heart has reasons

11. Lonergan, *Method in Theology*, 112.
12. Lonergan, *Method in Theology*.
13. Lonergan, *Method in Theology*, 105 and 106, respectively.
14. Lonergan, *Method in Theology*, 106; italics are mine.
15. Lonergan, *Method in Theology*, 105.
16. Lonergan, *Method in Theology*, 106 and 107, respectively.
17. Lonergan, *Method in Theology*, 106.
18. Lonergan, *Method in Theology*, 115.

which reason does not know," Lonergan construes "the heart's reasons" as "feelings that are intentional responses to values," in this case "an apprehension of transcendent value."[19] Unfortunately, in the response to transcendent value, he does not clearly distinguish between the feelings (the affective quality of consciousness) and the apprehension that we may have of them. Moreover, he does not spell out the components of that apprehension: the affective awareness that is felt, the meaning that is intuited without yet being formulated, and the two kinds of judgment (judgment of fact and judgment of value). His treatment of the intentional response, while creative, is too compact.[20]

Lonergan seems to situate faith halfway between the inner and the outer word. Faith is more explicit than the inner word and less explicit than the outer word. It is located in a sequence that could be expounded as follows: a basic state of being in love unrestrictedly (prior word, also called inner word) → faith (the knowledge born of religious love) → the word as expressed (outer word) → belief (judgments of fact and of value) → decision → action.

Does the fact that faith is first and foremost an affective knowledge demote the outer word to a secondary place? Not for Lonergan, who declares, "One must not conclude that the outward word is something incidental. For it has a constitutive role."[21] He makes it clear that "the constitutive role of meaning" is far from being marginal: "Acts of meaning inform human living."[22] Talking about two persons in love, he explains, "It is the love that each freely and fully reveals to the other that brings about the radically new situation of being in love and that begins the unfolding of its life-long implications."[23]

19. Lonergan, *Method in Theology*, 115; see 30–31 for the notion of intentional response.

20. For a critique of Lonergan's position on feeling and knowledge, see Terry J. Tekippe and Louis Roy, "Lonergan and the Fourth Level of Intentionality," *American Catholic Philosophical Quarterly* 70 (1996): 225–42; see also Roy, *Transcendent Experiences*, 135–37 and 162–64.

21. Lonergan, *Method in Theology*, 112; on constitutive meaning, see 78.

22. Lonergan, "Theology in Its New Context," in *A Second Collection*, ed. Robert M. Doran and John D. Dadosky, vol. 13 of *Collected Works of Bernard Lonergan* (Toronto: University of Toronto Press, 2016), 54.

23. Lonergan, *Method in Theology*, 113.

And applying this interpersonal situation to love between God and us, he submits:

One needs the word—the word of tradition that has accumulated religious wisdom, the word of fellowship that unites those that share the gift of God's love, the word of the gospel that announces that God has loved us first and, in the fulness of time, has revealed that love in Christ crucified, dead, and risen.[24]

Lonergan reinforces his point of not separating the inner and the outer word: "God's gift of his love has its proper counterpart in the revelation events in which God discloses to a particular people or to all mankind the completeness of his love for them."[25] The outer word facilitates a focusing: "In the paschal mystery the love that is given inwardly is focused and inflamed, and that focusing unites Christians not only with Christ but also with one another."[26]

Earlier in *Method*, Lonergan introduces a category that helps to situate the role of Christ in the emergence of a person's belief. Having quoted Newman's motto *Cor ad cor loquitur* ("Heart speaks to heart"), he defines "incarnate meaning" as "the meaning of a person, of his way of life, of his words, or of his deeds."[27] And a paper of his alludes to "the incarnate meaning to be contemplated in the life and ministry and, above all, in the suffering, death, and resurrection of Christ."[28]

Moreover, in a lecture delivered before *Method* was begun, he has recourse to the concept of mutual self-mediation to characterize a form of personal development that has two aspects; first, we mediate ourselves—that is, we actively constitute ourselves as human beings, especially in our religious dimension, thanks to the existential

24. Lonergan, *Method in Theology*.
25. Lonergan, *Method in Theology*, 283.
26. Lonergan, "Philosophy of God, and Theology: The Relationship between Philosophy of God and the Functional Specialty, Systematics," in *Collected Works*, vol. 17, *Philosophical and Theological Papers 1965–1980*, ed. Robert C. Croken and Robert M. Doran (Toronto: University of Toronto Press, 2004), 170.
27. Lonergan, *Method in Theology*, 73.
28. Lonergan, "The Response of the Jesuit as Priest and Apostle in the Modern World," in *A Second Collection*, 148.

decisions by which we make and transform ourselves; second, this process of growth unfolds with reference to Christ.

There is the mediation by our acts of what is immediate in us through the grace of God. Though the object of those acts is not exclusively Christ—it is everything—still, everything turns back to Christ in one way or another. That is, it is not merely a self-mediation in which we develop, but it is a self-mediation through another. One is becoming oneself, not just by experiences, insights, judgments, by choices, decisions, conversion, not just freely and deliberately, not just deeply and strongly, but as one who is carried along. One is doing so not in isolation, but in reference to Christ. The Father predestined us to be conformed to the image of his Son, through the merits of Christ, through the grace of Christ, through the example of Christ. Consequently, there is an element not merely of personal development, but of personal development in relation to another person.[29]

In a way similar to Lonergan's, William Desmond contrasts "self-mediation," typical of Hegelian dialectic, and "self-mediation through another," which he calls "intermediation." Far from being self-centered, intermediation allows a person to meet the other in the middle—namely, in Plato's *metaxu*, interpreted by Eric Voegelin's as the "in-between."

The agapeic self is for the other. In this respect its self-transcendence is decentered. It is decentered because its center is outside of itself in the between; this is shapes, not just for itself, but to free the other to be itself as other.... So if the agapeic self gives itself over, it is not the "I will" of decisive self-assertion; it is the "I am willing" that is also willing to be nothing, even in the plenitude of its power and in the excess of its original energy. The "I am willing" is the "Here I am," now ready to be sacrifice for the other. "Sacrifice" literally means to make sacred. The agapeic self seeks to sanctify the willingness that gives itself up as an offering for the good of the other.[30]

---

29. Lonergan, "The Mediation of Christ in Prayer," in *Collected Works*, vol. 6, *Philosophical and Theological Papers*, 180.

30. William Desmond, *Being and the Between* (Albany, N.Y.: SUNY Press, 1995), 409; see also xiv, 129, 178, and 408.

I think Lonergan would entirely concur with these lines by Desmond and would surely recognize here his own construal of Jesus and of all agapeic, self-sacrificing people as entirely committed to mutual self-mediation.

To wrap up this section, we can say that Lonergan situates religious conversion at the highest level of intentionality in its process of self-transcendence and that he nicely complements the inner word of infinite love with the role of the outer word and, for Christians, of the incarnate Word.

BELIEF

We can consider belief as an elaboration of the outer word. However, the importance of belief is far from being self-evident. So we must ask, how do people come to agree with religious beliefs? Lonergan answers, "Among the values that faith discerns is the value of believing the word of religion, of accepting the judgments of fact and the judgments of value that the religion proposes." The worth of belief derives from the fact that, far from being solitary, religious experience is shared and that "community invites expression."[31] Furthermore, countless believers acknowledge this: "Not only the inner word that is God's gift of his love but also the outer word of the religious tradition comes from God."[32]

Interestingly, in a previous section of *Method* on belief in general, Lonergan highlights the indispensable role of belief in daily life and observes that even scientists "do not suffer from a pointless mania to attain immanently generated knowledge of their fields."[33] "Immanently generated knowledge" refers to what individuals can verify for themselves—a very limited portion of science indeed.

Still, he maintains the primacy of faith over belief: "Beliefs do differ, but behind this difference there is a deeper unity. For beliefs result from judgments of value, and the judgments of value relevant for religious belief come from faith, the eye of religious love, an eye that can discern God's self-disclosures."[34]

What is absent here is the language of obligation, which we find in Aquinas and in Newman. In Aquinas's view, reported in chapter 3, believers see that some things are to be believed.[35] This "seeing" depends on the insight that Jesus Christ, the First Truth, must be believed. This is the formal aspect of faith. In a religious quest, at some point an individual comes to the conclusion that believing has now become a matter of obligation for her or him. As was noticed in chapter 4, Newman wrote to Mrs. William Froude, "Faith then is not a conclusion from premises, but the result of an act of the *will*, following upon a *conviction* that to believe is a *duty*."[36]

Does Lonergan disagree with his mentors Thomas Aquinas and Newman in this respect? Evidently his phrasings are less compelling than theirs. Nevertheless, if "the eye of religious love ... can discern God's self-disclosures," then the person makes judgments of fact and of value about those disclosures and must normally feel obliged to assent.[37] A few lines that precede on the same page in *Method* are clear about a divine revelation:

There is a personal entrance of God himself into history, a communication of God to his people, the advent of God's word into the world of religious expression. Such was the religion of Israel. Such has been Christianity.

Then not only the inner word that is God's gift of his love but also the outer word of the religious tradition comes from God.[38]

He adds, "Finally, the word of religious expression is not just the objectification of the gift of God's love; in a privileged area it also is specific meaning, the word of God himself."[39]

34. Lonergan, *Method in Theology*, 119.
35. *ST* II-II, q. 1, a. 4, ad 2 and ad 3; see also a. 5, ad 1.
36. Newman, *Letters and Diaries of John Henry Newman*, 12:228.
37. Lonergan, *Method in Theology*, 119; see the fuller quotation I gave, two paragraphs previously.
38. Lonergan, *Method in Theology*.
39. Lonergan, *Method in Theology*.

In fact, in chapter 2 of *Method*, in the section on beliefs, Lonergan uses the vocabulary of obligation. After the step in which a person judges that someone else's statement deserves to be believed, there comes the step in which the person reaches "the conclusion that the statement ought to be believed for, if believing is a good thing, then what can be believed should be believed."[40] Remarkably, the whole analysis of belief here is nonconfessional; it is applicable to any religious state or even to any purely moral situation.

If, in *Method*, Lonergan refrains from proposing the time-honored Roman Catholic view of faith as fashioned by Aquinas, it is, in my opinion, because his goal is not to expound a theology in conformity with a specific tradition. He himself declares, "I am writing not theology but method in theology. I am concerned not with the objects that theologians expound but with the operations that theologians perform."[41] His project is ecumenical, in the broadest sense, which includes even non-Christian theologies. "By distinguishing faith and belief we have secured a basis both for ecumenical encounter and for an encounter between all religions with a basis in religious experience."[42]

Toward the end of his chapter on religion, Lonergan writes, "In acknowledging a faith that grounds belief we are acknowledging what would have been termed the *lumen gratiae* or *lumen fidei* or infused wisdom."[43] He is right that such light of grace, light of faith, or infused wisdom amounts not to the outer word, but to the inner word—namely, to the subjective experience. The role of the outer word coming from the objective tradition is to explicate that religious experience and to situate it in a context of meaning. As he explains elsewhere, given that "meaning is the stuff of man's making of man," "a divine revelation is God's entry and his taking part in man's making of man. It is God's claim to have a say in the aims

40. Lonergan, *Method in Theology*, 46.
41. Lonergan, *Method in Theology*, xii.
42. Lonergan, *Method in Theology*, 119; see 332–33.
43. Lonergan, *Method in Theology*, 123.

and purposes, the direction and development of human lives, human societies, human cultures, human history."[44] Nevertheless, he prefers speaking of "word," rather than of "revelation," as a technical term, probably because the latter is commonly used metaphorically, whereas the former has a greater analogical potentiality (in the Thomist sense of analogy, in contradistinction to metaphor).

On this issue of the obligation to believe, Aquinas's, Newman's, and Lonergan's considerations will be helpful to us in chapters 6 and 7.

A FIRST OBJECTION TO LONERGAN

Let us now scrutinize two criticisms leveled at Lonergan's position on faith as deriving from religious love. The first comes from a Lutheran, partly neo-orthodox and partly Wittgensteinian theologian, whereas the second comes from a Roman Catholic, partly liberal and partly Lonerganian theologian.

In 1970, at the International Lonergan Congress, which took place in Florida, George Lindbeck gave a paper that was highly laudatory of Lonergan's views on the development of dogma.[45] However, in a book that was published about fifteen years later, *The Nature of Doctrine*, he became critical of Lonergan's method in theology as he denounced the adoption by liberal theologians of the concept of a generic human experience, which constituted a pseudo– common denominator among world religions. According to him, despite their best intentions, the liberals prefaced their theology with a notion of experience that preempted genuine revelation. We may think, for example, of Schleiermacher's feeling of absolute dependence, Tillich's ultimate concern, Wilfred Cantwell Smith's faith, Rahner's incomprehensible mystery, and Lonergan's being-in-love in an unrestricted fashion.

44. Lonergan, "Theology in Its New Context," 62.
45. George A. Lindbeck, "Protestant Problems with Lonergan on Development of Dogma," in *Foundations of Theology: Papers from the International Lonergan Congress 1970*, ed. Philip McShane (Notre Dame, Ind.: University of Notre Dame Press, 1972), 115–23.

Lindbeck attributes an "experiential-expressive model" not only to Schleiermacher and his successors, but also to Rahner and Lonergan, although he adds that the latter two have attempted, unsuccessfully, to correct that model by combining it with the cognitive model represented by Aquinas.[46] The double-barreled adjective "experiential-expressive" designates the view that religious meaning would be encapsulated in a direct experience of ultimacy, subsequently to be echoed in "a doctrine of belief," a *Glaubenslehre* in Schleiermacher's sense, with no claim to absolute truth. In Lindbeck's analysis, the mistake of both Rahner and Lonergan is to have tried to bring together two models that inevitably pull in opposed directions.

Presumably Lindbeck assumes that in Rahner and Lonergan the cross-cultural "transcendental" must be construed as logically derived from a rationalistic analysis of the human spirit and as a religious domain that stands by itself prior to any revelation and is independent of confessional belief. This would simply be a new version of the eighteenth-century "natural religion," which usurped the right to judge what it disparagingly called "positive religion." If we construe Rahner's and Lonergan's enterprise (in contradiction to their express aims) as driving a wedge between the transcendental and the categorial, or between faith and belief, and as unduly extolling the transcendental or faith, both described as unformulated knowledge, obviously we end up relativizing the content of Christian revelation. Consequently, the gospel would no longer be able to criticize any categorial expression in a particular culture, and no room would be left for evangelization.

Liberal theology's concept of a generic religion ought to be distinguished from a universal openness to revelation, grounded in concrete minds and uncovered by a faith-inspired theology that values, as Aquinas and Newman did, the realm of reason, which has been

---

46. Lindbeck, *The Nature of Doctrine: Religion and Theology in a Postliberal Age* (Philadelphia: Westminster Press, 1984), 16–17, 31–32.

created by God and healed by grace (at least for those who have positively responded to grace). In contradistinction to Schleiermacher's somewhat perceptualist interpretation of the God-consciousness,[47] Lonergan proposes a better account of the interactions between reason, religious experience, and belief.[48] The manifold question of God operates alongside religious experience and thus functions as a universal openness to revelation.[49] While human intentionality orients the seekers toward transcendent meaning and truth, the basic state of being-in-love recognizes transcendent value.

However, to answer the question of God requires more than religious experience. Far from merely deriving from the inner word, the outward word of a religious institution adds something significant to the inner word that is spoken to the heart. Halfway between silence and thinking, faith, in Lonergan's sense, is the linchpin that triggers the transition from mystical immediacy to the intellectual articulations typical of a world mediated by meaning. The word of a tradition facilitates this transition to belief by exercising a role that is both cognitive, since it refers to reality, and constitutive of a community that shares experiences, understandings, judgments, and commitments.[50]

Lindbeck wants to discount the inner word, construed as pseudo-private and unreal, since for him every human experience is mediated by language.[51] Methodologically, therefore, he begins and ends with an unchanging belief system that regulates a community's worship and thinking. In Lindbeck's proposal, theology has to do solely with what Lonergan calls the "outer word"; actually, Lindbeck sees the outer word of tradition in a very different light. In *The Nature*

---

47. See Roy, "Schleiermacher's Epistemology," *Method: Journal of Lonergan Studies* 16 (1998): 25–46.
48. See Roy, *Engaging the Thought of Bernard Lonergan*, study 3, esp. the section entitled "An Integration of Faith and Reason."
49. See Lonergan, *Method in Theology*, 101–3.
50. Lonergan, *Method in Theology*, 76–81 and 298–99.
51. This intricate issue is discussed in Roy, *Transcendent Experiences*, 137–39, 175–81.

of Doctrine the sources of Christian belief and the factors involved
in its development (in interaction with innumerable non-Christian
forms of thought) remain epistemologically unaccounted for.[52] Believers must obey linguistic rules, which shape their apprehension
of religious realities. Any particular tradition is equated with a fixed
datum, which cannot be rationally compared with the data of other
religious traditions, since their respective rules make them incom-
mensurable.

As Neil Ormerod perceptively notes, Lindbeck's vision is based
on "static conceptualist assumptions" and on a disregard of the dynamism of "questions, problems and answers." The consequence is
that "his [Lindbeck's] conceptualist assumptions have trapped the
subject within the horizon created by that tradition [his religious
tradition]."[53] And as Charles Hefling rightly states, Lindbeck overlooks Lonergan's recurrent insistence on the way we arrive at correct
judgments.[54]

By stressing the inner word, does Lonergan condone the anthropocentrism of Schleiermacher, of liberal Protestantism, or of Catholic modernism?[55] The answer to this question must take into consideration his methodological purpose. Accordingly, he underlines
the fact that his view of beliefs is open both to those currents and to
conservative versions of Christianity.

52. According to Michael H. McCarthy, *The Crisis of Philosophy* (Albany, N.Y.: SUNY
Press, 1990), Wittgenstein (who has deeply influenced Lindbeck) does not explain how
mathematicians adopt "variable rules of procedure" not merely "on pragmatic grounds"
(136); indeed, "the demand that we justify our linguistic practice is said to be superflu-
ous" (138). In "The Critique of Realism," *Method: Journal of Lonergan Studies* 10 (1992):
107–14, McCarthy calls attention to the same lacuna in the larger context of any community of language users.

53. Neil Ormerod, *Method, Meaning and Revelation: The Meaning and Function of
Revelation in Bernard Lonergan's "Method in Theology"* (Lanham, Md.: University Press of
America, 2000), 156 and 203; see also 29–32 and 192–204. See my laudatory review of that
book in *New Blackfriars* 82 (2001):597–98.

54. See Charles C. Hefling Jr., "Turning Liberalism Inside-Out," *Method: Journal of
Lonergan Studies* 3 (1985):68.

55. I address this issue more at length in *Engaging the Thought of Bernard Lonergan*,
study 5.

My account of religious beliefs does not imply that they are more than objectifications of religious experience. It is a view quite acceptable to the nineteenth-century liberal Protestant or to the twentieth-century Catholic modernist. But it is unacceptable to most of the traditional forms of Christianity, in which religious beliefs are believed to have their origin in charism, prophecy, inspiration, revelation, the word of God, the life, death, and resurrection of Christ. Obviously, to be applicable to this traditional type of religious belief, the skeleton model needs to be fleshed out, and fleshing it out calls for creativity.[56]

Lonergan maintains that he methodologically offers a model —which he also calls a construct or an ideal type—that must be completed by theological data and reflections, either in the direction of liberal or modernist standpoints or in the direction of long-established standpoints. Consequently, he concludes, "In that case religious beliefs would be objectifications not only of internal experience but also of the externally uttered word of God."[57]

However, he gives the impression of coming dangerously close to liberalism and modernism when he approves of Rahner for having written that "in theology theocentrism and anthropocentrism coincide. On this basis, he [Rahner] desires all theological statements to be matched by statements of their meaning in human terms." Nonetheless, Lonergan warns us against a false version: "Explicitly Father Rahner excludes a modernist interpretation of his view, namely, that theological doctrines are to be taken as statements about merely human reality."[58] Thanks to his critical realism, Lonergan's method decisively precludes any immanentism or subjectivism.[59]

56. Lonergan, "Faith and Beliefs," in *Philosophical and Theological Papers 1965–1980*, 46–47.

57. Ibid., 47.

58. Lonergan, "Theology and Man's Future," in *A Second Collection*, 148; see "The Future of Christianity," in *A Second Collection*, 161; also Karl Rahner, "Theology and Anthropology," trans. Graham Harrison, in *Theological Investigations* (New York: Herder, 1972) 9:28–45.

59. Much more successfully than Rahner; see Roy, *Engaging the Thought of Bernard Lonergan*, study 8. My strictures on Rahner in that study must be assessed in reference to my positive treatment of other aspects of his thought, in *Transcendent Experiences*, chap. 8.

Still, taking into account the justified criticisms leveled against the anthropocentrism that characterizes liberal Protestantism and Catholic modernism, I would suggest that in accord with chapter 1, in the section entitled, "Reading the Human Condition Theologically," we refrain to speak of Lonergan's method as an "anthropocentrism," and we rather call it "an anthropological method" (in the transcendental sense that he adopts), which is not a precipitate of some idealism, but an implementation of his critical realism.

I must reiterate that Lonergan sees no competition between the inner and the outer word. On the contrary, they reinforce each other. The inner word allows us to discern the beauty and luminosity of the outer word; the outer word encourages us to take to heart the effects of the inner word in us.

Consequently, on the one hand, he never belittles the validity of religious beliefs in the way Schleiermacher and liberal theologians do. Of course, it is not that, for them, all beliefs are unimportant: some are pronounced helpful. Still, in their eyes, beliefs are not considered to be normative in the sense that they would possess a permanent validity.

On the other hand, in *Method* he does not argue for specific beliefs. This decision of his belongs to his theological methodology. Consequently, as a methodologist, he brings in the role of Christ merely as a brief illustration. However, we have no indications that later in his life he abandoned his robust dogmatic stance in Catholic theology itself.[60] Having situated it in the dynamic context of the multiple developments of doctrines, he had no need to forego his dogmatic stance, as will be made manifest in the text to follow.

In this section, I have endeavored to fairly represent Lindbeck's view of theology and have contrasted it with Lonergan's. With the help of Ormerod and Hefling, connoisseurs who addressed Lindbeck's

60. An instance of that dogmatic stance is Lonergan's treatment of the Council of Chalcedon, in a lecture given in 1975 and entitled "Christology Today: Methodological Reflections," in *A Third Collection*, 74–99.

critique of Lonergan, I have replied to Lindbeck that a subjective approach to faith does not end up being subjectivist and does not necessarily set conditions that Christian revelation must obey, as if placing it in a procrustean bed. Instead, Lonergan's painstaking justification of the human person's universal intentionality provides a cross-cultural epistemology that can be put at the service of the divine outer word.

A SECOND OBJECTION TO LONERGAN

The second criticism that will be tackled has been voiced by David Tracy, interestingly at the same Lonergan congress in Florida, in which Lindbeck participated.[61] By and large, Tracy remains intellectually close to Lonergan, who was his mentor at the Gregorian University in Rome, so he upholds Lonergan's grounding of *intellectual* conversion.[62] What he questions is Lonergan's grounding of *religious* conversion, which appears to be merely dogmatic, whereas, according to Tracy, it ought to be critical. In reference to a couple of Lonergan's writings prior to *Method in Theology*, he is wary about a past attempt, on the part of Lonergan, to found his theological views "in the authoritative claims of the Roman Catholic tradition," although he opines that Lonergan, after having clarified his method, would no longer go this way.[63] Tracy is afraid that, as described by Lonergan, the functional specialty called "foundations" does not provide the required critical justification of theological discourse.

Given that the validity of Lonergan's theological method depends, to a large extent, on religious conversion, Tracy asks, don't we need "critical grounds for the enterprise itself—more precisely,

61. David Tracy, "Lonergan's Foundational Theology: An Interpretation and a Critique," in *Foundations of Theology: Papers from the International Lonergan Congress 1970*, ed. Philip McShane (Notre Dame, Ind.: University of Notre Dame Press, 1972), 197–222, esp. 214–22.
62. Tracy, "Lonergan's Foundational Theology," 215; see also Tracy's first book, *The Achievement of Bernard Lonergan*, with a foreword by Bernard Lonergan (New York: Herder and Herder, 1970).
63. Tracy, "Lonergan's Foundational Theology," 215; see also 255n12.

for the truth-value of the claims to ultimacy of religious and explicitly theological language?" Otherwise put, the question is, "What, then, are the conditions for the possibility of religious and explicitly theological meanings?"[64] As instances of "two presuppositions of a Christian foundational theology" that would need to be defended, Tracy mentions "the theistic thematisation of religious experience" and "the Christological claim to uniqueness as the thematisation of Christian religious experience."[65]

In his response, Lonergan agrees with Tracy that the specialty called "foundations" cannot be dogmatically established, since it cannot be built on dogmas. In a methodical theology, the dogmas will emerge later—namely, in the functional specialty called "doctrines." Nevertheless, Lonergan contends that foundations can be grounded in the believers' authentic subjectivity. To do so, theologians are helped by the first four functional specialties—research, interpretation, history, and dialectic—while the fifth specialty, foundations, explicates the threefold conversion.

Fittingly, then, we notice an objective and a subjective aspect to this theological grounding: "The method would ground foundations, objectively, in the situation revealed by dialectic and, on the side of subjective development, in intellectual, moral, and religious conversion."[66] Earlier in his response, Lonergan insists that "the [most basic] theological principle is religious conversion itself. It is not knowledge of religious conversion, awareness of religious conversion, interpretation of the psychological phenomena of conversion, propositions concerning conversion. It is simply the reality of the transformation named conversion."[67] Needless to say, such conversion should not be seen as an individualistic achievement, but shared by a community of scholars in dialogue both with

64. Tracy, "Lonergan's Foundational Theology," 214 and 216–17.
65. Tracy, "Lonergan's Foundational Theology," 255, endnote 14; see 256, endnote 27.
66. "Bernard Lonergan Responds," in *Foundations of Theology*, 231; see also 230.
67. "Bernard Lonergan Responds," 227.

past thinkers and among themselves. Hence, in Lonergan's eyes, the objective-subjective character of the theological enterprise.[68]

This "reality of the transformation named conversion" is a datum that may be registered and affirmed. In *Insight*, in the context of intellectual conversion, Lonergan declares, as he retraces his steps:

> Self-affirmation has been considered as a concrete judgment of fact. The contradiction of self-negation has been indicated. Behind that contradiction there have been discerned natural inevitabilities and spontaneities that constitute the possibility of knowing, not by demonstrating that one can know, but pragmatically by engaging one in the process. Nor in the last resort can one reach a deeper foundation than that pragmatic engagement.[69]

This project of establishing an *intellectual* foundation, which we find in *Insight*, recurs in a parallel and yet different manner when an *affective* foundation has to be established, at the time Lonergan was writing *Method in Theology*. There is no univocity but an analogy between uncovering an intellectual foundation (on the second and third levels of intentionality) and uncovering an affective foundation (on the fourth level), as Frederick Crowe observes in his brief remarks on the Tracy-Lonergan exchange in Florida.[70] Thus, in Lonergan's response of 1970, according to a viewpoint broader than *Insight*'s—a viewpoint that includes the moral and religious conversions as well as the intellectual—the knower's self-affirmation of *Insight* becomes *the entire person's* most fundamental option: "Foundations, then, consists in a decision that selects one horizon and rejects others."[71]

In an interview granted at the same congress, Lonergan reiterated his view:

68. Lonergan, *Method in Theology*, 235–44, 251–53, 262–66, and 292–93.

69. Lonergan, *Collected Works*, vol. 3, *Insight*, 356.

70. Frederick E. Crowe, "An Exploration of Lonergan's New Notion of Value," in *Appropriating the Lonergan Idea*, ed. Michael Vertin (Toronto: University of Toronto Press, 2006), 66–67.

71. "Bernard Lonergan Responds," 230.

Being in love is a fact, and it's what you are, it's existential. And your living flows from it. It's the first principle, as long as it lasts.... And critically grounding knowledge isn't finding the ground for knowledge. It's already there. Being critical means eliminating the ordinary nonsense, the systematically misleading images and so on; the mythical account.

To the question "might one not then be deceived?" he answers:

One can be deceiving himself. If one is deceiving oneself one is not in love. One is mistaking something for love. Love is something that proves itself. "By their fruits you shall know them," and "in fear and trembling work out your salvation" and all the rest of it. Love isn't cocksure, either.[72]

Perhaps spurred by that earlier discussion with Tracy, Lonergan writes, in *Method*, "Only God can give that gift [of his love], and the gift itself is self-justifying. People in love have not reasoned themselves into being in love."[73] About such being-in-love, he claims, "One has only to experience it in oneself or witness it in others, to find in it its own justification."[74] He explains:

In the realm of religious experience Olivier Rabut has asked whether there exists any unassailable fact. He found such a fact in the existence of love. It is as though a room were filled with music though one can have no sure knowledge of its source. There is in the world, as it were, a charged field of love and meaning; here and there it reaches a notable intensity; but it is ever unobtrusive, hidden, inviting each of us to join. And join we must if we are to perceive it, for our perceiving is through our own loving.[75]

Still, the exercise of this "unassailable fact" may be blocked by various types of bias:

Accordingly, while there is no need to justify critically the charity described by St. Paul in the thirteenth chapter of his first epistle to the Corinthians, there is always a great need to eye very critically any religious individual or

72. "An Interview with Fr. Bernard Lonergan, SJ," in Lonergan, *A Second Collection*, 229 and 230.

73. Lonergan, *Method in Theology*, 123.

74. Lonergan, *Method in Theology*, 283–84.

75. Lonergan, *Method in Theology*, 290. Lonergan is paraphrasing Olivier Rabut, *L'expérience religieuse fondamentale* (Tournai: Casterman, 1969), 168.

group and to discern beyond the real charity they may well have been grant-ed the various types of bias that may distort or block their exercise of it.[76]

A last excerpt deserves to be quoted, drawn from another inter-view accorded by Lonergan: "Necessary truths arise from the trans-formation of the subject—who is not necessary. Grace is given: it has to be fully accepted and lived. There is no intellectual founda-tion other than faith."[77] It must be recalled that for him, faith is "the knowledge born of religious love."[78] Notwithstanding the presence of such love and knowledge derived from it, there ever remains an uncertainty regarding our being in love. St. Thomas defends the the-sis that one can never know, in an apodictic manner, whether one is or is not in a state of grace. But he also holds that one may detect several signs that show the high probability of being in that state.[79] Such uncertainty is compatible with faith certainty, which our stud-ies of the biblical faith, of Thomas, and of Newman have clarified.

Diverging from a foundationalist search for a logically unassail-able point of departure, both *Insight* and *Method* begin not from pre-sumably self-evident premises taken either from the Bible, as in the old Protestant apologetic, or from the magisterium, as in the old Ro-man Catholic apologetic,[80] but with the intentional, conscious reality of the (at least half-converted) human subject who thinks, acts, and loves. Thus Lonergan does with religious data what scientists do with sense data: they do not try to ground the data, but they recognize that such data just happen to be present, that such data nonetheless provide indispensable information, and that science consists of ob-serving and analysing them in order to come to judgments of fact.

76. Lonergan, *Method in Theology*, 284; notice the quotation from Olivier Rabut, 290.

77. Quoted by Pierre Robert, "Theology and Spiritual Life: Encounter with Bernard Lonergan," in *Lonergan Workshop*, ed. Fred Lawrence (Boston: Boston College, 1994), 10:342.

78. Lonergan, *Method in Theology*, 115.

79. Aquinas, *ST* I-II, q. 112, a. 5; *The Disputed Questions on Truth*, q. 10, a. 10; *Super Secundam Epistolam ad Corinthios Lectura*, Caput 12, Lectio 1, no. 445, in *Super Epistolas S. Pauli Lectura*.

80. See Lonergan, *Method in Theology,* 270.

More than a century before Lonergan came to grips with this issue, Newman had adopted the same solution as he commented on two passages written by St. Paul:

And, it may be, this is something of the Apostle's meaning, when he speaks of the witness of the Spirit. Perhaps he is speaking of that satisfaction and rest which the soul experiences in proportion as it is able to surrender itself wholly to God, and to have no desire, no aim, but to please Him. When we are awake, we are conscious we are awake, in a sense in which we cannot fancy we are, when we are asleep. When we have discovered the solution of some difficult problem in science, we have a conviction about it which is distinct from that which accompanies fancied discoveries or guesses. When we realize a truth we have a feeling which they have not, who take words for things. And so, in like manner, if we are allowed to find that real and most sacred object on which our heart may fix itself, a fulness of peace will follow, which nothing but it can give. In proportion as we have given up the love of the world, and are dead to the creature, and, on the other hand, are born of the Spirit unto love of our Maker and Lord, this love carries with it its own evidence whence it comes. Hence the Apostle says, "The Spirit itself beareth witness with our spirit, that we are the children of God" (Rom 8:16). Again, he speaks of Him "who hath sealed us, and given the earnest of the Spirit in our hearts (2 Cor 1:22).[81]

This section has discussed Tracy's interesting objection to Lonergan's view of religious experience. Tracy is concerned with grounding theological method and discourse. In his reply, Lonergan asserts that religious experience cannot be *critically*—that is, epistemologically—grounded. Instead, it is simply as a matter of fact *present* in the religious experience of the theologian—an experience shared with other scholars in dialogue, both with past thinkers and among themselves. The task of the specialty called "foundations" consists in explicating a "being-in-love" that is in itself conscious without yet being known.

81. Newman, "The Thought of God," sermon 22, in part V, in *Parochial and Plain Sermons*, 1152.

INTELLECTUAL CONVERSION AND
CRITICAL REALISM

Intellectual conversion consists in the kind of self-knowledge whereby an individual affirms oneself as a knower. Lonergan calls such self-knowledge, as explicated, "cognitional theory."

Here is how he represents cognitional theory. Attentiveness to one's cognitive operations allows philosophers to notice the way those operations occur and interact. In intelligent minds, whether in practical matters or in any science, a series of operations spontaneously take place, along four basic steps, the first of which is perceptual experience, and the other three consisting of three types of questioning. Thus, sense data, once perceived, naturally become, in one's memory and imagination, images (in the broadest sense) about which one spontaneously asks, what is this? How has it happened? Why does it work this way? Insights are answers to this type of question. Yet insights remain hypotheses, and therefore the inquirer asks a second type of question: Is it so? Is it the case? Is reality as I have understood it? In response, one verifies, tests, weighs the evidence, one realizes that one has fulfilled the conditions for one's knowing that the hypothesis is true, and one makes judgments of fact about it. Finally, as a doer and not only as a knower, one asks a third type of question: How can I act in the present situation? Is it worthwhile to do this or that? What should I decide? This latter kind of question eventually results in judgments of value and in decisions.[82]

Lonergan's cognitional theory purports to be universal, and rightly so. As he notes in *Method*, any attempt to demolish it is self-defeating, since in order to do so, one cannot but perform the very acts one attempts to deny.[83] In any religious study, philosophy of religion, or theology, the process of formulation has no option but to implement the natural laws of the human mind. Admittedly,

---

82. Lonergan, *Method in Theology*, chap. 1, section 2, and chap. 2, sections 3–4.
83. Lonergan, *Method in Theology*, 19; see also Roy, *Mystical Consciousness*, 18.

we should not expect to achieve all the exact solutions at the beginning of an inquiry. Yet, both in principle and in practice, whenever people have the humility to recognize their shortcomings and biases, a self- and group-correcting process of scholarly learning spontaneously unfolds.

In its turn, cognitional theory generates right conceptions about the human person (philosophical anthropology), about intentionality, relatedness to the real, objectivity (epistemology), and about the several facets of being (metaphysics). Grounded in the self-knowledge that makes an adequate cognitional theory possible, Lonergan's fundamental position is a critical realism.

Intellectual conversion is a radical clarification and, consequently, the elimination of an exceedingly stubborn and misleading myth concerning reality, objectivity, and human knowledge. The myth is that knowing is like looking, that objectivity is seeing what is there to be seen and not seeing what is not there, and the real is what is out there now to be looked at.... Knowing, accordingly, is not just seeing; it is experiencing, understanding, judging, and believing. The criteria of objectivity are not just the criteria of ocular vision; they are the compounded criteria of experiencing, of understanding, of judging, and of believing. The reality known is not just looked at; it is given in experience, organized and extrapolated by understanding, posited by judgment and belief.[84]

Finally, we must detect the influence of religious conversion upon intellectual conversion (by way of moral conversion), which is neatly summed up in *Method* as follows:

From a causal viewpoint, one would say that first there is God's gift of his love. Next, the eye of this love reveals values in their splendor, while the strength of this love brings about their realization, and that is moral conversion. Finally, among the values discerned by the eye of love is the value of believing the truths taught by the religious tradition, and in such tradition and belief are the seeds of intellectual conversion. For the word, spoken and heard, proceeds from and penetrates to all four levels of intentional consciousness. Its content is not just a content of experience but a content

84. Lonergan, *Method in Theology*, 238.

of experience and understanding and judging and deciding. The analogy of sight yields the cognitional myth. But fidelity to the word engages the whole man.[85]

Lonergan highlights the fact that most of the time religious conversion comes chronologically first. We have seen that "being-in-love" in an unrestricted fashion generates faith as "the knowledge born of religious love." This faith spontaneously moves in the direction of moral conversion and of intellectual conversion, since these two kinds of conversion carry within themselves a desire to know truth and reality more adequately. However, Lonergan would not deny that moral and intellectual conversion also play a significant role in sustaining religious conversion that, after its inception, needs to be reinforced by right decisions and correct ideas about Christian commitments.

CONCLUDING REMARKS

As the preceding quotation states, religious conversion, which is principally affective, puts people in touch with great values and stirs up the desire to implement them (moral conversion). Among those values is the importance of belief, which is enhanced by attuning to the beauty and profundity of traditional writings, such as the Bible and the liturgy. Intellectual conversion consists in acquiring a kind of self-knowledge that is correctly expressed in cognitional theory, that yields an exact epistemology, and that unfolds into an accurate metaphysics. It is this intellectual conversion, prompted by religious conversion, that founds critical realism—namely, the reasoned hope that human beings can reach the real in a critical manner through the exercise of considered judgments.

Openness to divine revelation then depends on a quest for meaning and truth and on an affective experience. Authentic reception of revelation is considerably assisted by the fine balance, which Lonergan provides, between the affective and the intellectual aspects of

---

85. Lonergan, *Method in Theology*, 243.

human intentionality, between the inner and the outer word, and between experiential knowledge and tradition.

If we compare Lonergan with the two great thinkers he considered his mentors—namely, Thomas Aquinas and Newman—we can say that, having borrowed much from them, he has added the following contribution: situating religious experience in the broad context of human intentionality and of metaphysics, while employing the categories of interiority. So the language of psychology, which was not absent in Aquinas and Newman, is used by Lonergan in a manner that readily adjusts itself to the perspectives of Western audiences.

CHAPTER 6

Three Structuring
Dynamisms

ॐ

We have listened to reflections on the drama of hope, to the Bible, to exegetes, and to a good number of philosophers and theologians, principally Thomas Aquinas, John Henry Newman, and Bernard Lonergan. So I assume my readers are ready for an actualization of Christian faith in accordance with the concerns, hesitancies, worries, and questions about affective fulfillment, the meaning of human life, and truth, which were described in the introduction and in chapter 1. With respect to Lonergan's levels of intentionality, I situate affective fulfillment on the fourth level, meaning on the second, and truth on the third.

At least for a few decades, the faith of many believers—possibly the majority of them, at least in the West—has been plagued by individualism, subjectivism, and relativism. All beliefs seem to be relative to individual preferences.[1] At the same time a strong minority has fallen into objectivism.[2] They misinterpret and cling to certain biblical assertions or church pronouncements, taking no notice of the historical contexts and the intentions behind such statements, and construing them literally as these statements sound to modern

---

1. This position has been called "emotivism" by MacIntyre, *After Virtue*.
2. See Roy, *Engaging the Thought of Bernard Lonergan*, study 7.

ears obsessed with literal certainty at the expense of scripture's symbolic dimension.

Lonergan wrote that "genuine objectivity is the fruit of authentic subjectivity."[3] Authentic subjectivity is the key to answering the question "how can the faith experience be balanced and avoid falling into extremes?" On the one hand, how can it escape subjectivism—namely, the addiction to specific feelings, the pursuit of fanciful meanings, or the acting out of aberrant behavior? On the other hand, how can it shun objectivism—that is, the quasi-mindless acceptance of non-interiorized devotions, dogmatic formulas, or rules of conduct?

In the domain of faith, human subjectivity on the way to becoming objective faces a challenge. It is summoned to hold in a synergy three dynamisms or moments that are operative in the faith process: affective craving, quest for meaning, and aspiration for truth. This triad can also be called "heart, reason, and receptivity." It constitutes the anthropological substratum that accounts for the beginnings and the vitality of human hope. Needless to say, the operation of this active underpinning is enhanced by the Holy Spirit.

In this chapter, inspired by Augustine and Aquinas, and following Friedrich von Hügel, I will transpose John Henry Newman's famous Christological-ecclesiological triad into an anthropological triad. I hope that this transposition will throw some light upon the intermingling of the three fundamental forces in the lives of individuals and groups.

In order to do so, I will begin by characterizing the threefold human pursuit of fulfillment, meaning, and truth. Questions will be asked concerning the possibility that there obtains an interaction, a hegemony, or an alliance among these three dynamisms as they shape the actual situations in which believers find themselves. We shall also complete what was reported, in chapter 4, about Newman's views on distortions in the life of faith. Thereafter, we shall

3. Lonergan, *Method in Theology*, 292; see also 265.

take up the issue of self-deception, both within and without the faith. Last, we shall examine the central role of Jesus Christ in the process of coming to believe.

A MATTER OF EMOTION, OF REFLECTION, OR OF OBEDIENCE?

A number of believers would say that faith is first and foremost a matter of emotion. Religious experience, they would argue, consists of feelings, since it is the fulfillment of our aspirations. Affectivity asks questions such as, how can I satisfy my deep desires? Is it possible to be flawlessly loved and loving? How can my behavior be consistent with my purposes? Who can indefectibly confirm my fundamental worth as a human being? In the last analysis, what can I hope for? Transcendent trust certainly constitutes a response to these demands of our restless heart.

Other people, however, would maintain that faith is first and foremost a matter of reflection. For them, religion fundamentally consists in getting insights, since it is the answer that human thinking reaches in the course of its quest for meaning. Human understanding is troubled by questions such as, why is there this strange succession of pleasure, joy, suffering, evil, and death? May I identify meaning in any situation? Have my existence and my life a complete significance? Is the universe heading in the right direction? Experienced as knowing, faith projects some light onto these areas of interrogation.

Others, who belong in a third group, would contend that faith is first and foremost a matter of obedience to a self-revealing God. What is required is adherence to an authoritative religious message, since, as they would explain, religion is the human response to the question of truth. This question manifests a particularly noble preoccupation in the human person as he or she asks, regarding one's outlook on life: Is it so? Does my idea or hypothesis correspond with reality? Is there a source of truthfulness from which our very capacity to search for truth proceeds? This kind of question is perhaps less easily identified and less frequently voiced than those that have to do with affective needs or the urge to understand. Yet, if it is taken up seriously, it can lead to the free acknowledgment of the vision communicated by the word of God.

INTERACTION

Given that none of the three moments operates in an isolated manner, their relations vary according to typical situations. The first situation that can be sketched is the ideal one: the interaction thanks to which the three dynamisms aid each other. It may be represented by the schema of three equal circles (see figure 6-1A). The circles are equal because the three factors roughly have the same weight with respect to faith progression. In this case we observe an equilibrium among the three sources that foster the life of faith.

In a rich faith experience, the three factors—affective craving, quest for meaning, and aspiration for truth—exercise a long-range influence on each other, even though one of them may prove to be of more intense concern. The threefold longing for communion, understanding, and correct judgments of reality facilitates three kinds of progression that mutually reinforce one another: the more the heart commits itself, the more the intellect finds meaning, and the more the mind submits to truth.

The first aspect answers the question "*why* do I believe?" I am intent on assenting because the Holy Spirit has poured out divine love into my heart.[4] The second answers the question "*what* do I believe?" I make the Christian creed my own, ruling out contradictory alternatives. The third answers the question "*whom* do I believe?" God's truthfulness molds and undergirds my philosophy of life and my representation of world history.

Interestingly, the traditional Lutheran dogmatics is familiar with

4. Rom 5:5.

Figure 6-1A: Interaction

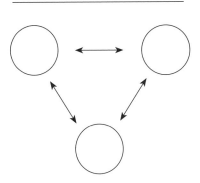

each of these three components. As said by Wolfhart Pannenberg, the first is called *fiducia*, trust; the second is called *notitia*, knowledge; and the third is called *assensus*, assent. He insists that each of these components plays an indispensable role.[5] In the modern Catholic world a comparable tripartite schema has been elaborated by Newman and von Hügel.

In the section of chapter 4 entitled, "Three Distortions of Faith," I expounded on Newman's Christological-ecclesiological triad. As Christ is priest, prophet, and king, so the church is endowed with three functions: sacerdotal, prophetical, and regal. Von Hügel takes up this triad and transforms it into an anthropological triad as he speaks of "the three great forces of the soul." These are "the sensational, the rational, the ethico-mystical." Since the latter two require no explanation, only a word will be said here about the first. By "the sensational," von Hügel means the receptivity of our sense apparatus, upon which the child's acceptance of external views is based.

The three forces operate in religion and are called "the three corresponding elements of religion," which are "the historical-institutional,"

---

5. Wolfhart Pannenberg, "Insight and Faith," in *Basic Questions in Theology* (Philadelphia: Westminster Press, 1971), 2:30–34.

"the critical-speculative," and "the mystical-operative," also labeled "the intuitive-emotional."[6] Von Hügel applies the tripartite schema to individual religious development. His interesting genetic presentation is nonetheless open to serious doubt: does the receptive (typical of the child, in von Hügel's opinion) entirely come before the rational (typical of the adolescent), and does the rational entirely come before the emotional (typical of the adult)? At any rate, my approach here is not genetic, but structural. Still, my treatment of the topic will reflect his notes—most useful, indeed—on the distortions that occur whenever one soul-force depreciates the other two.[7]

HEGEMONY OR ALLIANCE

So far we have paid attention to the first, ideal, situation, in which the three factors at work in faith interact. We still have to portray two other basic situations, this time unhealthy ones, with their subdivisions. The second, typical situation consists in a hegemony on the part of one force at the expense of the two other (see figure 6-1B). The big circle refers either to the heart, or to reason, or to receptivity—that is, to the specific force that happens to be winning over its competitors. Such a hegemony may imply three possibilities.

Whenever a person immoderately stresses the heart while neglecting the other two dynamisms, one risks falling into deviations such as sentimentalism or illuminism. Under such conditions, affectivity is interested solely in that which it can feel (sentimentalism).

6. Friedrich von Hügel, *The Mystical Element of Religion as Studied in Saint Catherine of Genoa and Her Friends*, 2nd ed. (London: J. M. Dent and Sons, 1923), 1:18, 56, 2:387, 393–94; see also 1:50–82, 2:367, 387–96. See also Lash, *Easter in Ordinary*, 154–62; I agree with Lash's remark that the full title of von Hügel's volume is misleading, since it is about issues more general than Catherine of Genoa and her time (135).

7. In "What Makes a Christology into a Christian Theology," *New Blackfriars* 77 (1996): 288–302, David Braine also introduces the three aspects of faith, albeit without the explicit intention to do so. He mentions the affective side (293) and dwells on the material side as he rightly states that doctrines must be understandable to a degree (288–93); yet he lays the main emphasis on the formal side (from 289 onward), for which he makes a very intelligent case.

Figure 6-1B: Hegemony

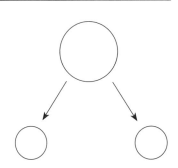

Or one entertains the illusory conviction that one's own lights or intuitions guarantee the truth of personal religious experience (illuminism, which can also be labeled "intuitionism"). Such believers are not sufficiently informed for one part by thinking and for another by revelation. Search for emotional security is accompanied with intellectual laziness, closed-mindedness, or self-deceit.

Whenever an inordinate emphasis is put on reason, human thinking wants to be too independent vis-à-vis emotion as well as tradition. It risks falling into deviations such as rationalism, pragmatism, and relativism. In the first of these three cases (rationalism), an individual accepts only what she understands or finds meaningful. In the second case (pragmatism), she holds as true what works, what is beneficial. In the third case (relativism), she resigns herself to the current opinion that religious beliefs are culturally determined.

Whenever a heavy stress is placed upon submission to authority—be it the Bible or the church, at the expense of *God's* authority[8]—one risks falling into deviations such as fideism, dogmatism,

8. See *ST* II-II, q. 1, a. 9, ad 5: "The phrase 'believing in the holy, catholic Church' should be understood in the sense that our faith is in the Holy Spirit who sanctifies the Church, thus as equivalent to, 'I believe in the Holy Spirit who makes the Church holy.'"

Figure 6-1C: Alliance

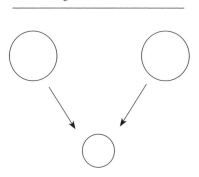

and authoritarianism. In this case the end result is a leap into the incomprehensible (fideism), or servile obedience, "*la foi du charbonnier*" (the charcoal-burner's faith) extolled by the French polemicist Louis Veuillot (1813–83), a form of religion that is blindly received, learned by rote, or imposed upon others (authoritarianism).[9] John Coventry pointedly criticizes this aberration: "It is inappropriate and misleading to speak of faith as 'a leap in the dark,' as is often done. It could better be called, and is at times experienced as, a leap into the light."[10]

As has just been mentioned, hegemony occurs in three distinct ways—to wit, whenever one dynamism occupies too much room and exceedingly predominates over the other two. Discernibly, this situation impoverishes the individual or the group wherein one of the factors crushes the other two.

Interaction and hegemony are the first two typical situations. The third one is alliance between two dynamisms against a third one. In figure 6-1C, the mid-size circles over the little one illustrate the fact

9. See Pierre Pierrard, *Louis Veuillot* (Paris: Beauchesne, 1998), 64–67.

10. John Coventry, *Christian Truth* (New York: Paulist Press, 1975), 5.

that two factors brush aside a third one. And again, in this third situation, a threefold subdivision obtains.

For example, affectivity and quest for meaning think of themselves as a self-sufficient couple and exclude the possibility that God might have revealed himself and might have made known his saving design to the world. Or affectivity and authority may join forces and generate a religiousness that is at once sentimental and submissive. In this instance there is no place for critical reflection. Finally, reason and loyalty to dogmas may establish a coalition that produces a dry and rigid attitude whereby the requests of the heart are rejected or just ignored.

THE ISSUE OF SELF-DECEPTION

Can we account for the persistence of those deformations of faith? How is it that a good number of believers fall into sentimentalism, rationalism, or fideism? One explanation singles out mere lack of religious knowledge. Thus a person may overly stress one of the three dimensions because he had no occasion to consider the significance of the other two, the import of which goes unnoticed. Biblical, catechetical, or theological formation can remedy such one-sidedness. Some psychological assistance may also be helpful. Lots of people are not open to owning up to their shortcomings; they fear that such recognition could entail they have a poor intellect, so that others would be entitled to look down on them. The thought does not cross their mind that admission of one's shortcomings betokens intelligence and honesty, hence cognitional nobility. Or else they fear the unknown because it requires changing, and they have painful doubts about their own capacity to change for the better.

A second explanation is the occurrence of wishful thinking. In this case, which concerns both believers and unbelievers, their basic outlook on life carries with it several lacunas, which they disregard. Such an outlook comprises prereflectively held, uncriticized beliefs. Insofar as affectivity is concerned, they make believe that actual fulfillment can be obtained in futile activities (for the secular people, much leisure time or, for religious people, infantile prayers and devotions). Insofar as rationality is concerned, they may have an unwarranted confidence in their personal judgment and be unwilling to observe its mistakes. Insofar as authority is concerned, they pretend that obedience to civil or ecclesiastical laws is invariably unproblematic. The signs that point to errors—on their part or on the part of the authorities—are available, and yet these people do not care to be told how they could deal with those signs. Hence their state of negligence and passivity.

A third explanation, over which we shall tarry, given its negative consequences for faith, is the influence of self-deception. Like in the case of wishful thinking, the phenomenon of self-deception is detectable in the lives of both believers and unbelievers. In contrast to wishful thinking, self-deception is a negation in the teeth of evidence.[11] In order to resist a particular truth, people focus on evidence that apparently supports their counterfeit beliefs and overlook evidence suggesting that those beliefs are erroneous. "Thus, we do not have the deliberate irrationality of believing something in the face of contrary evidence. Rather we have the refusal to collect or dwell on or appreciate the significance of evidence. In this case we may say that self-deception proceeds by the unwillingness to *look* or attend to."[12] It amounts to willful blindness.

The perceptive Blaise Pascal describes "deliberate self-delusion" as follows: Knowing itself to be "full of faults and wretchedness" or "full of imperfections," self-love

conceives a deadly hatred for the truth which rebukes it and convinces it of its faults. It would like to do away with this truth, and not being able to destroy it as such, it destroys it, as best it can, in the consciousness of itself

---

11. My contrast between wishful thinking and self-deception is dependent upon M. R. Haight, *A Study of Self-Deception* (Atlantic Highlands, N.J.: Humanities Press, 1980), chap. 1.

12. John W. Newman, *Disciplines of Attention: Buddhist Insight Meditation, the Ignatian Spiritual Exercises, and Classical Psychoanalysis* (New York: Peter Lang, 1996), 78.

and others; that is, it takes every care to hide its faults both from itself and others, and cannot bear to have them pointed out or noticed.[13]

A similar way in which made-up self-esteem is used to deny one's moral inadequacy is a cynical boasting of one's vices, proclaimed as virtues. The great Russian writer Leo Tolstoy very lucidly uncovers this mechanism:

Everybody, in order to be able to act, has to consider his occupation important and good. Therefore, in whatever position a person is, he is certain to form such a view of the life of men in general, as will make his occupation seem important and good.... People whom fate and their sin-mistakes have placed in a certain position, however false that position may be, form a view of life in general which makes their position seem good and admissible. In order to keep up their view of life, these people instinctively keep to the circle of those who share their views of life and of their own place in it. This surprises us where the persons concerned are thieves bragging about their dexterity, prostitutes vaunting their depravity, or murderers boasting of their cruelty. But it surprises us only because the circle, the atmosphere, in which these people live, is limited, and chiefly because we are outside it. Can we not observe the same phenomenon when the rich boast of their wealth—robbery; when commanders of armies pride themselves on their victories—murder; and when those in high places vaunt their power—violence? That we do not see the perversion in the views of life held by these people, is only because the circle formed by them is larger and we ourselves belong to it.[14]

Self-deception consists in an active eschewing of truth, a vigorous resistance, supported by ingenious tactics. One has learned where not to look.[15] As David Burrell explains, "We neglect to acquire the very skills which will test [our] profession of sincerity against our

---

13. Pascal, pensée 978.

14. Leo Tolstoy, *Resurrection*, trans. Louise Maude (New York: Dodd, Mead, 1927), 170.

15. Ten Elshof calls this "attention management," which, as he rightly maintains, is not a bad thing in itself, since we cannot but be selectively attentive; see Gregg A. Ten Elshof, *I Told Me So: Self-Deception and the Christian Life* (Grand Rapids, Mich.: Eerdmans, 2009), 31–40, 102–3; this short book offers very wise practical advice on how to handle self-deception.

current performance. On the contrary, we deliberately allow certain engagements to go unexamined, quite aware that areas left unaccountable tend to cater to self-interest."[16] Besides self-interest, animosity can play a role: "Sometimes a person may wish for something to be false simply because someone she dislikes is committed to it being true."[17] And what makes things worse is this: "Even when one is aware that one has a certain desire, one may still not be aware that that desire plays a causal role in one's own actions and in what one believes."[18]

Jean-Paul Sartre remarks that our consciousness is at the same time positional and nonpositional. It is positional whenever it focuses on objects that it has identified; it is nonpositional whenever it remains merely vaguely aware of its activities (lack of self-awareness) or of objects that are located on the periphery of its span of attention (lack of recognition of those objects). Self-deception (which Sartre calls *mauvaise foi*, "bad faith") consists in shunning the data (about one's beliefs, intentions, long-range fundamental project, self-identity or the identity of the group to which an individual has its place) that might throw light on oneself.[19]

As J. Kellenberger puts it, "In one sense self-deceived persons are aware but in another sense they are not aware: they are *implicitly* aware, but *explicitly* unaware."[20] They maintain an intention of blocking the explication of what is half-aware, in order to evade a displeasing truth. Strange paradox: using one's mind to remain mind-

---

16. David B. Burrell, "Self-Deception and Autobiography: Reflections on Speer's *Inside the Third Reich*," in *Truthfulness and Tragedy: Further Investigations in Christian Ethics*, ed. Stanley Hauerwas (Notre Dame, Ind.: University of Notre Dame Press, 1977), 82.

17. Kevin Kinghorn, "Spiritual Blindness: Self-Deception and Morally Culpable Nonbelief," *Heythrop Journal* 48 (2007):531.

18. Kinghorn, "Spiritual Blindness," 532.

19. See Jean-Paul Sartre, *The Transcendence of the Ego*, trans. Forrest Williams and Robert Kirkpatrick (New York: Farrar, Straus and Giroux, 1972), and *Being and Nothingness*, trans. Hazel E. Barnes (New York: Philosophical Library, 1956). About Sartre's account of consciousness, see Roy, *Mystical Consciousness*, 10–16.

20. J. Kellenberger, *The Cognitivity of Religion: Three Perspectives* (Berkeley: University of California Press, 1985), 121; see also 121–25.

less concerning facts that are vaguely familiar. A worse case is fore-closure, characterized by psychoanalysts as the rejection of unbear-able representations, without explicit awareness because there is no self-exploration.

Talking about "the case of most direct interest for self-deception," Herbert Fingarette writes:

This is the situation in which there is overriding reason *not* to spell-out some engagement [some stance of ours in the world], where we skilfully take account of this and systematically avoid spelling-out the engagement, and where, in turn, we refrain from spelling-out this exercise of our skill in spelling out. In other words, we avoid becoming explicitly conscious of our engagement, and we avoid becoming explicitly conscious that we are avoiding it.[21]

For instance, I may want not to see the unwelcome truth that my faith or my unbelief is blighted by a serious flaw in one or two of the three basic dynamisms. To justify my reluctance to scrutinize my unevenness, I latch upon some rationalization such as "Faith is not a matter of feelings" (against the role of affectivity), or "Faith is founded on the heart" (against the role of reason), or "Faith is a matter of personal experience; it does not depend on what other hu-man beings tell me" (against the role of authority). I then employ caricatures, be it of affectivity or of reason or of receptivity, in order to downgrade one or two among the three dynamisms.

Moreover, if self-deceit is so energetic, isn't it because it is usu-ally driven by fear? In the context of the three basic deviations de-picted in this chapter, a threefold fear can be evoked: of my emo-tions, which might carry me too far; of my questions, which might drag me onto slippery ground; of authority, which might enslave me. These are only illustrations, since self-deception is employed to counter several kinds of fear—for example, fear of discovering that my practice is contradicting my principles, or fear that such a dis-covery might tarnish my self-image, or that it would require weighty

21. Herbert Fingarette, *Self-Deception* (London: Routledge and Kegan Paul, 1969), 43.

changes in my conduct, changes that could entail giving up much. The Scottish philosopher John Macmurray observes that for Jesus, faith is the opposite of fear.[22] "Have faith" goes hand in hand with "fear not."[23] His point is well taken: "To 'believe,' or to 'have faith,' means not to be frightened. In that case, faith must mean something like courage, or confidence, or trust."[24]

Whereas the wishful thinker merely fails to notice his personal imperfections (or is only vaguely aware of them), the self-deceiver knows them all along in the recesses of his mind. Consequently he must endeavor to forget them, at least temporarily, or to delay examining them, by constantly turning his thoughts to other things. To escape disappointment and guilt about himself, he represses any memory or suggestion that would remind him of his dark shadow. Certain facts that are much to the point do not occur to him at all. Or, if they occur, he quickly pronounces them insignificant or irrelevant to the problem at stake, or else he obscures and misrepresents them in order to ignore the questions that might emerge from those facts.

Besides what I reported in chapter 2, Raymund Schwager explains the scribes' and Pharisees' hypocrisy in this way: they blame their ancestors' rejection of the prophets while behaving in exactly the same manner in face of Jesus. In addition to Matthew's chapter 23, texts by John the Evangelist illustrate the themes of darkness, of the world, of lying, of refusal to see. People do not come to the light, so that their deeds may not be exposed. As Schwager notes, at its worst "the cover-up is so complete that even the notion that something could be hidden there no longer comes up."[25]

Here we come across the highest degree of self-deception—namely, hypocrisy. Whereas ordinary self-deception is less dramatic, hypocrisy is accompanied by greater nervousness, owing to the fact

22. Mt 8:26, 14:30–31.
23. Mt 10:26.
24. Macmurray, *Ye Are My Friends*, 6.
25. Schwager, *Must There Be Scapegoats?*, 152.

that the hated and dreaded insight that one needs to dodge is just around the corner.[26] We may want to admit that there is a certain amount of bad will here; however, by itself, bad will utterly fails to account for the complexity of the phenomena, which turn out to be more complex than calculated lies. Thus Max Scheler's analysis of "organic mendacity":

Beyond all conscious lying and falsifying, there is a deeper "organic mendacity." Here the falsification is not formed in consciousness but at the same stage of the mental process as the impressions and value feelings themselves on the road of experience into consciousness. There is "organic mendacity" whenever a man's mind admits only those impressions and feelings which serve his "interest" or his instinctive attitude. Already in the process of mental reproduction and recollection, the contents of his experience are modified in this direction. He who is "mendacious" has no need to lie! In his case, the automatic process of forming recollections, impressions, and feelings is involuntarily slanted, so that conscious falsification becomes unnecessary.[27]

Other twentieth-century authors help us understand some of the tactics of self-deceit. For instance, the psychoanalyst Dan Merkur ascribes hypocrisy to "a reaction-formation, a configuration of splitting that allocates idealization to consciousness while maintaining derogation at a preconscious level." He comments, "The result is hypocrisy. A series of virtues are espoused consciously, but opposing vices are harboured preconsciously."[28]

Along parallel lines, inspired by Marx, Macmurray denounces religious idealism as entertaining noble beliefs disconnected from their actual influence in society, as closing our eyes to the role that our ideas do play within the nexus of economic, legal, political, and

---

26. See Newman, *Parochial and Plain Sermons*, part V, sermon 16, "Sincerity and Hypocrisy," 1092 and 1095.

27. Max Scheler, *Ressentiment*, trans. William W. Holdheim (New York: Free Press of Glencoe, 1961), 77–78.

28. Dan Merkur, *Crucified with Christ: Meditation on the Passion, Mystical Death, and the Medieval Invention of Psychotherapy* (Albany, N.Y.: SUNY Press, 2007), 81.

social relations.[29] He contends that, inasmuch as we succumb to moral or religious idealism, our underground motive is tantamount to the desire to protect interests contrary to our ideals. Our practice then gives the lie to our pretense.[30] Macmurray would concur with Lonergan, who remarks, "When knowledge is deficient, then fine feelings are apt to be expressed in what is called moral idealism, i.e. lovely proposals that don't work and often do more harm than good."[31]

Kellenberger touches upon this psychological lacuna: "The possibility of self-deception exists or may exist whenever there is a realisation-discovery that could have been made by a person but was not."[32] Lonergan is also interested in this strange phenomenon: the fact that a "realisation-discovery" that is highly desirable does not happen. This lack is the absence of an insight that ought to be there but is actually missing. In the introduction to his book *Insight*, he calls attention to "an oversight of insight" or, when it is the outcome of active ignoring, "a flight from understanding."[33] He takes it to be not a mere absence of insight, but a peculiar way of missing a potential insight. And in an allusion to a theme underlined in the Gospel of John, he declares, "Just as insight can be desired, so too it can be unwanted. Besides the love of light, there can be a love of darkness."[34]

In highly general terms, his solution runs as follows: "Insight into insight, then, will reveal what activity is intelligent, and insight into oversights will reveal what activity is unintelligent." Practically

29. See Roy, "Why Are Most Christians on the Defensive with Respect to Marxism?" *New Blackfriars* 64 (1983):29–34.

30. See Roy, "'The Form of the Personal': A Study of the Philosophy of John Macmurray with Particular Reference to His Critique of Religious 'Idealism,'" Ph.D. diss., Dissertation Abstracts International, 45, no. 12A (1984): 3667, available at Ann Arbor, Mich.: University Microfilms International, Order No. DA8501107.

31. Lonergan, *Method in Theology*, 38.

32. Kellenberger, *Cognitivity of Religion*, 121.

33. Lonergan, *Collected Works*, vol. 3, *Insight*, 21.

34. Jn 3:19–20; Lonergan, *Collected Works*, vol. 3, *Insight*, 3:214.

speaking, his prescription is that "if insight into insight is not to be an oversight of oversights, it must include an insight into the principal devices of the flight from understanding."[35]

One of those devices is the "scotosis" (from the Greek *skotōsis*, darkening), which Lonergan analyzes in chapter 6 of *Insight*. Being at once unconscious and conscious, hidden and not hidden, the scotosis is twofold:

> Fundamentally, the scotosis is an unconscious process. It arises, not in conscious acts, but in the censorship that governs the emergence of psychic contents. Nonetheless, the whole process is not hidden from us, for the merely spontaneous exclusion of unwanted insights is not equal to the total range of eventualities.[36]

He locates the scotosis, first in the attempt to prevent insights and questions that could lead to them, and second in a malfunctioning of the censor.

> The scotosis is an aberration, not only of the understanding, but also of the censorship. Just as wanting an insight penetrates below the surface to bring forth schematic images that give rise to the insight, so not wanting an insight has the opposite effect of repressing from consciousness a scheme that would suggest the insight. Now this aberration of the censorship is inverse to it. Primarily, the censorship is constructive; it selects and arranges materials that emerge in consciousness in a perspective that gives rise to an insight.... In contrast, the aberration of the censorship is primarily repressive; its positive activity is to prevent the emergence into consciousness of perspectives that would give rise to unwanted insights; it introduces, so to speak, the exclusion of arrangements into the field of the unconscious; it dictates the manner in which neural demand functions are not to be met.[37]

In consequence, images and affects that could be helpful are inhibited:

> The effect of the repression is an inhibition imposed upon neural demand functions. However, if we distinguish between demands for images and de-

35. Ibid., 8 and 5.
36. Ibid., 215.
37. Ibid., 215–16.

mands for affects, it becomes clear that the inhibition will not block both in the same fashion. For insights arise, not from the experience of affects, but rather from imaginative presentations. Hence, to prevent insights, repression will have to inhibit demands for images. On the other hand, it need inhibit demands for affects only if they are coupled with the undesired images.[38]

I would add that among the images that do pop up within sensitive awareness, some are harmful. Being associated with negative memories, they reinforce emotions that are hurtful—for instance, anxieties, regrets, grudges, resentments, vindictiveness, and so forth. Nevertheless, it is better to become aware of painful images and their attendant affects than to disregard them.

In the wake of Lonergan, Robert Doran has tackled the issue of surmounting the scotosis and has called the solution "psychic conversion." It has to do with the sensitive psyche—namely, that part of the human person that mediates between the body and intentionality. The psyche consists of "the sequence of sensations, memories, images, emotions, conations, associations, bodily movements, and spontaneous intersubjective responses."[39] Psychic conversion is the transformation of the censor from a basically repressive to a basically constructive function by providing the relevant images in which insights occur. In so doing, the psyche offers intentionality the sedulous collaboration of the feelings and images that are required for the emergence of pertinent questions and adequate answers.[40]

In this kind of liberation, the driving factor is the natural desire to be coherent, congruent, and harmonious. Obviously, in any inconsistent position (either theoretical or practical), a particular element remains obscure because, should it become conscious, the

38. Ibid., 216.

39. Robert M. Doran, *Psychic Conversion and Theological Foundations: Toward a Reorientation of the Human Sciences* (Chico, Calif.: Scholars Press, 1981), 28.

40. See Doran, "From Psychic Conversion to the Dialectic of Community," in *Lonergan Workshop*, ed. Fred Lawrence (Atlanta: Scholars Press, 1986), 6:91–93, and Doran, *Theology and the Dialectics of History* (Toronto: University of Toronto Press, 1990), 180–83.

self-contradiction would ostensibly manifest itself in a glaring fashion. Still, even the dimmest awareness of one's self-contradiction may be the beginning of a painful and yet liberating uncovering. Interestingly, Lonergan endorses Kierkegaard's view on the possible function of humor, irony, and satire in the transition from a drifting, aesthetic attitude to a committed, ethical one.[41]

The Danish loner does not underestimate the self-deceit that consists in thinking oneself immune from self-deceit. Writing about "the self-deceived person" who "has locked and is locking himself out of love," whom he characterizes as "the person who, very ingeniously, deceived himself by sagaciously walking into the trap of sagacity," he comments, "We can be deceived by appearances, but we certainly are also deceived by the sagacious appearance, by the flattering conceit that considers itself absolutely secure against being deceived."[42]

In Marx's, Nietzsche's, and Freud's critique of false consciousness, Paul Ricoeur perceives tools that can be used to dismantle it, at least in part. The religious illusion feeds on attachment to feelings, ideas, or ecclesiastical power in order to enjoy consolation and security. And yet Ricoeur claims that people can give up such immature consolation and security, typical of the youthful "first faith" or "first naiveté," and progressively adopt what he calls the mature "second faith" or "second naiveté."[43] They then discover another kind of consolation and security, which assists adults' responsible actions. Much personal and communal work is needed, however, if believers are to pass from the first to the second naiveté.

The purposes of this book do not require that we move more deeply into the intricate mechanisms of wishful thinking and self-deception. However, if I draw attention to them, it is in order to

41. Lonergan, *Collected Works*, vol. 3, *Insight*, 647.
42. Kierkegaard, *Kierkegaard's Writings*, vol. 16, *Works of Love*, ed. Howard V. Hong and Edna H. Hong (Princeton, N.J.: Princeton University Press, 1995), 5–6.
43. See Paul Ricoeur, *Freud and Philosophy: An Essay on Interpretation*, trans. Denis Savage (New Haven: Yale University Press, 1970).

sound a note of realism concerning the actual life of both believers and unbelievers.[44] It is incumbent on honest people to admit that their cherished stance is not immune from criticism and to envisage ways of at least partly overcoming their deficiencies. Thus Kant, talking about the conflict between morality and politics, writes:

> True courage . . . in the present case consists not so much in resolutely standing up to the evils and sacrifices that must be taken on; rather, it consists in detecting, squarely facing, and conquering the deceit of the evil principle in ourselves, which is the more dangerously devious and treacherous because it excuses all our transgressions with an appeal to human nature's frailty.[45]

I wish to conclude this section with an additional remark. The authors quoted here assume that most human beings are never totally entrapped in self-deceit. Indeed, among people whose mind functions at least minimally, complete self-deceit is impossible. The simple fact that someone can raise the issue of truth and untruth demonstrates that she intends the real. Intentionality is the intrinsic tendency to meet the requirements of reality. Therefore, any philosophy of "nothing but deception" is contradicted by its very effort to confirm itself intellectually. If this skeptical and narrow representation of human integrity were the last word on ethics, it could not be encompassed by our broader horizon of questions and answers, which are operative in terms of truth and reality. This broader horizon is always dynamically present. Of course, it may be replied that truth- or reality-talk is just a rationalization of our interests. Confronted with this extreme assertion, are we not entitled to ask, "Is your objection nothing but a rationalization of your interests?" If it

---

44. Among the numerous cases of denial, perhaps the most blatant is the disqualification of scientific evidence concerning the warning signs of a future ecological meltdown.

45. Immanuel Kant, "To Perpetual Peace: A Philosophical Sketch," in *Perpetual Peace and Other Essays on Politics, History, and Morals*, trans. Ted Humphrey (Indianapolis, Ind.: Hackett, 1983), 134 (Akademie ed., 8:379). For another indication that Kant was aware of the problem of self-deception, see Kant, "Religion within the Boundaries of Mere Reason," in *Religion and Rational Theology*, trans. Allen W. Wood and George Di Giovanni (Cambridge: Cambridge University Press, 1996), 83–84 (Akademie edition, 6:37–38).

were the case, this would imply that every form of human science and every experience of dialogue is an illusion! But how could we then be aware of that illusion?

Obviously, we must infer that besides the reasons people may have of concealing their inauthenticity, there are reasons to become aware of it and to defeat it at least partly. Such reasons emanate from intentionality, sense of dignity, and fundamental hope. Few individuals can entirely extinguish their desire to accept truth. One may take advantage of detailed studies of the religious illusion that are found both in the psychology of religion and in liberation theology. And if such readers are Christian, they may respond positively to the promise voiced by Jesus, "The truth will make you free."[46]

THE ENCOUNTER WITH JESUS CHRIST

Highlighting the three dynamisms operative in the faith process has allowed us to delineate schemas that in fact are valid for most of the world religions. We observe instances of interaction, hegemony, and alliance in Judaism, Christianity, Islam, Hinduism, and Buddhism. In any of those traditions, evidently, the three factors have been distinctively construed. Here I will simply sketch the way in which the encounter with Jesus Christ actualizes and concretizes the three factors. But let us note that scholars could find analogous applications in the case of a Hindu avatar or of the compassionate Buddha—all deemed worthy of devotion. However, the person of Jesus is all-important for Christians, as was illustrated in our previous chapters.

First, to what aspects of Jesus can human *affectivity* be sensitive? Along the centuries, scores of people have been attracted to and touched by the humanity of Jesus. One day, an eighteen-year-old woman portrayed Jesus as "the most human of humans." The nobility of his attitudes, a dignity ever permeated with simplicity, his

46. Jn 8:32b.

balance between gentleness and firmness, his sympathy for the little ones, the marginal, and the wayward have certainly conquered or reassured numberless hearts. Besides, when one is mindful of the fact that Christ was also divine, one cannot but be struck, first by his humility as he shared our human condition, and second by the infinite love manifested during his passion and made triumphant by the resurrection. "Now when they heard this, they were cut to the heart."[47] Such love in turn elicits love in truth and action on the part of those who trust in God.

Second, what does *reason* notice in Jesus? His orientations represent both a confirmation and a challenge for someone in quest of meaning. A confirmation insofar as one recognizes one's own aspirations in the values of Jesus; but also a challenge because, for instance, the Sermon on the Mount inexorably questions the sort of human wisdom that tries to be too reasonable.[48] Furthermore, as the locus of the divine response to the issue of suffering and evil, the passion that Jesus voluntarily suffered opens up a disconcerting path where believers are offered much meaning in the chiaroscuro of faith. Jesus' acceptance of the cross shows us that, in any situation marked by evil, faith in meaning and value is possible: God-given love can assert itself, and believers can grow as mature human beings. The resurrection is the key that unlocks the door to a most satisfying worldview proposed to the human race. Without being capable of mounting a full apodictic proof, the believing intelligence nevertheless catches a glimpse of the fact that both individual and collective existence is intensely illumined by the hope that God offers in Jesus. The Son reveals not only what the Father is, but at the same time what the human person really is and, despite its misery, can become.

Third, how does adherence to *truth* follow from the encounter

---

47. Acts 2:37.

48. Mt 5–7.; see also Roy, *Self-Actualization and the Radical Gospel*, introduction, chaps. 4–6, and conclusion.

with Jesus? Mark's Gospel provides a clue: "He taught them as one having authority."[49] In the human voice of Jesus, the believers hear a unique Voice, which deserves entire trust on their part.[50] And when Jesus asks his disciples if like the crowd they wish to go away, Simon Peter replies, "Lord, to whom shall we go? You have the words of eternal life. We have come to believe and know that you are the Holy One of God."[51] The voice of the Holy One is doubtless unsettling; but it is equally fascinating. As in the case of the prophets, although with a special accent, God speaks through Jesus: "Never has anyone spoken like this!"[52] In him the Father utters his definitive and normative Word. Nonetheless, this unveiling in no way puts an end to the interpretive process that takes place in the church. On the contrary, the Holy Spirit unceasingly stirs and orientates the emergence of new words bound to be faithful to the overall revelation.

CONCLUDING REMARKS

This chapter has tried to demonstrate that three approaches—the craving for affective fulfillment, the quest for meaning, and the commitment to truth—can all work together in the intentional movement of faith. My presentation first depicted each of these vectors. It then showed how they support one another inasmuch as they function in a harmonious interaction and bring about a certain equilibrium. It proceeded to expose the distortions that take place whenever one of those dynamisms strives toward hegemony, or whenever two of them enter into an alliance against a third factor. Thereafter, it probed the issue of self-deception for both believers and unbelievers. Finally, it considered how the discovery of Jesus Christ affects each of the three dynamisms.

49. Mk 1:22. In 1968, during an oral exchange, the Dominican Marie-Dominique Chenu pointed out that the first meaning of the Latin word *auctor* designates a person who makes others grow (*augere*).

50. See Jn 10:3–5 and 16.

51. Jn 6:68–69.

52. Jn 7:46.

Our threefold schema equally honors subjectivity, objectivity, and intersubjectivity. The subjective language, in terms of "I," expresses affective experience—one of the key factors in the search for God. The objective language, in terms of "it," has to do with another key factor—namely, the desire to understand the meanings disclosed in the faith process. And the intersubjective language, in terms of "you," responds to a third key factor—that is, the challenge of a dialogue and an interpersonal relationship with Christ and his church.[53]

Going back to the need to overcome subjectivism and objectivism, signaled at the beginning of this chapter, two conclusions can be drawn. First, the equation of authentic subjectivity with genuine objectivity reflects the complementarity of the subjective and the objective factors, which was mentioned several times in this book. According to Lonergan, authentic subjectivity becomes genuine objectivity every time it is faithful to its five transcendental precepts: be attentive, be intelligent, be reasonable, be responsible, be in love. What has been often called the objective side—namely, revelation (as different from the subjective side—that is, faith) is received on Lonergan's first level of intentionality—that is, as data. Those data are communicated to a quest for meaning (on the second level), for truth (on the third level), and for affective fulfillment that is sensitive to the aesthetic dimension of the Bible and of the Christian experience (on the fourth level).

Second, the achievement of objectivity by human subjectivity requires intersubjectivity. As evident in John's Gospel and in Aquinas's commentary on that gospel, the role of Jesus Christ as the supreme Witness and the role of his disciples as reliable witnesses are paramount. Believers live through intersubjectivity at once in

---

53. This paragraph is inspired by Martin Buber, *I and Thou*, trans. Ronald Gregor Smith, 2nd ed. (New York: Charles Scribner's Sons, 1958). Notwithstanding my agreement with him regarding the primacy of the *I-Thou* relationship, I value the *I* and the *It* more than he does.

their encounter with Jesus and in their bonds with others. These persons—namely, Jesus and other witnesses—evince testimonials that influence the seekers and powerfully draw the latter out of their subjectivist boundaries into an objectivity that explicates the relationship with Christ and the saints. Specifically founded upon Jesus the Truth and the Revealer, religious intersubjectivity also depends on the meaningfulness and the affective fulfillment attained in him.

CHAPTER 7

Confirming the
Tripartite Structure

༆

Our preceding chapter described the tripartite structure of living faith. I now intend to uncover more fully the grounds and the implications of that structure. So this chapter aims at enriching our account of the human progress toward faith.

The first section of this chapter will explain the importance of the distinctive roles that meaning and truth play in the attraction to God. Second, stages will be differentiated in the process of coming to believe. Third, some light will be thrown upon the complementarity of feelings and insights. Fourth, we shall ask whether religious experience is the main criterion of truth. Fifth, I will show how the Christian version of religious experience is mediated by Christ as well as by countless persons and events.

MEANING AND TRUTH

We now come to grips more directly with the arduous problem of truth, as we encounter it, first in human research in general and second in faith and theology.

Thomas Aquinas distinguished between the first and the second act of intellect. Bernard Lonergan explains that regarding the first, Aquinas held that "the question of truth or falsity is not as yet raised, because as yet one knows, not the thing, but only the idea of the thing." Lonergan adds that "the second operation of intellect— by the very nature of its reflective character, by the very fact that it raises the question of truth, which is conformity between mind and thing—introduces the duality of idea and thing."[1]

In light of Aquinas's distinction between the first and second operation of the mind, or of Lonergan's distinction between insight and judgment, it should be readily admitted that the desire for meaning is not the same as the concern for truth.[2] Basic to the human mind is not only the urge to understand, but equally the imperative to ascertain whether something understood is the case or not. Indeed, if acts of understanding are not followed by critical questions, such acts become pointless. The best minds—not superficial ones—will agree that simply accumulating meanings is tantamount to a futile exercise of curiosity, originality, acumen, or subtlety. Consequently, numerous meaningful propositions that are scrutinized must be discarded, simply for the sake of truth.

A healthy human intentionality is never satisfied until it has completed the final stage of an inquiry, the stage of verification and of intellectual commitment to that which is. A person's or a group's hunches, intuitions, opinions, or beliefs are not sufficient. In other words, the point of meaning is truth. Thus, commenting on the intellectual phenomenon taking place at the council of Nicea, Frederick Crowe speaks of "truth emerging as a separate concern" or "truth in the spotlight."[3]

---

1. Lonergan, *Collected Works*, vol. 2, *Verbum: Word and Idea in Aquinas*, ed. Frederick E. Crowe and Robert M. Doran (Toronto: University of Toronto Press, 1997), 20 and 21. Likewise, Bertrand Russell distinguishes between significance and truth. There is significance whenever a sentence possesses a signification; there is truth whenever an assertion corresponds to a fact. False sentences are not nonsense: they mean something; see Russell, *An Inquiry into Meaning and Truth* (London: Unwin Paperbacks, 1980), 171.

2. See Roy, *Coherent Christianity, passim*, and *Engaging the Thought of Bernard Lonergan*, study 6.

3. Frederick E. Crowe, *Theology of the Christian Word: A Study in History* (New York: Paulist Press, 1978), 49–57.

In sum, we detect in human intentionality a natural tendency to take questions for truth seriously and to try to answer them as best we can. As was said in our preceding chapter, authentic subjectivity heads for objectivity. It does so in all domains: daily living, the arts, the sciences, history, religion, and so forth. If we take account of this remarkable propensity of the human mind, we can acknowledge the fact that an authentic faith cannot bypass the issue of truth. How can someone believe Jesus without verifying whether the meanings and values about him that one would like to accept are not fictitious? Since Jesus' good news regarding God, salvation, and the future of humankind has been mediated by his disciples, one may very well hesitate before adhering to their views: do they accurately reflect Jesus' proclamation? But isn't such a hesitation the hallmark of intellectual integrity? In the end, whether an individual decides for or against giving credence to the person and message of Jesus transmitted by Christianity, one makes an assessment of truth— positive or negative—that purports to be not arbitrary, but backed by reasons. Inasmuch as we are authentic, our judgments aim at being objective—that is, at being in accordance with reality.

STAGES ON THE WAY TO FAITH

By speaking of "stages on the way to faith," I am taking a diachronic, or genetic, view of the faith process so as to complement the synchronic, or structural, scope of chapter 6, which dealt with the three faith dynamisms as concomitantly engaged.

The French Jesuit Pierre Rousselot (1879–1915) grasped with great perspicacity the role of intellectual light in the movement toward believing. He draws attention to "the synthetic activity of the intelligence," in which a person discovers the point in a phenomenon or in an event.[4] He mentions the frequent case of two scientists or two detectives, both possessing the same evidence, while only

4. Pierre Rousselot, *The Eyes of Faith*, trans. Joseph Donceel (New York: Fordham University Press, 1990), 26; see also 27–35.

one of them draws the right conclusion from the evidence. The manifold elements available for inspection become clues, the function of which is to allow a connection to be made between the data and their unifying signification. One sees the point and one exclaims, "I've got it!" At that moment, there is a synthesis between a somewhat unclear datum and the insight that apprehends its meaning.

Likewise, in the process of coming to faith, an insight or a series of insights must happen. The external signs afforded by Christianity are illumined from within the believer's mind. The light of grace enables the inquirer to discern the meaning conveyed by the signs and to become aware of the obligation to believe. Furthermore, to the existential subject already tugged along by the love of God, eyes to see are given by grace, as we saw in chapter 2, in the section on the Logos incarnate.

Unfortunately, Rousselot's genuine contribution is marred by his insistence that the various operations involved in the process of faith happen simultaneously. He collapses into one synthetic act first the understanding of the point in the signs, second the apprehension of the duty to believe, and third the assent, which is the act of faith proper. Based on Lonergan's differentiating of intentionality, we must say that Rousselot's account here is too compact because it does not differentiate adequately the distinct and ordered operations by which we apprehend meaning, truth, and value. For me, the first of those operations is an apprehension of meaning; the second amounts to the intense yearning to accept a divine proposal that is most worthwhile; the third consists in the decision to say "yes" to the truthfulness of this transcendent meaning-value.

We have to concede that sometimes these three operations occur at the same time because of a person's favorable preparation (her state of mind and heart), thanks to which a sudden insight precipitates a quick resolution and a decisive conversion. Nonetheless, even when they occur simultaneously, we can maintain the normative sequence of those distinct, ordered, and related operations. Such a sequence is preferable, since its distinctive steps make better sense than Rousselot's compact vision by accounting for the predicament of those who interrupt their progression toward the act of faith and do not succeed in giving their full assent. In my opinion, those of my readers who might find my differentiated account too scholastic ought to take into consideration its potential usefulness for pastoral guidance. Hence my attempt to represent the three stages as follows:[5]

First, the individual (in dialogue with others) gets interested in facts that intimate the desirability of faith. In any great religion, one can find features indicating that its basic message is worthy of esteem and admiration, aesthetically, intellectually, ethically, or religiously. Such features may be called "pointers," "clues," or "motives of credibility." In Christianity, they have to do with the beauty of the Bible, with "the signs of the times" set forth by Jesus,[6] with his life and orientations, his miracles, his promises, his passion, death, and resurrection, as well as with the church (its doctrines, feasts, saints, and martyrs) and with one's personal aspirations, questions, and transcendent experiences. At this first stage, one perceives a congruence between the gospel's values and one's own, so one reaches a judgment of *credibility*: the Christian message as a whole is deemed to be meaningful, beautiful, and beneficent, hence credible.

Second, the individual realizes that the basic religious message ought to be believed. This awareness is associated with the *credentity* of revelation. Building on the credibility, the credentity challenges practical reason by summoning it to respond positively to the divine offer of unrestricted, entirely trustworthy love. Because the judgment of credentity, to use Rousselot's scholastic categories, urges a resolute consent by the will, together with a steadfast assent by the

5. My stages are the same as Maurice Blondel's, reported by Dulles, *The Assurance of Things Hoped For: A Theology of Christian Faith* (New York: Oxford University Press, 1994), 108–9.

6. Mt 16:3.

mind, it happens halfway between the apprehension of credibility and the decision to believe; it adds much to the former and directly prompts the latter. Talking about the motives of credentity, Maurice Blondel states that "they are more intrinsic to the act of faith than the intellectual motives of credibility themselves."[7] Hence the role of the will, which we may prefer to call practical reason, thereby implying that the will, far from being arbitrary, is stimulated by a good number of insights. In fact, the duty to believe is accompanied and strengthened, as was underlined in the preceding chapter, by the attraction that the heart feels to Jesus, to his humanity and his divinity, and to his church.

Third, the individual makes the decision to believe and carries it out effectively. The decision is taken by the human subject on the fourth level of its intentionality (according to Lonergan's categories), and this decision triggers the act of receiving the truth proposed by God, including both its rich meanings and its enigmas. This act of faith, enunciated on the third level, thus assumes insights, which have emerged on the second level of intentionality; it formally belongs to the third level—that is, the level on which a person makes one's own the revealed truth, along with its implications. All these components are performatively unified in a single thrust of the person who happily (and sometimes painfully) agrees to a divine presence in one's life and to an amazing relationship graciously established by God.

Only at this third stage, however, is the faith certainty felt—a certainty grounded in God's very words and maintained as long as one keeps being committed to the living relationship with Jesus, the Father, and the Holy Spirit. Analogously, we can say that married partners experience the certitude that they are in love—a certitude that is not extraneous or independent from their sincere pledge.

The certainty derives from the very act of faith by which people

---

7. Maurice Blondel, "What Is Faith?" *Communio: International Catholic Review* 14 (1987): 185.

lovingly affirm the redeeming truth that they receive from God. In one of his notes, Ludwig Wittgenstein is groping toward a rendering of this insight:

But if I am to be really saved,—what I need is *certainty*—not wisdom, dreams or speculation—and this certainty is faith.... Perhaps we can say: Only *love* can believe the Resurrection. Or: It is *love* that believes the Resurrection. We might say: Redeeming love believes even in the resurrection; holds fast even to the Resurrection. What combats doubt is, as it were, *redemption*. Holding fast to *this* must be holding fast to that belief. So what that means is: first you must be redeemed and hold on to your redemption (keep hold of your redemption)—then you will see that you are holding fast to this belief.[8]

Rousselot's contention about the status of the synthetic act of faith is problematic for another reason, also. Contrary to his thesis, the apprehension of the point (in the motives of credibility) is natural (in the Thomist sense). Such a perception is facilitated not by an elevating grace, which would render supernatural all our activities toward God, but, as suggested in chapter 3, by a healing grace— namely, a transitory, actual grace—that ameliorates the working of our natural faculties. At the first stage, this healing grace sustains the apprehension of credibility. At the second stage, another healing grace draws the person toward God, in a foretaste of total happiness, with a vivid sense of credentity. And at the third stage, a more lasting grace (called "elevating" or "sanctifying") establishes a divinizing relationship with the Trinity. Strictly speaking, then, the first two stages implement the *natural* working of the human faculties, assisted by a healing grace, whereas the third stage consists in the *supernatural* event that is the act of faith proper.[9]

---

8. Ludwig Wittgenstein, *Culture and Value*, trans. Peter Winch (Chicago: University of Chicago Press, 1980), 33e.

9. Given the importance of Aquinas and Newman in this book, I recommend two articles: Étienne Vetö, "Rousselot and Thomas Aquinas: *The Eyes of Faith* as a Model of 'Suntheologein,'" and Nicolas Steeves, "Newman's Explicit Influence on Rousselot: Apparent Contrasts?," both in *Gregorianum* 96 (2015), respectively at 709–32 and 733–47.

During this faith process, we are not moving in a realm of proofs, as in mathematics. As Newman showed, it would be a mistake to pursue stringent evidence in the domain of religion. The signs of credibility are ambiguous; they coexist with formidable objections; the meanings to which they point are not self-evident. Surely they address human reason, and yet only a person concerned for ultimate truth and warmed up by love can perceive those meanings. Once weighed and appreciated, they may turn into signs of credentity by fostering the conviction that they have been set forth by God and consequently must be believed. And at this final stage, the religious meanings are held as referring to actual history—principally the Incarnation—to wit, the living and enduring relationship or covenant between the triune God and the human race. The meanings are then received as judgments of fact, accompanied by judgments of value, all coming from a God who is Truth.

FEELINGS AND INSIGHTS

We have just seen how crucial insights take place in the movement toward faith. Feelings, too, play a prominent role; indeed, they are vital. Therefore, the affective side of this three-stage process of believing must now be highlighted. Given the many times in which affectivity was presented in this book, which began with human hope and repeatedly mentioned the role of feelings, it should suffice to note that affectivity is influential during all segments of the faith journey.

Several kinds of concerns, wishes, and emotional factors are at play in the ability to grasp motives of *credibility*. Whereas self-deception militates against grasping those motives, the openness of the heart to values enhances the search for meanings. Similarly, a blunted, unrefined conscience would never perceive motives of *credentity*; on the contrary, the judgment of credentity is the fine outcome of a severe test of intellectual probity and of moral authenticity. Last, a proper ethical development upholds the capacity to make choices of great moment for the person. The *decision to believe*—namely, the fundamental option—involves taking all sorts of risks (intellectual, moral, psychological, practical), accompanied by lack of full evidence, the demands of conversion, and the (not unnatural) fear of the divine mystery. As a result, even when the attractiveness of Jesus and the obligation to believe are felt, an individual remains free to say "no" to the divine gift.

The contemporary philosopher Jean-Luc Marion views the role of the will as subsequent to the judgments reached by apologetics:

> Apologetics plays the role of clearly indicating the place where the decision of the will must intervene, so that the will might know what it must, without avoidance, accept or refuse, and above all that the will might know the One whom it must repudiate or confess. Paradoxically, apologetics should aim only *to reinforce* the difficulty, by situating it at its real and genuine dignity: faith neither compensates for the lack of evidence nor resolves itself in arguments, but decides by the will for or against the love of Love.[10]

Thanks to its clarity, an intelligent apologetics highlights the difficulty of consenting to Love.

Rousselot justly reminded his readers that faith presupposes a striking discovery of meaning, a unifying synthesis concerning what Jesus is all about, an insight into the significance and coherence of some central points of the New Testament, in connection with an individual's or a group's profound quest. The spiritual voyage is punctuated by episodes of disclosure on the part of the Holy Spirit, to which episodes one may respond with a definite commitment to being a loving person. In the Catholic view salvation becomes effective by virtue of the grace that enables someone to make such a commitment, whether in a confessional or in a secular mode. In either of these two modes, we can observe a receptivity and a creativity. The recipients of transcendent experiences have the strong impression of having touched an ungraspable Reality whose influ-

---

10. Jean-Luc Marion, *Prolegomena to Charity*, trans. Stephen E. Lewis (New York: Fordham University Press, 2002), 61–62; on apologetics, see 67–69.

ence has reached them. And having appreciation for this happening, they undertake to express their discovery and innovatively shape it according to their anticipating images and categories.

Nonetheless, creativity is only one facet of the faith journey. Josef Pieper stresses the disparity between belief based on one's own spiritual intuitions and belief based on Jesus Christ's testimony.

It presumably happens fairly often that something which in reality is not belief is nevertheless regarded as belief—possibly even by the "believers" themselves. Thus someone may accept the doctrines of Christianity as truth *not* because they are witnessed and warranted by the revealing Logos of God, but because he is impressed by their "coherence," because the boldness and depth of the conception fascinates him, because those doctrines fit in with his own speculations on the mystery of the universe. This man would then regard the content of Christian religious doctrines as true, but *alio modo quam per fidem*, "in a different way from that of belief."[11] He might without any qualms consider himself a "believing Christian"; and others might likewise so regard him. Possibly the error would only come to light in a crisis; then it would become apparent that what was "collapsing" might have been various things: a kind of "philosophy of life," or "ideological" wishful thinking, or respect for tradition—but not at all belief in the strict sense.[12]

Undoubtedly Pieper is right in specifying the formal determinant of faith: believing not one's own conclusions in one's search for meaning, but God's word. However, what we have learned from Rousselot enables us to nuance Pieper's statement. We should avoid a stark opposition between relying on one's personal understanding (being impressed by the motives of credibility) and fully acknowledging divine testimony as entirely trustworthy (being impressed by the motives of credentity). They work hand in hand.

11. *ST* II-II, 5, 3; compare ad 1.
12. Pieper, *Belief and Faith*, 19–20.

THE ROLE OF RELIGIOUS EXPERIENCE

And this brings us to the role of religious experience with respect to truth. Since Schleiermacher, countless books have been written for or against theology being grounded in experience.[13] The question that must be tackled is: May we have recourse to our experience in order to test our beliefs? Does intellectual integrity require that our faith confessions be measured by religious experience? Some Buddhists say, "Do not believe blindly, but verify if the path you're engaged in really works for you." Can we reconcile this recommendation with receptivity to a revelation coming from God? Should Christian belief be considered adequate only if it corresponds to people's inner visions? Is being true to one's sentiments and insights the greatest of duties?

How those questions are answered hinges on how experience is defined. On the one hand, by "experience" most authors mean the affective and cognitive discoveries that lead to a person's or a group's religious convictions. Such discoveries are the motives of credibility. Nevertheless, while there is no Catholic faith without motives, the motives do not possess the rational power to ground faith. If, on the other hand, faith follows upon the motives of credentity, it is indeed grounded in them, since they consist precisely in the awareness that God, who is First Truth, has spoken and still speaks to humankind. Then we can say that religious experience includes this awareness.

Among the three elements of faith that Aquinas spelled out as *credere in Deum*, to believe in God (= the affective aspect), *credere Deum*, to believe that God is such (= the cognitive aspect), and *credere Deo*, to believe God (= the aspect of trust in God as in the One who reveals truth), liberal Protestantism has dispensed with the third one. The reason for this departure from patristic and medieval theology was already put forward by Lessing: there are too many

13. See, for instance, Roy, *Mystical Consciousness*, chap. 6; *Engaging the Thought of Bernard Lonergan*, study 5; and "Viability of the Category of Religious Experience."

fallible mediators between Jesus and modern Christians. The issue we are dealing with at the moment is this one: if exegetes, historians, theologians, and bishops cannot propose truth, then it seems that faith must rely first and foremost on subjective experience.

For instance, the seventeenth-century visionary Jacob Boehme asserted, "I do not wish to set down anything strange which I did not myself experience so that I do not find myself as a liar before God.... I do not write of my own accord but by the witness of the Spirit which no one can withstand."[14] His translator, Peter Erb, comments, "The being of God that Boehme experienced and wished to describe was primarily a burning love, the light of which illuminated God's image to which man had been created. Once illuminated, Boehme believed, a man knows his proper direction."[15] Evidently, individual experience is ambiguous, since it may easily fall into illuminism—that is, into trusting solely one's own individual light. However, as a matter of fact, Boehme's personal experience is not that different from Lonergan's account, as noted in chapter 5; both insist on the affective aspect of faith. Nonetheless, Boehme lacks the third aspect—namely, trust in God as in the One who reveals truth.

In light of the distinction between truth and meaning, it is not too difficult to realize that in modern philosophy of religion the distinction has been progressively blurred, as truth has been swallowed up by meaning. Perhaps we could enunciate one of modernity's dogmas as follows: in religious matters, truth is that which makes sense for an individual or a group. Truth ever remains what we choose, instead of what we discover. Those who espouse this stance are excessively preoccupied with being masters and controllers of their thoughts. Clinging to one's experience can blot out any challenge or questioning that would come from the word of God. Unwittingly perhaps, people thus preclude any genuine confrontation

14. Quoted by the translator in his introduction to Jacob Boehme, *The Way to Christ*, trans. Peter Erb (New York: Paulist Press, 1978), 8.

15. Translator's introduction, in Boehme, *Way to Christ*, 9.

with divine revelation, which would make them revise their personal or collective tenets.

If I adopt this attitude, I, as an individual, never totally enter into the vast symbolic world of a profound religious tradition. I don't allow revealed doctrines to stretch my mind beyond its limits toward an unheard-of divine design. There is no actual encounter with the infinite Other. Paradoxically, by absolutizing *my experience*, I cannot *experience* a complete intellectual trust in the incarnate Son of God, thanks to which I would have access to the intimate truths he has received from his Father and now wishes to share with me. God is forbidden from saying, "Let me introduce myself!"[16] Furthermore, lack of actual listening to Christ's teaching may entail being lukewarm as a disciple. Then Jesus and his followers are not permitted to awake and confirm what is best in me by preventing me from being somehow static and by opening me up to something radically new. Under those conditions, a defective orthodoxy—that is, no entire acceptance of divine revelation—may damage orthopraxis—namely, right action.

What should be denied, then, is not the role of experience in faith, but experience as the principal criterion of Christian truth. The First Vatican Council rejected the assertion "that divine revelation cannot be made credible by outward signs, and that, therefore, men ought to be moved to faith solely by each one's inner experience or by personal inspiration."[17] The mistake that the council underscores is to pit inner experience over against outward signs.

Rousselot, who comments on this canon of Vatican I, offers a very helpful clarification. He finds his cue in Blondel, where the

---

16. In René Latourelle, ed., "Testimony," in *Dictionary of Fundamental Theology* (New York: Crossroad, 1994), 1046. Latourelle writes, "We have access to the inner life of persons only through their freely given testimony about themselves, through confidences that are in the strict sense revelations or unveilings of their inner mystery." And he applies this analogy to "confidences" that come from the trinitarian persons.

17. Canon 3 on Chapter III, DS 3033; English translation from *The Christian Faith*, ed. J. Neuner and J. Dupuis (New York: Alba House, 1982), 44.

latter highlights "the encounter of the interior fact (grace, practical good will, righteous living, docility to infused aspirations) and the exterior fact of positive revelation."[18] Rousselot sums up his own position in this way:

A certain voluntary disposition produced by grace is indispensably required for every legitimate act of faith and for every certain perception of credibility, *not as a perceived internal fact, but as eyes to perceive the external fact.* Thus the "internal fact" is "illuminating rather than illuminated, intelligent rather than intelligible," to borrow a few excellent expressions of M. Mallet [pseudonym for M. Blondel].... Hence the supernatural love inspired by grace ... is not consciously *represented*; the eyes of faith do not look at themselves. We are aware of them only insofar as we see the object through them, insofar as we open them, insofar as we use them.[19]

In other words, far from being an object, what is internal is the subjective light that enables someone to perceive the external fact, which is the object of faith.

For all the incisiveness of this clarification, it appears that its author has been misled by his metaphor of "the eyes of faith." *Pace* Rousselot, the love inspired by grace, although most of the time alluded to symbolically rather than conceptually, *can* nevertheless be represented because it is conscious, as we saw Lonergan demonstrate in chapter 5. However, like Rousselot, Lonergan appropriately emphasizes the reciprocity between what he calls the "inner" and the "outer" word. Besides, we should not forget that for him the outer word par excellence or the incarnate meaning par excellence is Jesus Christ himself.

In his endeavor to make sense of Vatican I's previously quoted canon, Rousselot adds, "I would sum up in the following way the difference between the Protestant understanding intended by the Council and the Catholic understanding as I comprehend it: the former requires a perceptible grace; the latter, a *perceiving* grace."[20] I

18. Blondel, "What Is Faith?," 187.
19. Rousselot, *Eyes of Faith*, 38.
20. Rousselot, *Eyes of Faith*, 38.

suppose that this characterization applies to many Protestants (and many Catholics today), inasmuch as they basically rely on their own experience construed as "a perceptible grace" instead of relying on the authoritative word of God.

Faith knowledge is the best case for testing any construal of the relations between subjectivity and objectivity. In its efforts at repudiating subjectivism, the First Vatican Council tended toward objectivism. Still, despite this epistemological one-sidedness, it correctly spotted the threat of religious individualism. Today, with the nuances introduced by Blondel, Rousselot, and Lonergan, we are in a position to aver this point: human subjectivity becomes most authentic and objective by virtue of its total openness to the word of God, which it acknowledges in Jesus Christ and greets as coming from the First Truth, who guarantees its truthfulness. If the concept of religious experience embraces not only motives of credibility, but equally this motive of credentity, then it is perfectly legitimate to say that Christian faith is rooted in religious experience.

Furthermore, some measure of verification regarding particular beliefs is highly desirable, for two reasons at least. In the first place, given the risks of interpretative error, a certain fear of being misled by self-deceiving church authorities happens to be quite justified. Hence a moderately critical attitude, coupled with a good knowledge of biblical exegesis and of the ecumenical councils, is to be recommended in the face of bishops' and priests' teachings. Because of the ambiguous character of the particular religious accretions that influence us, for better or worse, what ought to be developed is an adult, not infantile, respect for church authorities.

In the second place, given the dangers of self-deception, having a clear grasp of what is meaningful and what is meaningless for us plays a positive role in maturing. In effect, this kind of honesty concerning one's personal situation in the faith journey is entirely well suited to doctrinal fidelity. Indeed, in the best of cases, each of these two concerns—honesty and fidelity—reinforces the other. For example, if a person is aware of dark spots in his flawed assimilation of the gospel, this humble lucidity may render his prayer life more sincere and more authentic. A critique of the way an individual has construed religious meanings liberates her and quickens her movement toward personal integration, both intellectual and affective. So any increase in terms of meaning normally strengthens the adhesion to Christ. And if someone can do this without questioning the truths of my Catholic heritage, it is because the issues of personal sincerity and authenticity have to do with *meaning* more or less successfully appropriated, whereas matters of *truth* are determined by the word of God.

THE CHRISTIAN MEDIATION OF
RELIGIOUS EXPERIENCE

In this last section, I will illustrate how any well-oriented religious experience is mediated.[21] Intentional interiority and relatedness are interactive. On the one hand, since it is a dynamism unfolding in activities, intentional interiority is the condition of possibility for the coming to be of the mediations. On the other hand, interiority is mediated by our relations with what is other than our own selves, since these relations provide the occasions needed if intentional interiority is to operate at all.

The complementarity between interiority and relatedness becomes evident as soon as we cast even a cursory glance on the manner in which three forms of human interiority—intentionality, psychic life, and religious experience—are mediated. Let us note that these forms *of interiority* are not meant to match the triad of the preceding chapter, which functions both internally and externally.

First, intentionality, as relating to human persons and finite objects, appropriates itself in the mediating contexts of interpersonal encounter and of book-reading; one can also profit from a sound

---

21. See Roy, *Transcendent Experiences*, 175–81.

education, from assignments and conversations with teachers and fellow students. Second, psychic life becomes more transparent as feelings and images are talked about in various self-correcting and therapeutic environments; healing takes place inasmuch as integration of meaning replaces disconnectedness and misconception in a person's biography.[22] Finally, religious experience—the apex of human consciousness—can be symbolically operative, owing to the outside stimulation that comes from a particular tradition. In all of these three cases—intentionality, psychic life, and religious experience—interiority needs external input in order to become symbolically and verbally aware of itself.

We are now in a better position to raise this question: Given that the inner word of God is tantamount to the unrestricted love that typifies religious interiority, is the inner word nonetheless mediated? If so, through what mediations do humans hear and respond to the voice of God? In order to answer this question, three steps are required. I shall successively present the mediations of daily life, the mediations of Christian witnesses, and the mediation of Jesus Christ.

In the first place, during the long process by which human beings constitute themselves, primary human relationships are paramount. Thanks to parents, educators, and peers, children—and later, adolescents—are coaxed and guided as they engage in a multifaceted play: paying attention to what presents itself in terms of percepts, affects, images, and feelings; taking interest in questions and enjoying insights; discovering the importance of verifying and judging; discriminatingly trusting or distrusting feelings; making free decisions; and communicating with others in the sharing of all these features of experience. Nothing can replace the presence of those who encourage us as we learn to engage and withdraw, to unite love for others and love of self, to explore the outside world and probe the inner world.

22. See Herbert Fingarette, *The Self in Transformation: Psychoanalysis, Philosophy, and the Life of the Spirit* (New York: Harper and Row, 1965).

In the second place, a decisive step is possible whenever human beings come across the human excellence that is grounded in religious experience. They are attracted to the value of intellectual, moral, psychic, and religious conversion. In the face of a spiritual excellence that surpasses theirs, they can either recoil in resentment or accept the challenge it poses. Furthermore, most of the time, the accomplished individuals that they admire refer to a faith community of some sort, be it artistic, intellectual, activist, or explicitly religious.

Anything concrete can be an opportunity for apprehending absolute value or raising a question regarding ultimacy: happy, painful, or intriguing events; human encounters; words, sermons, narratives, literary or religious texts; prayers, sacraments, liturgies. On such occasions, human beings directly or indirectly express themselves. Throughout their activities, stories, works of art, and in their own personalities, they embody meanings and values. As they bear witness to something momentous in their own eyes, they trigger questioning. Someone who observes them may ask, should I agree with the meanings they convey? Should I adopt the values they live? So questions of truth and commitment bring about the existential moment in which faith becomes a concrete possibility.

In the third place, Christian witnesses draw attention to a history that goes back to Abraham, the prototype of living faith. Beginning with Abraham, shaped by Moses, elucidated by the prophets, commented upon by the wisdom writers, the history of the Lord's dealings with the chosen people discloses the meaning of humankind's existence. The focal point in which such meaning becomes clearest is the life, passion, death, and resurrection of Jesus. In the Jesus-event, the key to the riddle of evil is offered. Humanity is revealed as its potentialities are manifested; divinity is revealed as God's fundamental stance with respect to the world is made known.

It would be too ambitious to try to unpack in a few paragraphs the total meaning of the Christ-event. In addition to what was said before, especially in the last section of chapter 6, suffice it to highlight briefly, from the point of view adopted here, its experiential side, by asking the question, how does the Christ-event mediate religious immediacy? How does the outer word of God mediate the inner word of God? I shall take my cue from Sebastian Moore, who has constructed, out of psychoanalytic and mystical literature, a heuristic structure of conscious interiority that sheds light on the Easter event. The rationale of the heuristic structure is that the Christ-event is seen as the key experience both for the early and the contemporary disciples of Jesus.[23]

A psychoanalytical examination of desire shows that the human being feels a tension between two poles of attraction, one toward oneness and one toward individuality. Many writers tell us that the human journey leading to full maturity consists of three fundamental stages: awakening, crisis, and renewal of desire. The conjunction of the two poles with the three stages of Christian discipleship should make sense in light of an analysis of interiority.

In stage one, human desire, which presses out both in feelings and in questions, relentlessly interrogates itself and other people regarding the validity of its experience of oneness and separation. Since they are separate and unique individuals, people want to hear that their beauty is confirmed by the Author of the universe. And because they are fascinated by the mystery of the whole, they hope to be reassured that they are not at odds with the ground of being. During his ministry in Galilee, Jesus evoked and supported, in his disciples' consciousness, a healthy tension between oneness and separation. They felt this tension, in Jesus himself, enhanced to a high degree, because he was sinless.

In stage two, the scandal of evil, already present in nature's seem-

---

23. See Sebastian Moore, *Jesus the Liberator of Desire* (New York: Crossroad, 1989). Specific references to other books and articles by this author can be found in Roy, "Human Desire and Easter Faith," in *Jesus Crucified and Risen: Essays in Spirituality and Theology in Honor of Dom Sebastian Moore*, ed. Vernon Gregson and William P. Loewe (Collegeville, Minn.: Liturgical Press, 1998), 53–67.

ingly capricious destructiveness, in society's aberrations, in the individual's physical, psychic, and moral sicknesses, reaches its climax in the crucifixion of Jesus. The collapse of the disciples' dreams and their betrayal of Jesus make them realize that in this drama both their enemies and they actually negate their own fundamental desire. During this painfully wrenching phase, they can no longer believe in their intentionality or affectivity; at the same time their human relationships are cut off. Thus the Holy Spirit empties them of any finite support as they are being readied for a further phase.

In stage three, the mediation of the crucified and risen Christ displays all its effectiveness.[24] The highest form of transcendent experience is given to those who have lost their faith in love. The merciful and forgiving love of the Father is disclosed as reaching out to the loveless in Jesus' earthly life and resurrection. The reconciling movement from God toward the sinners appears in the manifestation of divine forgiveness, embodied in Jesus' self-sacrificing passion and in his resurrection. The destructive direction of sinfulness is reversed as the disciples receive a forgiving love, which restores and enhances their conscious tension between oneness and separation. In their encounter with the risen Christ, they experience their relational intentionality as no longer basically sinful, but decidedly loving and self-transcending. To recreate their being, the Father grants them both the outer word of the Son and the inner word of the Holy Spirit.

From this peak experience of the resurrection, the believers link up the three kinds of mediation in a sacramental way: the mediation of Jesus Christ is seen as operative at once in the mediating of the Christian witnesses (the church) and in the mediating of the persons, events, and discoveries that are formative in someone's life (the world). When graced intentionality fully responds to these mediations, nothing is experienced as more real than the love, faith,

---

24. See Lonergan, "The Mediation of Christ in Prayer," in *Collected Works*, vol. 6, *Philosophical and Theological Papers 1958–1964*, 160–82.

and hope with which it relates itself to the mystical body of Christ in all its interpersonal and cosmic dimensions.

This model is indeed basic and transcendental because it correlates human relationality, religious immediacy, and the mediating of religious immediacy by human relationality. In correlating religious immediacy with the web of mediations offered by Christianity, the model values both immediacy and mediatedness. As the outcome of the Holy Spirit's mission, religious immediacy is neither more nor less significant than mediated revelation, which is Christ's mission, prolonged by all the members of his body.

CONCLUDING REMARKS

All the way through this chapter, several conclusions have been suggesting themselves emphatically. The first one is that faith may be intelligent and healthy by virtue of its insights, which are nourished by feelings. It is not blind; it requires asking questions, searching, and taking account of one's affective demands and intuitions. So faith is both reasonable and affective.

Moreover, in its intent of truth, faith may be respectful of reality. It consists in more than adopting meanings generated by mere human thinking or by a religious experience that would be indifferent to the possibility of a revelation coming from God. Faith's knowledge is not merely a compound of individual opinions, which should be conserved if they pragmatically work or which can be modified according to personal and cultural situations.

The next point that has been made is about immediacy and mediatedness. Faith is the grateful acceptance of a divine offer that has been recognizably presented in the biblical traditions and mediated by Christ as well by numerous witnesses and events.

Finally, twice in this chapter, various stages on the way to faith were delineated. The first description of stages was inspired by modern scholasticism, especially by Pierre Rousselot, and consequently was rather logical; the second description was inspired by Sebastian

Moore, and consequently was rather psychological. I thereby tried to illustrate how, far from consisting of a blanket, static, and undramatic acceptance of truth, the movement in hope toward faith is dynamic, progressive, albeit with hesitations and at times apparent regressions, which could turn into future progressions. It is in the dialectic of people's lives that the Holy Spirit operates.

A Pastoral Conclusion

༄

"Come then, Lord my God, teach my heart where and how to seek You, where and how to find You."[1] Thus St. Anselm of Canterbury addresses God in the prayer that launches his celebrated allocution on the existence and the nature of God. In our twenty-first century, can we localize this "where and how" somewhat differently, in accord with cultural situations that are not the same as those that prevailed in the eleventh century? In response to this query, this book has situated the beginnings of Christian faith in the anthropological locus constituted by uncertainties and doubts regarding human hope.

A first chapter spelled out some of the ambiguities of that hope, which may either foreclose any openness to God (as in Hobbes and Bloch) or constitute the sphere in which basic concerns and questions emerge. That chapter also disowned a hierarchical model of religion, with its exaggerated emphasis on ecclesiastical mediators as guardians of orthodoxy and orthopraxis. Dionysius's suggestion that *all* religious light comes from the episcopal hierarchy is preposterous. The bishops' function as exercising the magisterium is not to be decried, but placed within the broad environment made up of the abundant mediations put in place by God in the created world. Right in the thick of human experience, the problem of hope triggers a search, which finds assistance in those numberless mediations: people, events, narratives, art-forms, writings, and so forth.

---

1. St. Anselm, *Proslogion*, trans. M. J. Charlesworth (Notre Dame, Ind.: University of Notre Dame Press, 1979), chap. 1.

From a Christian point of view, all those presences derive from Jesus Christ, the Mediator, the Sacrament par excellence, the Source of all light and motivation.[2]

The Roman Catholic Church belatedly admitted, at the Second Vatican Council, the validity of Luther's insight into the priesthood of the faithful, which is a biblical assertion.[3] However, my nonhierarchical treatment of faith by no means cancels out authority—namely, the function of the pope and bishops, as well as the church's infallibility in special circumstances. After all, the democracies based on representation include some kind of hierarchy in the sense that duly elected deputies are entitled to legislate on behalf of the people. The Christian churches do not need an all-out democratic system, but some mechanisms of real, not skewed, consultation, which would ensure that the hierarchy take seriously the desires and misgivings of the faithful, as well as their offers of competent advice, in line with Vatican II's model of the church as a communion.

All the way through history, the menace of religious officials enacting unenlightened absolutist policies has recurred. A negative assessment of human nature, presumably not restored to health by grace, deceptively attempts to legitimize the policy of stifling original thinking. If the churches are to avoid incurring more losses than gains, it is better to put up with errors, while declaring them as such, and assisting believers and theologians to search out more responsibly and more methodically. This study has affirmed the vital function of authority in the church. The faithful need the support of authority—not authoritarianism—if they are to develop a space of intellectual freedom under the assaults of commercial advertisements and political brainwashing. Undeniably we are confronted with an ominous secular authoritarianism, whose manipulative performance is

2. See John Paul II, Encyclical Letter *Redemptoris Missio* (1990), no. 5.
3. See the "Dogmatic Constitution on the Church" (*Lumen Gentium*), nos. 9 and 10. It quotes 1 Pt 2:9–10 and Rv 1:6, and refers to Rv 5:9–10—the very texts adduced by Luther (!), as Wolfhart Pannenberg observes in *Systematic Theology*, trans. Geoffrey W. Bromiley (Grand Rapids, Mich.: Eerdmans, 1998), 3:127n89.

backed by the inexhaustible power of money. Our resistance cannot rely on mere opinions; it must be buttressed by Catholic convictions grounded in divine revelation.

In any case, I hope it has become obvious to my readers that this book has not praised Christianity in a naïve manner. Instead, it has taken as demonstrated the fact that the faith experience is always partly inauthentic. In particular, various deviations in religious experience have been portrayed. As James Marsh rightly contends, whenever belief and suspicion work in tandem, they are in a position to draw from complementary resources to surmount inauthenticity.

When we consider the Old and New testaments, … we note already a prophetic critique that anticipates what is going on in Freud, Nietzsche, and Marx. Such a biblical critique is complemented, filled out, and rendered more intellectually rigorous and contemporary by the masters of suspicion. On the other hand, religious belief helps such suspicion to keep from being overly cynical or despairing or hypercritical in itself, in the sense that I direct my suspicion toward others but leave myself off the hook. Rich complementarity, then, rather than mutual exclusion, seems to be the most adequate stance.

Properly understood, then, religious belief requires suspicion, and suspicion requires religious belief. Suspicion can and must become a kind of spirituality that believers employ in order to move themselves and society from inauthentic to authentic religious belief and practice, from mere religion to faith.[4]

Any religious authority must be tempered. And in this respect, another disquieting phenomenon must be adverted to: the fact that Catholics who think they are entirely faithful to the church nonetheless misread its doctrinal positions, highlight aspects *they* deem central, and one-sidedly make them more important and authoritative than they actually are, while ignoring other, often more decisive, teachings. At times, such people go so far as to affix the stigma of dis-

---

4. James L. Marsh, *Process, Praxis, and Transcendence* (Albany, N.Y.: SUNY Press, 1999), 159.

loyalty upon other Catholics who do not share their views in matters that are open to diverse interpretations. This intolerance prevents them from having access to a rich and balanced account of Christian demands. Their dogmatism amounts to an objectivism that, because it leaves out significant church doctrines (usually in the field of social ethics), ends up being another form of subjectivism. For them, the pope is more important than individual conscience, whereas Newman declared that one should toast conscience before toasting the pope. They fail to realize that conscience is more fundamental than the pope, since it is conscience that decides to obey the pope.

In chapter 6, we have observed that a well-rounded faith experience combines three factors: affectivity, rationality, and receptivity. First, insofar as affectivity is concerned, by commencing with the issue of hope, chapter 1 presented the readers with reflections drawn from sociology and from the radicalism of those who are sensitive to the plight of the poor and who struggle for a just world. Second, I have considered rationality, which has been a major theme throughout the book, as the great core value of a sound liberalism (hence as different from the liberalism that Newman combated): freedom to pose the most difficult questions, out of inquisitiveness and intellectual integrity. Given the role of the reasons people have to believe (called "motives of credibility" and "motives of credentity"), my position steers clear of fideism. Third, receptivity has been viewed as based on a high respect for God's revelation.

From chapter 2 onward, faith has been construed as an experience, a journey, a moving viewpoint. This vision has been supported by texts from the Bible, Thomas Aquinas, Newman, and Lonergan. Moreover, human subjectivity has been construed as summoned to hold in an effective synergy the three dynamisms that are operative in the faith process: affective craving, quest for meaning, and aspiration for truth. What has been envisaged is that, prompted by the Holy Spirit, a person may become aware that one's home coincides with love and that one's horizon coincides with belief.

A PASTORAL CONCLUSION

In making a case for a dynamically encompassing standpoint, I had to rule out both dogmatism and extreme liberalism—the former being anti-freedom and the latter being anti-authority. As a response to these false solutions, I have proposed an integrative dialectic, which I boast is richer than either of the dismissed pseudo-solutions.[5] In terms of practical wisdom, this concern for a dynamic equilibrium entails letting the heart play its part, allowing reason to ask all its questions and explicate its insights, and honoring belief as the result of an intelligent option. Thus we can avoid succumbing to emotivism, rationalism, or authoritarianism—phenomena that develop when the three fundamental aspects of religious experience are torn asunder. Even though these factors are not semantically the same as Freud's famous triad, the id, the ego, and the superego, this triad may help us beware of three devastating phenomena: the hedonism of the id, the willfulness of the ego, and the tyranny of the superego. As is well known, much too often religion has been harnessed and used for the sake of mediocre happiness, individual pride, or repression. All three distortions are unhealthy: self-indulgence, self-assertion, and self-accusation. And they shed light on the three deviations that this book has tackled.

That said, it is legitimate and wise to grant a moderate priority to one of the three dynamisms, either during a particular stage in a person's religious itinerary or even permanently. After all, faith is equally offered to people who respond to life in a feeling manner, to people who need detailed explanations, and to people who insist on the transcendent origin of revealed doctrine. Yet we must be wary of imbalance—namely, of a disproportionate preference for one of the three factors or for two of them at the expense of a third.

As far as religious education is concerned, the three basic situations that have been described—interaction, hegemony, alliance—constitute a typical set of human patterns that is likely to facilitate

5. A similar dialectic is deployed in Roy, *Self-Actualization and the Radical Gospel.*

the identification of concrete tendencies in a person or a group. This
threefold typology can be of service to diagnose and remedy the
believers' weaknesses in their faith orientation. It may also be useful in an inventory of existing strengths. Such pastoral tools will be
of assistance provided they are utilized in an ambience of humility,
mutual understanding, and critical encouragement.

Sound pedagogy requires that we first pay close attention to our
contemporaries' craving for fulfillment and meaning so as to reach
progressively a position in which a case can be made for revealed
truth. Propelled by emotional and rational factors, Christian faith
consists in a personal choice stemming from a willingness to trust
religious witnesses, mostly Jesus and his disciples. Thanks to such
trust, human freedom enters into the dynamic context of a credible
community to which they want to belong. Mature believers "know"
(as in St. John's Gospel and Letters) that their own particular religious stance suits them. They are content with their manner of living the three dynamisms—that is, with the way they believe toward
God (*credere in Deum*), they believe in what he says (*credere Deum*),
and they believe God (*credere Deo*), as his message is mediated by
human leaders (apostles, missionaries, pastors, friends, or other
stimulating figures). They have tested their belief system as embed-
ded in a reference group that inspires them and points to Jesus and
to the beauty of his revelation.

Faith certainty becomes easier whenever the faithful consider
any other religious path, either as fitting other people's spiritual
needs or as the best path that those other people can hit upon at the
moment. My reflections here on the certainty attained in a reference
group are inspired by the sociologist Christian Smith. In a study of
the religious vitality of evangelicalism, he argues that most evangeli-
cals rather successfully achieve a "subcultural identity" that is not
undermined by society's pluralism.[6] Readers may remember that in

6. See Christian Smith, *American Evangelicalism: Embattled and Thriving* (Chicago:
University of Chicago Press, 1998), chap. 4. For a similar study, this time on Catholics,

210

my first chapter I approvingly referred to Peter Berger's "heretical imperative"—to wit, the necessity to make basic personal choices— a necessity that is now observable worldwide. Nevertheless, following Smith, I disagree with Berger's thesis that the modern plurality of views inevitably generates anomie, skepticism, and relativism. My foregoing paragraphs have just explained how it is that countless believers (who should be considered "mature") develop strong convictions and are capable of firm religious assents.

I repeat my own proposal that most of the time such strong convictions and firm assents do not and cannot derive from an authoritarian approach. I say "most of the time" because there will ever be people whose psychology calls for a peremptory exercise of an allegedly inerrant authority, especially those who accept "a surrender to an external authority which overcomes the self-destructive drives in oneself."[7] At any rate, the kind of theology and philosophy of education offered in these pages is addressed to those whose appreciation for the dignity of the person has been molded by the Western ideals of freedom and sincerity—ideals that have been embraced, especially by the youth, in many non-Western regions.

At first sight, the paramount values of freedom and sincerity seem to exclude any religious authority. On account of this cultural fact, I have argued for the indispensability of an authority approached from the point of view of the search for fulfillment and meaning. Whenever authority is presented as coming before fulfillment and meaning, it will be accepted only by a minority of educated adults. This applies even to children who respond positively to offers of fulfillment and meaning. As a matter of fact, even when this minority of faithful appeal to authority, it is not without concomitant discoveries in terms of fulfillment and meaning. For the major-

---

see Richard W. Flory and Donald E. Miller, *Finding Faith: The Spiritual Quest of the Post-Boomer Generation* (New Brunswick, N.J.: Rutgers University Press, 2008).

7. Charles Taylor, *A Secular Age* (Cambridge, Mass.: Harvard University Press, 2007), 512.

ity, the significance of authority must be found within the concerns of affectivity and reason, as the liberating Truth, which is none other than Jesus Christ. Human beings are attracted, not to propositional revelation in the first place, but to the Revealer himself, Jesus, the one who makes them free affectively and intellectually.

Inculturation demands that educational steps be ordered along sequences that fit particular social settings. Only in this manner can we minimize the misconstrual of Christian belief—misconstrual that is likely to take place often, as the New Testament states. For instance, Jesus "sternly ordered and commanded them [his disciples] not to tell anyone" that he was the Messiah, knowing that this affirmation would be misapprehended at that phase of his ministry.[8] As a matter of fact, because of his misunderstanding, Peter energetically disagreed with Jesus.[9]

Commenting on St. Paul's speech before the Areopagus in Athens, Newman praises him for having shown "that the Gospel was rather the purification, explanation, development, and completion of those scattered verities of Paganism than their abrogation."[10] He goes on to write:

It was not his [St. Paul's] method to represent the faith, to which he exhorted his hearers, as a state of mind utterly alien from their existing knowledge, their convictions, and their moral character. He drew them on, not by unsettling them, but through their own system, as far as might be,—by persuasives of a positive nature, and which, while fitted to attract by their innate truth and beauty, excluded by their very presence whatever in Paganism was inconsistent with them. What they already were, was to lead them on, as by a venture, to what they were not; what they knew was to lead them on, upon presumptions, to what they as yet knew not.[11]

Newman felicitously stresses how assents can build on both real apprehension and informal inference and go beyond the latter in

8. Lk 9:21.
9. Mk 8:29–33.
10. Acts 17:22–34; John Henry Newman, *Fifteen Sermons*, sermon XII, 247.
11. Newman, *Fifteen Sermons*, sermon XII, 248.

their final and certain assertions. Moreover, he highlights the role of "antecedent probability." It is the duty of pastors to address with precision such antecedent probability of believing, found in the concerns, desires, questions, and religious experiences of men and women of today. They must also pay attention to the antecedent probability of *not* believing, owing to a cultural placement in which "belief in God ... is understood to be one option among others."[12] This novel antecedent probability, more and more widespread in the West and elsewhere, is tied up with a sturdy prejudice against authority, with its myriad objections. Given that this anti-authoritarianism stems from a concern for the authenticity of the self, the apologetic task I am advocating has become more urgent than ever.

Thus the subjective—not subjectivist—approach to faith can demonstrate its fruitfulness. We observe it in the Bible and in the patristic age, albeit without the modern stress of the individual. Among scriptural and early Christian authors, questions about human happiness and the meaning of collective events are prominent. On this issue, we have seen how Lonergan's epistemology is very helpful, since it displays the fact that subjectivity and objectivity need one another.

An education based on human subjectivity is far more promising than one based on authoritarianism. In the latter, pastors insist on an immediate faith decision, which requires little reflection and little religious experience. Then only a minimum of fulfillment and meaning suffices. What counts is explicit belief, which, in that perspective, must be put in place as early as possible, since salvation requires faith (construed as being primarily belief). Catechesis becomes a matter of indoctrination: funneling information into people's minds instead of assisting them in achieving relevant insights. By contrast, if we adopt a gradual pedagogy, marked by patience, then the decision of entirely surrendering to Christ and his message may occur

---

12. Taylor, *Secular Age*, 3. In this remarkable book the author calls this new situation "the nova effect" while elaborating its implications; see index, "nova effect."

after a while. What counts is an honest process of inquiry and conversion in which the definitive act of faith becomes possible and authentic when the person actually receives the divine light.

The distinction between meaning and truth, introduced in chapter 7, may help to differentiate two features of Christian pedagogy. On the one hand, meaning is found on the level of understanding. When human beings query about the signification of the believers' texts and practices, they raise questions for understanding. Catechesis and theology have the duty to respect this urge to know: whenever relevant questions are posed regarding Christian teachings, sound information or elucidation must be provided. Honoring the search for meaning makes for creativity in the churches.

On the other hand, apprehensions of meaning cannot settle the question of whether Catholic doctrines are true. People of good will should be guided toward raising this question for themselves and consider the option of responding affirmatively in light of their awareness of the movement from above downward (according to Lonergan's central metaphor). That is to say, if they have an experience of a transcendent love, brought home to them by Christian mediators and by the greatest of mediators, Jesus Christ, then faith as the knowledge born of religious love will allow them to discern the value of believing in the judgments of value and of fact proposed by the church. They will have to face squarely the dilemma of assenting to divine revelation. They will make a decision that is founded not only on the meaningfulness of what they understand, but, more crucially, on the credibility of God.

In addition to these tasks, Christian educators must face widespread irrationalism—namely, the lack of logic and coherence that we observe in the mass media—for instance, in rock songs, music videos, movies, imageries on websites, and other popular creations. I am not implying that those productions lack intelligible content. On the contrary, they often convey perspicacious or profound insights, combined with the overwhelming force of symbolism. Instead of looking down on the approaches to faith provided by those channels of communication, we should critically scrutinize and appraise them as potentially leading their addressees toward faith. Such is the task of pastoral or practical theology—the theological specialty that Lonergan calls "communications."[13]

A study shows that 80 percent of young American Catholics consider themselves "spiritual persons," while 65 percent of them agree that "an individual should arrive at his or her own religious beliefs independent of any churches or synagogues."[14] To this 65 percent we must add the percentage of those who would say that, in interaction with the teachings of the Catholic Church, they want to have the final word about their own religious beliefs. This fact proves that even in Catholic circles, believing God (*credere Deo*) and intellectually trusting God's church are far from self-evident.

Therefore, in this second decade of the third millennium, the present book has delineated an approach that reconciles our contemporaries' craving for fulfillment and meaning and their hesitant openness to a revelation that transcends human capabilities. This theology is no longer solely Thomist because, while it builds upon the rich insights and values of the past, it also takes the diverse cultural settings into consideration. It incorporates a subjective apologetics, with its emphasis on hope and significance—an emphasis that usually precedes the preoccupation with truth. In all ages, most people who get seriously interested in Christianity discover orthodoxy within their orthopraxis itself. If orthopraxis is to dodge compromises, it needs a solid basis in truth. At some point in the journey, prayerful intuitions such as those we can find in the Johannine writings enable believers to interiorize the word of God and eventually to no longer envision dogma as extrinsic. In Lonergan's catego-

---

13. Lonergan, *Method in Theology*, chap. 14.

14. Dean R. Hoge et al., *Young Adult Catholics: Religion in the Culture of Choice* (Notre Dame, Ind.: University of Notre Dame Press, 2001), 154 and 61. Even if it was carried out some fifteen years ago, this survey is still representative.

ries, one moves from religious and moral conversions to intellectual conversion.

Thus will present-day believers be able to take up, as previous generations did, the ever valid injunction "Always be ready to make your defense to anyone who demands from you an accounting for the hope that is in you; yet do it with gentleness and reverence."[15]

---

15. 1 Pt 3:15–16.

Bibliography

Aquinas, Thomas. *The Academic Sermons*. Translated by Mark-Robin Hoogland. Washington, D.C.: The Catholic University of America Press, 2010.

———. *Commentary on Saint Paul's Epistle to the Ephesians*. Translated by Matthew L. Lamb. Albany, N.Y.: Magi, 1966.

———. *Commentary on Saint Paul's Epistle to the Galatians*. Translated by F. R. Larcher. Albany, N.Y.: Magi, 1966.

———. *Commentary on the Gospel of St. John*. Translated by James A. Weisheipl and Fabian R. Larcher. 2 vols. Albany, N.Y.: Magi, 1980 (also Petersham, Mass.: St. Bede's Publications, no date).

———. *The Disputed Questions on Truth*. Vol. 3. Translated by Robert W. Schmidt. Chicago: Regnery, 1954.

———. *Expositio Primae Decretalis*. In *Opuscula Theologica*, edited by Raymundo A. Verardo. Turin: Marietti, 1954.

———. *Faith, Reason and Theology*. Translated by Armand Maurer. Toronto: Pontifical Institute of Mediaeval Studies, 1987.

———. *In Librum Beati Dionysii de Divinis Nominibus Expositio*. Edited by Ceslai Pera. Turin: Marietti, 1950.

———. *Quaestiones Quodlibetales*. Edited by Raymundo Spiazzi. Turin: Marietti, 1956.

———. *Scriptum super Libros Sententiarum*. Edited by Maria Fabianus Moos. Paris: Lethielleux, 1933.

———. *Sermon-Conferences on the Apostles' Creed*. Translated by Nicholas Ayo. Notre Dame, Ind.: University of Notre Dame Press, 1988.

———. *Summa Contra Gentiles*. Translated by Anton C. Pegis. 5 vols. Notre Dame, Ind.: University of Notre Dame Press, 1975.

———. *Summa Theologica*. Translated by the Fathers of the English Dominican Province. 3 vols. New York: Benziger Brothers, 1947.

———. *Super Epístolas S. Pauli Lectura*. Edited by Raphael Cai. 2 vols. Turin: Marietti, 1953.

Augustine. *Confessions*. Translated by F. J. Sheed. Rev. ed. Indianapolis, Ind.: Hackett, 1993.

———. *The Enchiridion on Faith, Hope, and Love*. Edited by Henry Paolucci. Translated by J. F. Shaw. Chicago: Regnery Gateway, 1961.

———. *Homilies on the Gospel of John*. In *Nicene and Post-Nicene Fathers*, vol. 7, edited by Philip Schaff. First Series. 2nd printing. Peabody, Mass.: Hendrickson, 1995.

———. *Letters 100–155*. Translated by Roland Teske. Hyde Park, N.Y.: New City Press, 2003.

———. *Sermons III/4 on the New Testament*. Translated by Edmund Hill. Edited by John E. Rotelle. Brooklyn, N.Y.: New City Press, 1992.

Barciauskas, Jonas. *Landscapes of Wisdom: In Search of a Spirituality of Knowing*. Lanham, Md.: University Press of America, 2000.

Barth, Karl. *Witness to the Word: A Commentary on John 1*. Edited by Walther Fürst. Translated by Geoffrey W. Bromiley. Grand Rapids, Mich.: Eerdmans, 1986.

Beaudoin, Tom. *Virtual Faith: The Irreverent Spiritual Quest of Generation X*. San Francisco: Jossey-Bass, 1998.

Berger, Peter L. *The Heretical Imperative: Contemporary Possibilities of Religious Affirmation*. Garden City, N.Y.: Doubleday, 1979.

Bloch, Ernst. *The Principle of Hope*. Translated by Neville Plaice, Stephen Plaice, and Paul Knight. Cambridge, Mass.: MIT Press, 1986.

Blondel, Maurice. *Dialogue avec les philosophes: Descartes, Spinoza, Malebranche, Pascal, Saint Augustin*. Paris: Aubier, 1966.

———. What Is Faith?" *Communio: International Catholic Review* 14 (1987): 162–92.

Boehme, Jacob. *The Way to Christ*. Translated by Peter Erb. New York: Paulist Press, 1978.

Boismard, M.-E. "La connaissance dans l'Alliance Nouvelle d'après la Première Lettre de Saint Jean." *Revue Biblique* 56 (1949):366–91.

Braine, David. "What Makes a Christology into a Christian Theology." *New Blackfriars* 77 (1996):288–302.

Brodie, Thomas L. *The Gospel according to John: A Literary and Theological Commentary*. New York: Oxford University Press, 1993.

Brown, Raymond E. *The Gospel according to John*. 2 vols. Garden City, N.Y.: Doubleday, 1966.

———. *The Critical Meaning of the Bible*. New York: Paulist Press, 1981.

Buber, Martin. *I and Thou*. Translated by Ronald Gregor Smith. 2nd ed. New York: Charles Scribner's Sons, 1958.

Burrell, David B. "Self-Deception and Autobiography: Reflections on Speer's *Inside the Third Reich*." In *Truthfulness and Tragedy: Further Investigations in Christian Ethics*, edited by Stanley Hauerwas, 82–98. Notre Dame, Ind.: University of Notre Dame Press, 1977.

Butler, Joseph. *The Analogy of Religion, Natural and Revealed, to the Constitution and Course of Nature*. London: George Bell and Sons, 1878.

Cessario, Romanus. *Christian Faith and the Theological Life*. Washington, D.C.: The Catholic University of America Press, 1996.

Citrini, Tullio. "The Principle of 'Christocentrism' and Its Role in Fundamental Theology." In *Problems and Perspectives of Fundamental Theology*, edited by René Latourelle and Gerald O'Collins, translated by Matthew J. O'Connell, 168–85. New York: Paulist Press, 1982.

Clement of Alexandria. *Christ the Educator*. Translated by Simon P. Wood. New York: Fathers of the Church, 1954.

———. *The Exhortation to the Greeks*. Translated by G. W. Butterworth. Cambridge, Mass.: Harvard University Press, 1982.

Cottier, Georges M.-M. *Le conflit des espérances*. Paris: Desclée de Brouwer, 1977.

Coventry, John. *Christian Truth*. New York: Paulist Press, 1975.

Crowe, Frederick E. *Theology of the Christian Word: A Study in History*. New York: Paulist Press, 1978.

———. "An Exploration of Lonergan's New Notion of Value." In *Appropriating the Lonergan Idea*, edited by Michael Vertin, 51–70. Toronto: University of Toronto Press, 2006.

de la Potterie, Ignace. "L'onction du Chrétien par la foi." In *La vie selon l'Esprit: Condition du Chrétien*, by Ignace de la Potterie and S. Lyonnet. Paris: Cerf, 1965.

———. *La vérité dans Saint Jean*. 2 vols. Rome: Biblical Institute Press, 1977.

Desmond, William. *Being and the Between*. Albany, N.Y.: SUNY Press, 1995.

Dessain, C. Stephen. "Cardinal Newman on the Theory and Practice of Knowledge: The Purpose of the *Grammar of Assent*." *Downside Review* 75 (1957): 1–23.

"Dogmatic Constitution on the Church" (*Lumen Gentium*). In *Documents of Vatican II*, edited by Austin P. Flannery. New rev. ed. Grand Rapids, Mich.: Eerdmans, 1984.

Doran, Robert M. *Psychic Conversion and Theological Foundations: Toward a Reorientation of the Human Sciences*. Chico, Calif.: Scholars Press, 1981.

———. "From Psychic Conversion to the Dialectic of Community." In *Lonergan Workshop*, edited by Fred Lawrence, 6:91–93. Atlanta: Scholars Press, 1986.

———. *Theology and the Dialectics of History.* Toronto: University of Toronto Press, 1990.

Dulles, Avery. *The Assurance of Things Hoped For: A Theology of Christian Faith.* New York: Oxford University Press, 1994.

———. *The Craft of Theology: From Symbol to System.* New expanded ed. New York: Crossroad, 1995.

———. *Newman.* New York: Continuum, 2002.

Dumais, Marcel. "Sens de l'Écriture: Réexamen à la lumière de l'herméneutique philosophique et des approches littéraires récentes." *New Testament Studies* 45 (1999):310–31.

Dumas, Marc. "Corrélations d'expériences?" *Laval Théologique et Philosophique* 60 (2004):317–34.

Dupré, Louis. "Hope and Transcendence." In *The God Experience*, edited by Joseph P. Whelan, 217–25. New York: Newman Press, 1971.

Ernst, Cornelius. *The Theology of Grace.* Notre Dame, Ind.: University of Notre Dame Press, 1974.

———. *Multiple Echo: Explorations in Theology.* Edited by Fergus Kerr and Timothy Radcliffe. London: Darton, Longman, and Todd, 1979.

———. Introduction. In *Theological Investigations*, by Karl Rahner, 1:xvi–xvii. New York: Crossroad, 1982.

Erikson, Erik H. *Identity and the Life Cycle.* New York: W. W. Norton, 1980.

Ferreira, M. Jamie. *Doubt and Religious Commitment: The Role of the Will in Newman's Thought.* Oxford: Clarendon Press, 1980.

Fingarette, Herbert. *The Self in Transformation: Psychoanalysis, Philosophy, and the Life of the Spirit.* New York: Harper and Row, 1965.

———. *Self-Deception.* London: Routledge and Kegan Paul, 1969.

Flory, Richard W., and Donald E. Miller, eds. *GenX Religion.* New York: Routledge, 2000.

Flory, Richard W., and Donald E. Miller. *Finding Faith: The Spiritual Quest of the Post-Boomer Generation.* New Brunswick, N.J.: Rutgers University Press, 2008.

Gadamer, Hans-Georg. *Truth and Method.* Translated by Joel Weinsheimer and Donald G. Marshall. 2nd rev. ed. New York: Crossroad, 1989.

Gaffney, James. "Believing and Knowing in the Fourth Gospel." *Theological Studies* 26 (1965):215–41.

Gandhi, Mahatma. *The Essential Writings of Mahatma Gandhi.* Edited by Raghavan Iyer. Delhi: Oxford University Press, 1993.

Gauchet, Marcel. *The Disenchantment of the World.* Translated by Oscar Burge. Princeton, N.J.: Princeton University Press, 1997.

Gibbon, Edward. *The History of the Decline and Fall of the Roman Empire*. Vol. 1. New York: Allen Lane and Penguin, 1994.

Giddens, Anthony. *The Consequences of Modernity*. Stanford, Calif.: Stanford University Press, 1990.

Grant, Robert M., and David Tracy. *A Short History of the Interpretation of the Bible*. 2nd ed., rev. and enlarged. Philadelphia: Fortress Press, 1984.

Grondin, Jean. "The New Proximity between Theology and Philosophy." In *Between the Human and the Divine: Philosophical and Theological Hermeneutics*, edited by Andrzej Wiercinski, 97–101. Toronto: Hermeneutic Press, 2002.

Guitton, Jean. *Critique religieuse*. Paris: Desclée de Brouwer, 1968.

Haight, M. R. *A Study of Self-Deception*. Atlantic Highlands, N.J.: Humanities Press, 1980.

Harrison, Peter. "Correlation and Theology: Barth and Tillich Re-examined." *Studies in Religion/Sciences Religieuses* 15 (1986):65–76.

Hazard, Paul. *The European Mind (1680–1715)*. Translated by J. Lewis May. Cleveland: World, 1967.

Hefling, Charles C., Jr. "Turning Liberalism Inside-Out." *Method: Journal of Lonergan Studies* 3 (1985):51–69.

———. "Newman on Apprehension, Notional and Real." *Method: Journal of Lonergan Studies* 14 (1996):55–84.

Hesiod. *Works and Days*. Edited by H. G. Evelyn-White. Cambridge, Mass.: Harvard University Press, 1950.

Hick, John. *Faith and Knowledge*. Cleveland: Fontana, 1974.

Hobbes, Thomas. *Leviathan*. Edited by Edwin Curly. Indianapolis: Hackett, 1994.

Hoge, Dean R., et al. *Young Adult Catholics: Religion in the Culture of Choice*. Notre Dame, Ind.: University of Notre Dame Press, 2001.

Holyer, Robert. "Religious Certainty and the Imagination: An Interpretation of J. H. Newman." *Thomist* 50 (1986):395–416.

Horkheimer, Max, and Theodor W. Adorno. *Dialectic of Enlightenment: Philosophical Fragments*. Edited by Gunzelin Schmid Noerr. Translated by Edmund Jephcott. Stanford, Calif.: Stanford University Press, 2002.

Howe, Neil, and William Strauss. *Millennials Rising: The Next Great Generation*. New York: Vintage, 2000.

John Paul II. Encyclical Letter *Redemptoris Missio* (1990).

———. Encyclical Letter *Fides et Ratio* (1998); see http://www.vatican.va

Johnson, Luke Timothy. *Religious Experience in Earliest Christianity*. Minneapolis: Fortress Press, 1998.

Kant, Immanuel. *Religion and Rational Theology.* Translated by Allen W. Wood and George Di Giovanni. Cambridge: Cambridge University Press, 1996.

———. *Critique of Pure Reason.* Translated by Paul Guyer and Allen W. Wood. Cambridge: Cambridge University Press, 1998.

Kellenberger, J. *The Cognitivity of Religion: Three Perspectives.* Berkeley: University of California Press, 1985.

Ker, Ian. *The Achievement of John Henry Newman.* Notre Dame, Ind.: University of Notre Dame Press, 1990.

Kierkegaard, Søren. "The Expectancy of Faith." In *Eighteen Upbuilding Discourses,* edited and translated by Howard V. Hong and Edna H. Hong, 7–29. Princeton, N.J.: Princeton University Press, 1990.

———. *Works of Love.* Edited by Howard V. Hong and Edna H. Hong. Princeton, N.J.: Princeton University Press, 1995.

Kinghorn, Kevin. "Spiritual Blindness: Self-Deception and Morally Culpable Nonbelief." *Heythrop Journal* 48 (2007):527–45.

Kreeft, Peter, and Ronald K. Tacelli. *Handbook of Christian Apologetics: Reasoned Answers to Questions of Faith.* San Francisco: Ignatius Press, 2009.

Lafont, Ghislain. *Histoire théologique de l'Église catholique.* Paris: Cerf, 1994.

Lash, Nicholas. *Theology on Dover Beach.* London: Darton, Longman and Todd, 1979.

———. *A Matter of Hope: A Theologian's Reflections on the Thought of Karl Marx.* London: Darton, Longman and Todd, 1981.

———. *Easter in Ordinary: Reflections on Human Experience and the Knowledge of God.* Charlottesville: University Press of Virginia, 1988.

Latourelle, René, ed. "Testimony." In *Dictionary of Fundamental Theology,* 1044–51. New York: Crossroad, 1994.

LeGrys, James. "The Christianization of Modern Philosophy according to Maurice Blondel." *Theological Studies* 54 (1993):455–84.

Lindbeck, George A. "Protestant Problems with Lonergan on Development of Dogma." In *Foundations of Theology: Papers from the International Lonergan Congress 1970,* edited by Philip McShane, 115–23. Notre Dame, Ind.: University of Notre Dame Press, 1972.

———. *The Nature of Doctrine: Religion and Theology in a Postliberal Age.* Philadelphia: Westminster Press, 1984.

Locke, John. *An Essay concerning Human Understanding* (1700). Edited by Peter H. Nidditch. 4th ed. Oxford: Clarendon Press, 1975.

Lonergan, Bernard J. F. *Caring about Meaning: Patterns in the Life of Bernard Lonergan.* Edited by Pierrot Lambert, Charlotte Tansey, and Cathleen Going. Montreal: Thomas More Institute, 1982.

———. *A Third Collection: Papers by Bernard J. F. Lonergan.* Edited by Frederick E. Crowe. New York: Paulist Press, 1985.

———. *Collected Works of Bernard Lonergan.* Vol. 2, *Verbum: Word and Idea in Aquinas,* edited by Frederick E. Crowe and Robert M. Doran. Toronto: University of Toronto Press, 1997. Vol. 3, *Insight: A Study of Human Understanding.* Edited by Frederick E. Crowe and Robert M. Doran. Toronto: University of Toronto Press, 1992. Vol. 4, *Collection.* Edited by Frederick E. Crowe and Robert M. Doran. Toronto: University of Toronto Press, 1988. Vol. 6, *Philosophical and Theological Papers 1958–1964,* edited by Robert C. Croken, Frederick E. Crowe, and Robert M. Doran. Toronto: University of Toronto Press, 1996. Vol. 13, *A Second Collection.* Edited by Robert M. Doran and John D. Dadosky. Toronto: University of Toronto Press, 2016. Vol. 17, *Philosophical and Theological Papers 1965–1980,* edited by Robert C. Croken and Robert M. Doran. Toronto: University of Toronto Press, 2004.

———. *Method in Theology.* Toronto: University of Toronto Press, 2003.

MacDonald, Neil B. *Metaphysics and the God of Israel: Systematic Theology of the Old and New Testaments.* Grand Rapids, Mich.: Baker Academic, 2006.

MacIntyre, Alasdair. *After Virtue.* 2nd ed. Notre Dame, Ind.: University of Notre Dame Press, 1984.

Macmurray, John. *Ye Are My Friends* and *To Save from Fear.* London: Quaker Home Service, 1979.

Marion, Jean-Luc. *Prolegomena to Charity.* Translated by Stephen E. Lewis. New York: Fordham University Press, 2002.

Marsh, James L. *Process, Praxis, and Transcendence.* Albany, N.Y.: SUNY Press, 1999.

Marshall, Bruce D. "Aquinas as Postliberal Theologian." *Thomist* 53 (1989): 353–402.

Martin, Francis. *The Feminist Question: Feminist Theology in the Light of Christian Tradition.* Grand Rapids, Mich.: Eerdmans, 1994.

McCarthy, Michael H. *The Crisis of Philosophy.* Albany, N.Y.: SUNY Press, 1990.

———. "The Critique of Realism." *Method: Journal of Lonergan Studies* 10 (1992):89–125.

Meissner, W. W. *Life and Faith: Psychological Perspectives on Religious Experience.* Washington, D.C.: Georgetown University Press, 1987.

Mercadante, Linda A. *Belief without Borders: Inside the Minds of the Spiritual but Not Religious.* New York: Oxford University Press, 2014.

Merkur, Dan. *Crucified with Christ: Meditation on the Passion, Mystical Death, and the Medieval Invention of Psychotherapy.* Albany, N.Y.: SUNY Press, 2007.

Metz, Johannes Baptist. *Christliche Anthropozentrik: Über die Denkform des Thomas von Aquin.* Munich: Kösel Verlag, 1962.

Meyer, Ben F. *The Aims of Jesus.* London: SCM Press, 1979.

Mitchell, Basil. *The Justification of Religious Belief.* London: Macmillan, 1973.

Moleski, Martin X. *Personal Catholicism: The Theological Epistemologies of John Henry Newman and Michael Polanyi.* Washington, D.C.: The Catholic University of America Press, 2000.

Moltmann, Jürgen. *Theology of Hope: On the Ground and the Implications of a Christian Eschatology.* Translated by James W. Leitch. New York: Harper and Row, 1967.

Moore, Sebastian. *Jesus the Liberator of Desire.* New York: Crossroad, 1989.

Nabe, Clyde. *Mystery and Religion: Newman's Epistemology of Religion.* Lanham, Md.: University Press of America, 1988.

Neuner, J., and J. Dupuis, eds. *The Christian Faith.* New York: Alba House, 1982.

Newman, Jay. *The Mental Philosophy of John Henry Newman.* Waterloo, Ont.: Wilfrid Laurier University Press, 1986.

Newman, John Henry. *A Letter Addressed to His Grace the Duke of Norfolk on Occasion of Mr. Gladstone's Recent Expostulation.* London: Pickering, 1875. Also published in *Conscience, Consensus, and the Development of Doctrine: Revolutionary Texts by John Henry Cardinal Newman,* edited by James Gaffney, chap. 5. New York: Doubleday, 1992.

———. *Discourses Addressed to Mixed Congregations.* 6th ed. London: Burns and Oates, 1881.

———. "On the Introduction of Rationalistic Principles into Revealed Religion." In *Essays Critical and Historical.* Vol. 1. London: Longmans, Green, 1910.

———. *The Idea of a University.* London: Longmans, 1912. Also edited by Martin J. Svaglic. Notre Dame, Ind.: University of Notre Dame Press, 1982.

———. *Faith and Prejudice and Other Unpublished Sermons.* Edited by the Birmingham Oratory. New York: Sheed and Ward, 1956.

———. *On Consulting the Faithful in Matters of Doctrine.* Edited by John Coulson. New York: Sheed and Ward, 1961.

———. *The Letters and Diaries of John Henry Newman.* Edited by Charles Stephen Dessain et al. Oxford: Clarendon Press, 1961–84.

———. *Meditations and Devotions.* London: Burns and Oates, 1964.

———. *Apologia pro Vita Sua: Being a History of his Religious Opinions.* Edited by Martin J. Svaglic. Oxford: Clarendon Press, 1967.

———. *The Philosophical Notebook of John Henry Newman.* Edited by Edward Sillem. Revised by A. J. Boekraad. 2 vols. Louvain: Nauwelaerts, 1970.

———. *The Theological Papers of John Henry Newman on Faith and Certainty*. Edited by J. Derek Holmes. Oxford: Clarendon Press, 1976.

———. *An Essay in Aid of a Grammar of Assent*. Edited by I. T. Ker. Oxford: Clarendon Press, 1985.

———. *Parochial and Plain Sermons*. San Francisco: Ignatius Press, 1987.

———. *An Essay on the Development of Christian Doctrine*. Notre Dame, Ind.: University of Notre Dame Press, 1989.

———. *The "Via Media" of the Anglican Church*, edited by H. D. Weidner. Oxford: Clarendon Press, 1990.

———. *Three Latin Papers of John Henry Newman*. Translated by Carleton Jones. Rome: Pontifical University of Saint Thomas Aquinas, 1995.

———. *Fifteen Sermons Preached before the University of Oxford*. Notre Dame, Ind.: University of Notre Dame Press, 1997.

Newman, John W. *Disciplines of Attention: Buddhist Insight Meditation, the Ignatian Spiritual Exercises, and Classical Psychoanalysis*. New York: Peter Lang, 1996.

Nietzsche, Friedrich. "The Antichrist." In *The Portable Nietzsche*, translated by Walter Kaufmann. New York: Penguin, 1976.

Oakes, Kaya. *The Nones Are Alright: A New Generation of Believers, Seekers, and Those In Between*. Maryknoll, N.Y.: Orbis, 2015.

O'Collins, Gerald, and Daniel Kendall. *The Bible for Theology: Ten Principles for the Theological Use of Scripture*. New York: Paulist Press, 1997.

O'Connor, Edward D. *Faith in the Synoptic Gospels: A Problem in the Correlation of Scripture and Theology*. Notre Dame, Ind.: University of Notre Dame Press, 1961.

Ormerod, Neil. *Method, Meaning and Revelation: The Meaning and Function of Revelation in Bernard Lonergan's "Method in Theology."* Lanham, Md.: University Press of America, 2000.

Pannenberg, Wolfhart. "Insight and Faith." In *Basic Questions in Theology*. Vol. 2. Philadelphia: Westminster Press, 1971.

———. *Systematic Theology*. Translated by Geoffrey W. Bromiley. 3 vols. Grand Rapids, Mich.: Eerdmans, 1998.

Pascal, Blaise. *Oeuvres complètes*. Edited by Louis Lafuma. Paris: Seuil, 1963.

———. *Pensées*. Translated by A. J. Krailsheimer. Rev. ed. New York: Penguin, 1995.

Peirce, Charles Sanders. "A Neglected Argument for the Reality of God (1908)." In *The Essential Peirce: Selected Philosophical Writings*, edited by the Peirce Edition Project. Vol. 2. Bloomington: Indiana University Press.

Pieper, Josef. *Belief and Faith*. Chicago: Regnery, 1963.

———. *Hope and History*. Translated by Richard Winston and Clara Winston. New York: Herder and Herder, 1969.

Pierrard, Pierre. *Louis Veuillot*. Paris: Beauchesne, 1998.

Polanyi, Michael. *The Tacit Dimension*. Garden City, N.Y.: Doubleday, 1966.

Procureur, Daniel. "Parler de l'espérance aujourd'hui." In *La sagesse, une chance pour l'espérance?*, edited by Adolphe Gesché, 13–26. Paris: Cerf, 1998.

Pseudo-Dionysius. *The Complete Works*. Translated by Colm Luibheid. New York: Paulist Press, 1987.

Rabut, Olivier. *L'expérience religieuse fondamentale*. Tournai: Casterman, 1969.

Rahner, Karl. "Einführender Essay" to Johannes Baptist Metz, *Christliche Anthropozentrik: Über die Denkform des Thomas von Aquin*. Munich: Kösel Verlag, 1962.

———. "Thoughts on the Possibility of Belief Today." In *Theological Investigations*, translated by Karl-H. Kruger, 5:3–22. Baltimore: Helicon Press, 1966.

———. "Theology and Anthropology." Translated by Graham Harrison. In *Theological Investigations*, 9:28–45. New York: Herder, 1972.

Ricoeur, Paul. *Freud and Philosophy: An Essay on Interpretation*. Translated by Denis Savage. New Haven: Yale University Press, 1970.

———. "The Critique of Religion." In *The Philosophy of Paul Ricoeur: An Anthology of His Work*, edited by Charles E. Reagan and David Stewart, 213–22. Boston: Beacon Press, 1978.

———. "The Hermeneutics of Testimony." In *Essays on Biblical Interpretation*, edited by Lewis S. Mudge, 119–54. Philadelphia: Fortress Press, 1980.

———. "Manifestation and Proclamation." In *Figuring the Sacred: Religion, Narrative, and Imagination*, edited by Mark I. Wallace, translated by David Pellauer. Minneapolis: Fortress Press, 1995.

———. "A Philosophical Hermeneutics of Religion: Kant." In *Figuring the Sacred: Religion, Narrative, and Imagination*, edited by Mark I. Wallace, translated by David Pellauer. Minneapolis: Fortress Press, 1995.

Robert, Pierre. "Theology and Spiritual Life: Encounter with Bernard Lonergan." In *Lonergan Workshop*, edited by Fred Lawrence, 10:333–43. Boston: Boston College, 1994.

Roof, Wade Clark. *A Generation of Seekers: The Spiritual Journeys of the Baby Boom Generation*. San Francisco: Harper and Row, 1993.

Rosenzweig, Franz. *Der Mensch und sein Werk: Gesammelte Schriften*. Vol. 1. The Hague: Martinus Nijhoff, 1979.

Rousselot, Pierre. *The Eyes of Faith*. Translated by Joseph Donceel. New York: Fordham University Press, 1990.

Roy, Louis, OP. "Why Are Most Christians on the Defensive with Respect to Marxism?" *New Blackfriars* 64 (1983):29–34.

———. "'The Form of the Personal': A Study of the Philosophy of John Macmurray with Particular Reference to His Critique of Religious 'Idealism.'" Ph.D. diss. Dissertation Abstracts International, 45, no. 12A (1984):3667. Available at Ann Arbor, Mich.: University Microfilms International, Order no. DA8501107.

———. "Interpersonal Knowledge according to John Macmurray." *Modern Theology* 5 (1989): 349–65.

———. "Bruce Marshall's Reading of Aquinas." *The Thomist* 56 (1992):473–80, with a rejoinder from Bruce D. Marshall, 499–524.

———. "Toward a Psychology of Grace: W. W. Meissner's Contribution." *Theological Studies* 57 (1996):322–31.

———. "Human Desire and Easter Faith." In *Jesus Crucified and Risen: Essays in Spirituality and Theology in Honor of Dom Sebastian Moore*, edited by Vernon Gregson and William P. Loewe, 53–67. Collegeville, Minn.: Liturgical Press, 1998.

———. "The Passion of Jesus: A Test Case for Providence." *New Blackfriars* 79 (1998):512–23.

———. "Schleiermacher's Epistemology." *Method: Journal of Lonergan Studies* 16 (1998):25–46.

———. *Le sentiment de transcendance, expérience de Dieu?* Paris: Cerf, 2000.

———. "Neither within nor outside Time: Plotinus' Approach to Eternity." *Science et Esprit* 53 (2001):419–26.

———. *Transcendent Experiences: Phenomenology and Critique*. Toronto: University of Toronto Press, 2001.

———. "Notes on Thomas Aquinas." *Budhi: A Journal of Culture and Ideas* 6 (2002):235–43.

———. *Self-Actualization and the Radical Gospel*. Collegeville, Minn.: Liturgical Press, 2002.

———. *Mystical Consciousness: Western Perspectives and Dialogue with Japanese Thinkers*. Albany: SUNY Press, 2003.

———. "Cornelius Ernst's Theological Seeds." *New Blackfriars* 85 (2004): 459–70.

———. "Why Is the Death of Jesus Redemptive?" In *Pondering the Passion: What's at Stake for Christians and Jews*, edited by Philip A. Cunningham, 129–39. Lanham, Md.: Rowman and Littlefield, 2004.

———. *Coherent Christianity: Toward an Articulate Faith* (Eugene, Ore.: Wipf & Stock, 2017).

———. "Does Christian Faith Rule out Human Autonomy?" *Heythrop Journal* 53 (2012): 606–23.

———. *Engaging the Thought of Bernard Lonergan.* Montreal: McGill-Queen's University Press, 2016.

———. "The Viability of the Category of Religious Experience in Bernard Lonergan's Theology." *Method: Journal of Lonergan Studies,* New Series, no. 6 (2015):99–117.

Russell, Bertrand. *An Inquiry into Meaning and Truth.* London: Unwin Paperbacks, 1980.

Sartre, Jean-Paul. *Being and Nothingness.* Translated by Hazel E. Barnes. New York: Philosophical Library, 1956.

———. *The Transcendence of the Ego.* Translated by Forrest Williams and Robert Kirkpatrick. New York: Farrar, Straus and Giroux, 1972.

Scheler, Max. *Ressentiment.* Translated by William W. Holdheim. New York: Free Press of Glencoe, 1961.

Schillebeeckx, Edward. *Jesus: An Experiment in Christology.* Translated by Hubert Hoskins. New York: Crossroad, 1979.

———. *Christ: The Experience of Jesus as Lord.* Translated by John Bowden. New York: Crossroad, 1980.

Schlier, Heinrich. "Glauben, Erkennen, Lieben nach dem Johannesevangelium." In *Besinnung auf das neue Testament,* 2:279–93. Freiburg: Herder, 1964.

Schwager, Raymund. *Must There Be Scapegoats? Violence and Redemption in the Bible.* Translated by Maria L. Assad. New York: Crossroad, 2000.

Smith, Christian. *American Evangelicalism: Embattled and Thriving.* Chicago: University of Chicago Press, 1998.

Smith, Wilfred Cantwell. *Faith and Belief.* Princeton, N.J.: Princeton University Press, 1979.

St. Anselm. *Proslogion.* Translated by M. J. Charlesworth. Notre Dame, Ind.: University of Notre Dame Press, 1979.

Stark, Rodney. *The Rise of Christianity: A Sociologist Reconsiders History.* Princeton, N.J.: Princeton University Press, 1996.

Steeves, Nicolas. "Newman's Explicit Influence on Rousselot: Apparent Contrasts?" *Gregorianum* 96 (2015):733–47.

Taylor, Charles. *A Secular Age.* Cambridge, Mass.: Harvard University Press, 2007.

Tekippe, Terry J., and Louis Roy. "Lonergan and the Fourth Level of Intentionality." *American Catholic Philosophical Quarterly* 70 (1996):225–42.

Ten Elshof, Gregg A. *I Told Me So: Self-Deception and the Christian Life.* Grand Rapids, Mich.: Eerdmans, 2009.

Tenner, Edward. *Why Things Bite Back: Technology and the Revenge of Unintended Consequences.* New York: Knopf, 1996.

Theissen, Gerd. *Psychological Aspects of Pauline Theology.* Translated by John P. Galvin. Philadelphia: Fortress Press, 1987.

Thérèse de Lisieux. *Conseils et souvenirs recueillis par Soeur Geneviève de la Sainte Face.* Paris: Cerf and Desclée de Brouwer, 1979.

Thompson, William M. *Bérulle and the French School: Selected Writings.* Translated by Lowell M. Glendon. New York: Paulist Press, 1989.

Tillich, Paul. *Systematic Theology.* 3 vols. Chicago: University of Chicago Press, 1951.

———. *The Courage to Be.* New Haven: Yale University Press, 1952.

———. *Dynamics of Faith.* New York: Harper and Row, 1957.

———. *Theology of Culture.* Edited by Robert C. Kimball. New York: Oxford University Press, 1959.

Tolstoy, Leo. *Resurrection.* Translated by Louise Maude. New York: Dodd, Mead, 1927.

Tracy, David. *The Achievement of Bernard Lonergan.* Foreword by Bernard Lonergan. New York: Herder and Herder, 1970.

———. "Lonergan's Foundational Theology: an Interpretation and a Critique." In *Foundations of Theology: Papers from the International Lonergan Congress 1970,* edited by Philip McShane, 197–222. Notre Dame, Ind.: University of Notre Dame Press, 1972. See also in the same volume "Bernard Lonergan Responds," 223–34.

Turner, Denys. *The Darkness of God: Negativity in Christian Mysticism.* Cambridge: Cambridge University Press, 1995.

Vetö, Étienne. "Rousselot and Thomas Aquinas: *The Eyes of Faith* as a Model of 'Suntheologein.'" *Gregorianum* 96 (2015):709–32.

von Balthasar, Hans Urs. *The Moment of Christian Witness.* Translated by Richard Beckley. San Francisco: Ignatius Press, 1994.

von Hügel, Friedrich. *The Mystical Element of Religion as Studied in Saint Catherine of Genoa and Her Friends.* 2nd ed. London: J. M. Dent and Sons, 1923.

Wainwright, Geoffrey. *Doxology: The Praise of God in Worship, Doctrine and Life.* London: Epworth, 1980.

Wittgenstein, Ludwig. *Culture and Value.* Translated by Peter Winch. Chicago: University of Chicago Press, 1980.

Wolterstorff, Nicholas. "Can Belief in God Be Rational If It Has No Foundation?" In *Faith and Rationality: Reason and Belief in God,* edited by Alvin Plantinga and Nicholas Wolterstorff, 135–86. Notre Dame, Ind.: University of Notre Dame Press, 1983.

Wright, N. T. *The Climax of the Covenant: Christ and the Law in Pauline Theology*. Minneapolis: Fortress, 1992.

Wu, John Jr. "Centennial Vignettes: Life with Father." In *Merton and the Tao: Dialogues with John Wu and the Ancient Sages*, edited by Christóbal Serrán-Pagán y Fuentes, 367–97. Louisville, Ky.: Fons Vitae, 2013.

Index of Names

℘

Adorno, Theodor, 31
Anselm of Canterbury, 205
Aristotle, 29, 78, 84, 105–6
Augustine of Hippo, 4n11, 17, 25, 42, 62, 68, 71, 88, 117n117, 158

Barciauskas, Jonas, 18n25
Barth, Karl, 13, 14, 16n20, 39n8, 63–64
Beaudoin, Tom, 2
Berger, Peter, 9, 10, 211
Bloch, Ernst, 28–31, 205
Blondel, Maurice, 15, 16n18, 187n5, 188n7, 195–97
Boehme, Jacob, 194
Boismard, M.E., 67n163
Braine, David, 162n7
Brodie, Thomas, 58
Brown, Raymond, 40, 56n84
Buber, Martin, 180n53
Burrell, David, 167, 168n16
Butler, Bishop Joseph, 104, 108, 119

Cajetan, 76n22
Calvin, John, 119
Caswall, Edward, 91
Cessario, Romanus, 76n20
Chenu, Marie-Dominique, 179n49
Childs, Brevard, 39n8
Citrini, Tullio, 16
Clement of Alexandria, 35, 47
Clifford, W.K., 99
Cottier, Georges M.-M., 28n56
Coventry, John, 164
Crowe, Frederick, 13n9, 106n62, 131n6, 148, 184

Dante, 18n25
de Bérulle, Pierre, 18
de Finance, Joseph, 130
de la Potterie, Ignace, 61n120
de Sales, Francis, 94n13
Desmond, William, 136n30
Dessain, Charles Stephen, 91n1
Doran, Robert M., 13n9, 39n7, 106n62, 130, 134n22, 135n26, 174, 184n1,
Dulles, Avery, 107, 113, 114n99, 124, 187n5
Dumas, Marc, 16n21
Dumais, Marcel, 40n10
Dupré, Louis, 29
Dionysius, 17–18, 82, 205

Eckhart, 4, 22
Eliade, Mircea, 19
Elshof, Gregg A. Ten, 167n15
Erikson, Erik H., 32
Ernst, Cornelius, 20, 38

Ferreira, M. Jamie, 96n18
Fingarette, Herbert, 169n21, 199n22
Flew, Antony, 103
Flory, Richard W., 2n5, 210n6
Fra Angelico, 126
Froude, Mrs. William, 109

Gadamer, Hans-Georg, 32, 105n55, 107, 108n71, 114
Gaffney, James, 68, 125n145
Gandhi, Mahatma, 79–80
Gauchet, Marcel, 18
Gibbon, Edward, 115, 118
Giddens, Anthony, 25

231

Subject Index

꤮

affectivity, heart, will, 5, 12, 66, 71–78, 86, 89, 94, 122, 133, 138, 188, 145, 160, 169, 177, 191, 202, 208, 212. *See also* love
alliance, 44, 67n163, 122, 158, 164, 177, 179, 209
anthropological, 10, 14–17, 21–23, 33, 145, 158, 161
apologetics: apologists, apology, 11, 23, 91, 99, 113, 191
apprehension: real and notional, 92–99, 126. *See also* insight; understanding
assent, consent, 73, 93, 96–97, 105, 107, 187
authoritarianism, 163–64, 209
authority, 5, 124, 125, 165–66, 206, 211. *See also* obedience

belief, 6, 11, 41, 84, 88, 92, 96, 103, 108, 126, 134, 137–39, 142. *See also* doctrine; dogma
blindness, 6, 36, 47, 50–51, 64. *See also* self-deception

certainty, certitude, 6, 29, 81–82, 101–2, 152, 188
Christ. *See* Jesus Christ
Church, 17–18, 20, 120, 202, 206
commitment, 184, 191, 200
conversion, 6, 48, 73, 116, 129–30, 132, 137, 146–48, 152–54, 174
covenant, 30, 48, 190
credibility, credentity, 68, 73, 76, 81, 187, 190, 197, 208

distortions of faith, 119–25
doctrine, 17n23, 119, 121, 192, 208–9. *See also* belief; dogma
dogma, 120, 122, 124. *See also* belief; doctrine
doubt, 79, 82, 110, 189

emotion, emotionalism, 120, 121, 126, 159–60. *See also* feeling
Enlightenment, modernity, 6, 25, 30–31, 92, 100, 194

faith, 43–68; and distortions, 119–25; and love; 71–75; and three dynamisms, 158, 160, 177, 179, 208–10
feeling, 169, 171–75, 190–92. *See also* affectivity
Fideism, 164–65
faithful, 44, 89, 95, 120, 154, 165, 197, 206
first principles, 78
First Truth, 71, 75–82. *See also* meaning and truth
freedom, 76, 124, 130, 210–11
functional specialities, 37, 43, 146–47

God the Father, 59, 74
Good News, Gospel, 48, 52, 135, 185, 179, 212,
grace, 4, 36, 38, 74, 136, 139, 150, 189, 191, 196

happiness, 22–33
heart. See affectivity
hegemony, 162–165, 179
history, 15, 20, 24, 29, 112, 116, 190, 206

SUBJECT INDEX

Holy Spirit, 42, 61, 63, 69, 73, 76, 87,
124n143, 158, 160, 163n8, 179, 191, 203
hope, 9–33

illumination, 36, 46, 47–55. *See also* blindness; light of faith
improbability. *See* probability
incarnate, incarnation, 56–68, 86–87, 135,
195–96
inference: proof, formal and informal, 83,
91, 93, 99–101, 102–3, 105, 106, 108–11,
119, 126
inquiry and investigation, 71, 81, 105,
109–10
insight, 92, 150, 172–73, 184, 186. *See also*
apprehension; understanding
intentionality, 131–137, 180, 184–86, 188,
202
interaction, 158, 160–162
investigation. *See* inquiry

Jesus Christ, 16, 42, 44, 47, 51, 87, 89–90,
138, 177, 179
judgment of fact and of value, 33, 134,
138

knowledge, knowing, 51–52, 54, 56, 69, 73,
78–79, 82–86, 101, 133–34, 153, 159, 197

liberalism, 91, 121, 208–9
light of faith, 72, 75, 139
Logos, 56–68. *See also* Word of God
love, 64, 66–67, 113–14, 117, 132–35, 149–51,
189. *See also* affectivity

meaning and truth, 183–85, 217
mediation, 54, 136–37, 198–203
Messiah, 46, 212
miracles, 11n5, 57, 106, 187
modernity. *See* Enlightenment
motives of faith, 187–90, 197, 208. *See also*
credibility
mysticism, 17, 18n25

natural and supernatural, 77–78, 80, 189
natural reason. *See* reason

obedience, 17, 52, 54, 159, 164, 166. *See also*
authoritarianism; authority
object of faith, 75, 89, 196
objectivity. *See* subjectivity
objectivism. *See* subjectivity
orthodoxy, 42, 195, 205
orthopraxis, 195, 205, 215

pluralism, 39, 210
probability: antecedent probability, accumulation of probabilities and improbability, 101–4, 106–8, 114–15, 122, 126, 213
proof. *See* inference
proposition, 72n5, 75, 89, 92–93, 96–99,
109–11, 147, 184. *See also* judgment

rationalism, 91, 120–22, 126, 163
realism: critical realism, 144–45, 152–54,
176
reason, 15, 26, 40–41, 77, 84–85, 116, 121,
178, 209. *See also* meaning and truth
religion(s), 1–4, 13, 20–21, 26, 41–42, 80,
97, 111–12, 114, 122, 125, 133, 141, 164
religious experience, 7, 20–21, 31, 151, 183,
193–204

Savior, 46, 60, 116, 127
scholasticism, 203
Scripture, 35, 37–38, 40–43, 55, 58, 86–87,
122–23. *See also* Word of God
self-deception, 27, 47, 50, 55, 64, 69, 159,
166–70, 176, 179, 197. *See also* blindness
skepticism, 1, 32, 211
Son of God, 61, 69, 78, 83
Spirit. *See* Holy Spirit
subjectivity: objectivity, subjectivism,
objectivism, 10–16, 33, 77, 144, 147, 153,
157–58,180–81, 197, 208, 213
supernatural. *See* natural
symbol, symbolic, 30, 38, 49, 57, 89, 126
systematic theology, systematics, 37, 39,
40–41,

testimony, 58–61, 109, 121, 192, 195
tradition, 4, 36, 135, 137–39, 142–43
transcendence, 29, 131, 137

✠

The Three Dynamisms of Faith: Searching for Meaning, Fulfillment & Truth was designed in Arno Pro, and composed by Kachergis Book Design of Pittsboro, North Carolina. It was printed on 60-pound Sebago IV B18 Cream and bound by Maple Press of York, Pennsylvania.